Evolutionary Game Theory

Evolutionary Game Theory

Jörgen W. Weibull

The MIT Press
Cambridge, Massachusetts
London, England

This book was set in Times Roman by Windfall Software using ZzTEX and was printed and bound in the United States of America.

Library of Congress Cataloging-in-Publication Data

Weibull, Jörgen W., 1948–
 Evolutionary game theory / Jörgen W. Weibull.
 p. cm.
 Includes bibliographical references and index.
 ISBN 0-262-23181-6 (alk. paper)
 1. Game theory. 2. Evolution–Mathematical models. I. Title
QA269.W45   1995
519.3–dc20

                              94-44425
                              CIP

for Sofia and Anna

Contents

Foreword

Ken Binmore

When von Neumann and Morgenstern's *Theory of Games and Economic Behavior* appeared in 1944, it was greeted with great enthusiasm. It was thought that a complete theory of strategic behavior had sprung into existence from nowhere, as Athena burst fully armed from the forehead of Zeus. However, it soon became apparent that von Neumann and Morgenstern had provided only the beginnings of a theory, and those seeking quick applications became disillusioned. Game theory then spent a long period in the doldrums. The mathematics of the theory of two-person, zero-sum games continued to be studied. Much effort was also devoted to developing cooperative game theory. But the problems of noncooperative game theory in general were left largely untouched.

Von Neumann and Morgenstern being no more, the Nobel Prize for Economics was recently awarded to three game theorists, John Nash, John Harsanyi, and Reinhard Selten. Nash's work was published in the early 1950s, but it was not until the early 1970s that it was fully realized what a powerful tool Nash had provided in formulating the equilibrium concept that bears his name. Game theory then enjoyed a renaissance as economists applied the idea to a wide range of problems. However, a fly in the ointment was awaiting discovery. Games typically have many Nash equilibria. In two-person, zero-sum games, this creates no problem because all equilibria are then interchangeable and payoff-equivalent. But the equilibrium selection problem for more general games has no such easy solution.

At first it was thought that the problem could be tackled by refining the Nash equilibrium concept. Despite Nash's remarks in his thesis about a possible evolutionary interpretation of the idea of a Nash equilibrium, attention at that time was focused almost entirely on its interpretation as the only viable outcome of careful reasoning by ideally rational players. Various bells and whistles were therefore appended to the definition of rationality. These allowed some Nash equilibria to be discarded as inadequately rational according to whatever new definition of rationality was being proposed. However, different game theorists proposed so many different rationality definitions that the available set of refinements of Nash equilibrium became embarrassingly large. Eventually, almost any Nash equilibrium could be justified in terms of someone or other's refinement. As a consequence a new period of disillusionment with game theory seemed inevitable by the late 1980s.

Fortunately the 1980s saw a new development. Maynard Smith's book *Evolution and the Theory of Games* directed game theorists' attention away from their increasingly elaborate definitions of rationality. After all, insects can hardly be said to think at all, and so rationality cannot be so crucial if game theory somehow manages to predict their behavior under appropriate conditions. Simultaneously the advent of experimental economics brought home the fact that human subjects are no great shakes at thinking either. When they find their way to an equilibrium of a game, they typically do so using trial-and-error methods.

As the appearance of this book indicates, the 1990s have therefore seen a turning away from attempts to model people as hyperrational players. The new approach to the equilibrium selection problem emphasizes the almost tautological assertion that the equilibrium selected will be a function of the equilibrating process by means of which it is achieved. The process may be slow, as in biological evolution. It may be fast, as in social evolution, when the mechanism for the transmission of superior strategies from one head to another is imitation. It may be almost instantaneous, as when the price adjusts to equate supply and demand in the Chicago wheat market. However, we have learned that all these different processes have features in common that make it worthwhile considering evolutionary processes in the abstract.

Such studies teach us some painful lessons. We learn that there is nearly always evolutionary pressure against the various types of behavior labeled as "irrational" in the refinements' literature, but these pressures can vary enormously in their relative strengths. If the pressure against one type of irrationality is weak, the pressures against other types of irrationality may rush the system to an equilibrium before the pressure against the first type of irrationality has a chance to have much effect. For example, weakly dominated strategies need not be eliminated. Even strongly dominated strategies can survive in certain special cases.

We also learn that historical and institutional factors cannot be ignored. This is not a hard lesson for biologists, for whom the realities of genetic inheritance and the accidents of geography are brute facts that cannot be overlooked. But economists remain resistant to the idea that the same game might receive a different analysis if the players have a different history of experience, or live in different societies, or operate in different industries. One sometimes even reads that theories that ignore such considerations are "superior" to those that do because they are able to generate predictions with less data! However, if there is one fact that work on evolutionary games has established beyond doubt, it is that some details of the equilibriating process can have a major impact on the equilibrium selected. One of the major tasks awaiting us is to identify such significant details so that applied workers know what to look for in the environments within which the games they care about are played.

However, such a program is for the future. Jörgen Weibull's book is a compendium of progress so far in the area in which biology and economics overlap. Much of the material is his own work and that of his collaborators. It is distinguished by the clarity of the exposition and the elegance of the mathematics. He does not pretend to cover the whole field. One must look elsewhere for the nitty-gritty of population genetics or the properties of evolutionary processes with a strong stochastic component. But within his chosen area, his coverage is satisfyingly comprehensive.

Evolutionary game theory is here to stay, and I suspect this book will be a staple of its literature for many years to come. Its author is to be congratulated on having done such a fine job.

Introduction

The standard interpretation of noncooperative game theory is that the analyzed game is played exactly once by fully rational players who know all the details of the game, including each other's preferences over outcomes. Evolutionary game theory, instead, imagines that the game is played over and over again by biologically or socially conditioned players who are randomly drawn from large populations.[1] More specifically, each player is "pre-programmed" to some behavior—formally a strategy in the game—and one assumes that some evolutionary selection process operates over time on the population distribution of behaviors. What, if any, are the connections between the long-run aggregate behavior in such an evolutionary process and solution concepts in noncooperative game theory? More specifically: Are dominated strategies wiped out in the long run? Will aggregate behavior tend toward a Nash equilibrium of the game? Are some Nash equilibria more likely to emerge in this fashion than others? What is the nature of long-run aggregate behavior if it does not settle down on some equilibrium? These are the kinds of questions addressed in this book.

Similar questions have, of course, been raised in the domains of economics and biology. Market competition is usually thought to weed out firms that are not profit maximizers and to bring about the equilibrium outcomes predicted by economic theory. This is the basis for the so-called "as if" defense of economic theory, which claims that it is not important that managers think the way microeconomic theory says they do; what counts is whether they behave as if they did (Friedman 1953). Likewise natural selection is usually thought to result in animal behavior that is well adapted to the environment. In the simplest cases this environment is exogenously fixed, while in other cases the environment of an individual is itself composed of other individuals who are subject to the same forces of natural selection (this is also true for market selection). What is optimal for an individual or firm in such an interactive setting is endogenous in the sense of depending on the distribution of behaviors in the population with which the individual or firm interacts. Evolutionary game theory is designed to enable analysis of evolutionary selection in precisely such interactive environments.

---

1. In his unpublished Ph.D. dissertation (Nash 1950a) John Nash suggests a population-statistical interpretation of his equilibrium concept in which he imagines that players are randomly drawn from large populations, one for each player position in the game. These players were not assumed to "have full knowledge of the total structure of the game, or the ability and inclination to go through any complex reasoning process" (op. cit., p. 21); see Leonard (1994), Weibull (1994), and Björnerstedt and Weibull (1993).

Plan of the Book

Evolutionary game theory provides a tool kit of wide applicability. Its potential domain ranges from evolutionary biology to the social sciences in general and economics in particular. This book does not try to cover all the developments in the field, not even all the most important ones. Instead, it strives to give a self-contained treatment of a selected set of core elements, focused on conceptual and technical connections between evolutionary and noncooperative game theory.

Chapter 1 gives a concise introduction to noncooperative game theory. Notation, definitions, and results of relevance to the subsequent discussion are introduced, along with a number of examples that are used throughout the book. Chapters 2 through 4 deal with single-population evolutionary models of pairwise interactions represented as a symmetric two-player game. Chapter 2 considers a few static models, centered around the key concept of an evolutionarily stable stragegy. Chapter 3 focuses on a particular dynamic model of evolutionary selection in continuous time, the so-called replicator dynamics. Chapter 4 develops a few variations on the theme in chapter 3, including dynamic models of social evolution. Chapter 5 develops both static and dynamic models of multipopulation interactions represented as an n-player game. The dynamic models developed in chapters 3 through 5 use systems of ordinary differential equations to describe the evolution of aggregate behavior over time. Chapter 6 provides a concise introduction to the theory of ordinary differential equations. All chapters contain examples that illustrate the workings of the discussed methods.

The presentation of the material in many instances proceeds from the special to the general. Several themes first appear in simple examples, thereafter in specific but broader contexts, and finally in more general and abstract settings. It may annoy some mathematically well-versed readers to first see a claim proved in a special case and later in a more general case. However, it is hoped that this procedure will facilitate an operational "hands on," and not only abstract, understanding of the methods used.

The reader is assumed to have some familiarity with standard notions in mathematics (basic set theory, topology, and calculus) at about the level achieved after the first year of graduate studies in economics. Although chapter 1 provides the tools needed from noncooperative game theory, this treatment will most likely appear terse for a reader who is not acquainted with the basic ideas in noncooperative game theory. Also here the reader is presumed to have a knowledge at about the level achieved after first-year graduate studies in economics.

How to read the book, and how to use it in class? One obvious way is to read chapter 1, selected parts of chapter 2, make a short excursion into selected parts of chapter 6, and finally read selected parts of chapters 3 through 5. A shorter course could focus on parts of chapters 1, 2, 3, and 5 (e.g., sections 1.1–1.3, 1.5, 2.1–2.3, 3.1–3.3, 3.5, and 5.2).

To enable a self-contained and yet concise treatment, only deterministic models of games in normal form are discussed in this book, despite the fact that there now are a few promising evolutionary stochastic models and evolutionary models of extensive-form games. Each of these two extensions of the scope would require additional technical machinery. The reader who is interested in these and other developments in evolutionary game theory not covered here may consult the bibliography at the end of the book. For example, stochastic models are discussed in Foster and Young (1990), Kandori, Mailath, and Rob (1993), and Young (1993). Models of games in extensive form may be found in Selten (1983), van Damme (1987), and Nöldeke and Samuelson (1993) A number of other important contributions can be found in recent issues of economics and biology journals.

Acknowledgments

During the writing of this book I benefited greatly from conversations with colleagues and students. I am particularly grateful for comments on various drafts of the manuscript from Jonas Björnerstedt, Anette Bjørsted, Immanuel Bomze, Ross Cressman, Eric van Damme, Martin Dufwenberg, Josef Hofbauer, Oliver Kirchkamp, Johan Lindén, Oleg Malafeyev, Per Molander, Peter Norman, Jörg Oesschler, Klaus Ritzberger, Larry Samuelson, Karl Schlag, Björn Segendorff, Birgitte Sloth, Tony E. Smith, Joakim Sonnegård, Johan Stennek, David Strömberg, and Karl Wärneryd.

I would also like to thank Assar Lindbeck, Janos Kornai, and Lars E. O. Svensson for their moral and intellectual support during my transition from applied mathematics to economics, and for generously sharing their profound insights. Especially stimulating for the present project was a course I took many years back in dynamic modeling of ecological systems, taught by Ingemar Nåsell, as well as conversations I had with Janos Kornai, also a long time ago, about the evolution of firm behavior in markets with varying degrees of state intervention.

Terry Vaughn of The MIT Press was a great support during the preparation of the manuscript. Special thanks go to Dana Andrus of The MIT Press for her fine editing, and in Stockholm, Sweden, to Jonas Björnerstedt for all computer illustrations in the book, to Molly Åkerlund for her excellent help with page proofs, and to Karl Wärneryd for his contribution to the cover illustration.

I am grateful to the Industrial Institute for Economic and Social Research (IUI), Stockholm, for its sponsoring of part of the research behind this text.

Mathematical Notation

Lowercase letters are mostly used for real numbers, vectors of real numbers, and for functions, while capital letters usually signify matrices and sets. Euclidean spaces are typically denoted R^n, where n is a positive integer—the dimension of the space. The subset of vectors x in R^n that have all coordinates x_i nonnegative is denoted R^n_+, and the subset of vectors that have all coordinates positive is written R^n_{++}. The *inner* (or *scalar*) *product* of two vectors x and y in R^n is a real number (scalar) written $x \cdot y = \sum_{i=1}^n x_i y_i$. The euclidean *norm* (or length) of a vector $x \in R^n$ is denoted $\|x\| = \sqrt{x \cdot x}$, and the *distance* between two points (vectors) x and y in R^n is written $d(x, y) = \|x - y\|$. The transpose of an $n \times n$ matrix A is denoted A^T.

In this book $\subset$ denotes *weak* set inclusion. Hence $X \subset Y$ signifies that all elements of X are also elements of Y. The *complement* of a set $X \subset R^n$ is written $\sim X$. By a *neighborhood* of a point (vector) x in R^n is meant an open set $U \subset R^n$ containing x. The *interior* of a set $X \subset R^n$ is written $\text{int}(X)$; this is the subset of points x in X such that X also contains some neighborhood of x. The *boundary* of a set $X \subset R^n$ is written $\text{bd}(X)$; this is the set of points $y \in R^n$ such that every neighborhood of y contains some point from X and some point from $\sim X$. The *closure* of a set $X \subset R^n$ is denoted $\overline{X}$; this is the union of X and its boundary. A *function* f from a set X to a set Y is viewed as a rule that to each element x of X assigns precisely one element, $f(x)$, of Y. Likewise a *correspondence* φ from a set X to a set Y is a rule that to each element x of X assigns precisely one nonempty subset, $\varphi(x)$, of Y.

Evolutionary Game Theory

1 Elements of Noncooperative Game Theory

This chapter provides an introduction to the concepts and results in noncooperative game theory that will be used in the subsequent evolutionary analysis. The material in this chapter is organized as follows: In section 1.1 the structure of finite normal-form games is outlined. In particular, the geometry of strategy spaces and multilinearity of payoff functions is emphasized. Section 1.2 discusses dominance orderings of a player's strategy space and formalizes the notion of "best replies." Section 1.3 considers Nash equilibria as fixed points of the best-reply correspondence, and studies some properties of the set of Nash equilibria. Section 1.4 gives a brief account of some point- and setwise refinements of the Nash equilibrium concept. Section 1.5 introduces some special notation for, and properties of, symmetric two-player games; the basic setting in chapters 2 through 4. Many of the examples introduced in the chapter will be used later to illustrate evolutionary concepts.

The reader who wishes to have a fuller treatment of noncooperative game theory is advised to consult Fudenberg and Tirole (1991) or, for a more concise and technical treatment, van Damme (1987).

1.1 Strategies and Payoff Functions

The analysis in this book is restricted to *finite games in normal form*. More precisely, let $I = \{1, 2, \ldots, n\}$ be the set of *players*, where n is a positive integer. For each player $i \in I$, let S_i be her finite set of *pure strategies*. For notational convenience, we will label every player's pure strategies by positive integers. Hence the pure-strategy set of any player $i \in I$ is written $S_i = \{1, 2, \ldots, m_i\}$, for some integer $m_i \geq 2$. A vector s of pure strategies, $s = (s_1, s_2, \ldots, s_n)$, where s_i is a pure strategy for player i, is called a *pure-strategy profile*. The set of pure strategy profiles in the game is thus the cartesian product $S = \times_i S_i$ of the players' pure strategy sets, sometimes to be called the *pure-strategy space* of the game.

For any strategy profile $s \in S$ and player $i \in I$, let $\pi_i(s) \in R$ be the associated payoff to player i. In economics the payoffs are usually firms' profits or consumers' (von Neumann-Morgenstern) utility, while in biology payoffs usually represent individual fitness (expected number of surviving offspring). The finite collection of real numbers $\pi_i(s)$ defines the ith player's *(pure-strategy) payoff function* $\pi_i : S \to R$, for each player $i \in I$. The combined pure-strategy payoff function of the game, $\pi : S \to R^n$, assigns to each pure-strategy profile s the full vector $\pi(s) = (\pi_1(s), \ldots, \pi_n(s))$ of payoffs.

In terms of pure strategies, a game in normal form may be summarized as a triplet $G = (I, S, \pi)$, where I is its player set, S its pure-strategy space, and π its combined payoff function. In the special case when there are only two players, one may conveniently write each of the two payoff functions π_1 and π_2 in tabular form as an $m_1 \times m_2$ matrix. We will usually denote the first player's payoff matrix $A = (a_{hk})$, where $a_{hk} = \pi_1(h, k)$ for each $h \in S_1$ and $k \in S_2$, and will likewise denote the second player's payoff matrix $B = (b_{hk})$, where $b_{hk} = \pi_2(h, k)$. Each row in both matrices thus corresponds to a pure strategy for player 1, and each column to a pure strategy for player 2. Any two-player game can be fully represented by the associated payoff matrix pair (A, B), where player 1 is understood to be the "row player" and player 2 the "column player."

Example 1.1   The most widely known game is probably the Prisoner's Dilemma Game, a two-player game in which each player has only two pure strategies. A typical configuration of payoffs is given in the matrix pair

$$A = \begin{pmatrix} 4 & 0 \\ 5 & 3 \end{pmatrix}, \quad B = \begin{pmatrix} 4 & 5 \\ 0 & 3 \end{pmatrix}. \tag{1.1}$$

Evidently player 1's second pure strategy ("defect") gives a higher payoff than her first pure strategy ("cooperate"), irrespective of which strategy is used by player 2; each entry in the second row of matrix A exceeds the corresponding entry in the first row. Likewise player 2's second pure strategy always gives her a higher payoff than her first pure strategy; each entry in B's second column exceeds the corresponding entry of its first column. Hence individual rationality leads each player to select her second pure strategy (defect). The dilemma consists in the fact that both players would earn higher payoffs if they were to select their first pure strategy (cooperate).

1.1.1   The Geometry of Mixed-Strategy Spaces

A *mixed strategy* for player i is a probability distribution over her set S_i of pure strategies. Since for each player $i \in I$ the set S_i is finite, we can represent any mixed strategy x_i for player i as a *vector* x_i in m_i-dimensional euclidean space R^{m_i}, its hth coordinate $x_{ih} \in R$ being the probability assigned by x_i to the player's hth pure strategy.

The set of pure strategies that is assigned *positive* probabilities by some mixed strategy x_i is called the *support* (or *carrier*) of x_i, and it will be denoted

$$C(x_i) = \{h \in S_i : x_{ih} > 0\}. \tag{1.2}$$

Since all probabilities x_{ih} (for $h = 1, 2, \ldots, m_i$) are nonnegative and sum up to one, the vector $x \in R^{m_i}$ belongs to the *unit simplex* Δ_i in m_i-space, defined as

$$\Delta_i = \{x_i \in R_+^{m_i} : \sum_{h=1}^{m_i} x_{ih} = 1\}, \tag{1.3}$$

see figures 1.1 (a) and (b) for illustrations of the cases $m_i = 2$ and $m_i = 3$, respectively.

The mixed-strategy simplex Δ_i of player i has dimension $m_i - 1$ (one may write any one of the probabilities x_{ih} as 1 minus the other probabilities). Without loss of information we may thus instead study some *projection* of the simplex $\Delta_i \subset R^{m_i}$ to a euclidean space with dimension $m_i - 1$. Figures 1.2 (a) and (b) show projections in the cases $m_i = 2$ (to the x_{i1}-axis) and $m_i = 3$ (to the (x_{i1}, x_{i2})-plane), respectively.

The *vertices* (or *corners*) of the simplex Δ_i are the *unit vectors* in m_i-space, denoted $e_i^1 = (1, 0, 0, \ldots, 0)$, $e_i^2 = (0, 1, 0, \ldots, 0)$, $\ldots$, $e_i^{m_i} = (0, 0, 0, \ldots, 1)$. Each such vertex e_i^h represents the mixed strategy for player i which assigns probability one to her hth pure strategy. From this viewpoint pure strategies are just special, "extreme," mixed strategies.

The mixed-strategy simplex Δ_i is the *convex hull* of its vertices; every mixed strategy $x_i \in \Delta_i$ is some convex combination of the unit vectors, or pure strategies, e_i^h:

$$x_i = \sum_{h=1}^{m_i} x_{ih} e_i^h. \tag{1.4}$$

If a subset $X_i \subset \Delta_i$ is the convex hull of some nonempty subset of pure strategies (vertices of Δ_i), then X_i is called a *face* of Δ_i. In particular, $X_i = \Delta_i$ is a face, and so is each pure-strategy singleton $\{e_i^h\}$, for $h \in S_i$.

The subset

$$\text{int}(\Delta_i) = \{x_i \in \Delta_i : x_{ih} > 0 \ \forall h\} \tag{1.5}$$

(a)

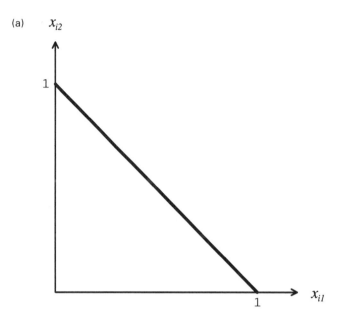

(b)

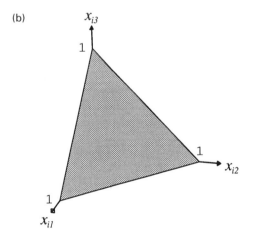

Figure 1.1
(a) The unit simplex Δ_i when $m_i = 2$. (b) The unit simplex Δ_i when $m_i = 3$.

(a)

(b) $x_{i\,2}$

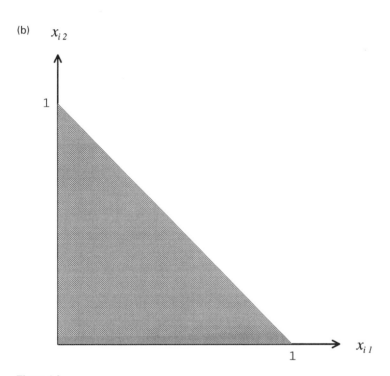

Figure 1.2
(a) Projection of the unit simplex Δ_i when $m_i = 2$. (b) Projection of Δ_i when $m_i = 3$.

is called the *(relative) interior* of Δ_i.[1] Accordingly the mixed strategies in this subset are called *interior* or *completely mixed*; they assign positive probabilities to *all* the player's pure strategies and so have full support, $C(x_i) = S_i$ for all $i \in I$. The set of noninterior strategies in Δ_i is called the *boundary* of Δ_i, denoted

$$\mathrm{bd}(\Delta_i) = \{x_i \in \Delta_i : x_i \notin \mathrm{int}(\Delta_i)\}. \tag{1.6}$$

---

1. The attribute "relative" is used here since Δ_i has an empty interior when viewed as a subset of R^{m_i} but a nonempty interior $\mathrm{int}(\Delta_i)$ when viewed as a subset of the hyperplane $H_i = \left\{x_i \in R^{m_i} : \sum_{h=1}^{m_i} x_i^h = 1\right\}$.

Note that the boundary of Δ_i is the set of strategies x_i for which the support $C(x_i)$ is a *proper* subset of the strategy set S_i. Alternatively one may view $bd(\Delta_i)$ as the union of boundary faces of Δ_i, where a *boundary* face is a face spanned by some *proper* subset of S_i. (Hence Δ_i is the only face that is not a boundary face.)

A *mixed-strategy profile* is a vector $x = (x_1, x_2, \ldots, x_n)$, where each component $x_i \in \Delta_i$ is a mixed strategy for player $i \in I$. A mixed strategy profile x is hence a point in the *mixed-strategy space*

$$\Theta = \times_{i \in I} \Delta_i \tag{1.7}$$

of the game. Being the cartesian product of the n unit simplexes Δ_i, one $(m_i - 1)$-dimensional set for each player $i \in I$, the set Θ is a $(m - n)$-dimensional *polyhedron* in R^m, where $m = m_1 + m_2 + \ldots + m_n$ is the total number of pure strategies in the game.[2] See figure 1.3 (a) for a two-dimensional projection of the two-dimensional polyhedron $\Theta \subset R^4$ in the case $n = 2$ and $m_1 = m_2 = 2$. Likewise figure 1.3 (b) shows a three-dimensional projection (projected to two dimensions on the page) of the three-dimensional polyhedron $\Theta \subset R^5$ in the case $n = 2$, $m_1 = 3$ and $m_2 = 2$.

A strategy profile x is called *interior* (or *completely mixed*) if each of its component strategies x_i is interior. The subset of such profiles is denoted

$$\text{int}(\Theta) = \times_{i \in I} \text{int}(\Delta_i). \tag{1.8}$$

Writing $C(x) = \times_{i \in I} C(x_i) \subset S$ for the support of any profile $x \in \Theta$: $x \in \text{int}(\Theta)$ if and only if $C(x) = S$. The boundary of Θ, $bd(\Theta)$, is the set of non-interior profiles $x \in \Theta$. A subset $X \subset \Theta$ is called a *face* of Θ if X is the cartesian product of faces of the players' simplexes. In particular, $X = \Theta$ is a face of Θ, its maximal face. All other faces of Θ are called *boundary* faces. In particular, each pure strategy profile, viewed as a singleton subset of Θ, is a boundary face. The union of boundary faces of Θ is identical with the set $bd(\Theta)$.

We will write (x_i, y_{-i}) for the strategy profile in which player $i \in I$ plays strategy $x_i \in \Delta_i$, while all other players j play according to the profile $y \in \Theta$. More precisely, the strategy profile $z = (x_i, y_{-i}) \in \Theta$ is defined by $z_i = x_i$, and $z_j = y_j$ for all $j \neq i$. This notation is particularly convenient when a single player i considers "deviations" $x_i \in \Delta_i$ from a given profile $y \in \Theta$.

---

2. $m - n > 0$, since, by hypothesis, each player has at least two pure strategies.

(a)

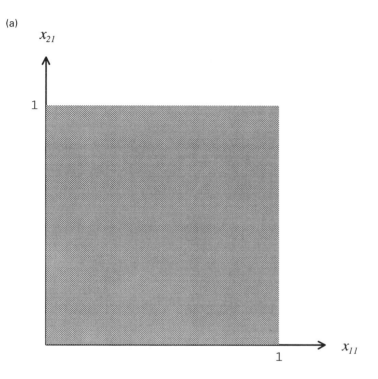

(b)

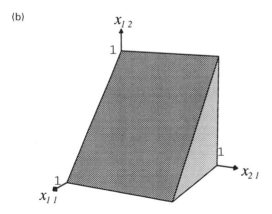

Figure 1.3
(a) Projection of the polyhedron Θ when $n = 2$ and $m_1 = m_2 = 2$. (b) Projection of Θ when $n = 2$, $m_1 = 3$, and $m_2 = 2$.

1.1.2 Mixed-Strategy Payoff Functions

In the standard approach of noncooperative game theory, to which we adhere in this book, all players' randomizations are statistically independent.[3] Hence the probability that a particular pure strategy profile $s = (s_1, \ldots, s_n) \in S$ will be used, when a mixed-strategy profile $x \in \Theta$ is played, is simply the associated *product*

$$x(s) = \prod_{i=1}^{n} x_{is_i} \tag{1.9}$$

of the probabilities assigned by each player's mixed strategy $x_i \in \Delta_i$ to her pure strategy $s_i \in S_i$. Consequently the (statistically) *expected value* of the payoff to player i associated with a mixed-strategy profile $x \in \Theta$ is

$$u_i(x) = \sum_{s \in S} x(s) \pi_i(s). \tag{1.10}$$

The real number $u_i(x)$ will simply be called the ith player's *payoff* from strategy profile x. Note that this payoff is a linear function of each player's mixed strategy (taken individually). To see this, first note that since playing a pure strategy $s_j = k \in S_j$ is probabilistically equivalent to playing the (extreme) mixed strategy $e_j^k \in \Delta_j$, we can write $u_i(e_j^k, x_{-j})$ for the payoff that player i obtains when player j uses her kth pure strategy. Hence for any $x \in \Theta$ and $i, j \in I$,

$$u_i(x) = \sum_{k=1}^{m_j} u_i(e_j^k, x_{-j}) x_{jk}. \tag{1.11}$$

In other words, the payoff $u_i(x)$ can be computed as the weighted sum of the payoffs that player i obtains for each of j's pure strategies (all other players' mixed strategies being fixed), where the weights are the probabilities assigned by player j in his mixed strategy to each of his pure strategies. Equation (1.11) shows that $u_i(x)$ is linear in $x_j \in \Delta_j$.

Furthermore equation (1.10) defines $u_i(x)$ as a real number for *all* vectors x in R^m, not only for those in the subset $\Theta \subset R^m$. Hence this equation defines u_i as a *multilinear* mapping, that is, linear in each vector component $x_j \in R^{m_j}$,

---

3. Otherwise, the resulting collective randomization is correlated; see, for example, Fudenberg and Tirole (1991) for definitions and examples along this line.

of R^m to R. This extended function $u_i : R^m \to R$ will be called the (mixed-strategy) *payoff function* of player i. The combined function $u : R^m \to R^n$, defined by $u(x) = (u_1(x), u_2(x), \dots, u_n(x))$, will accordingly be called the *combined mixed-strategy payoff function* of the game.

As an alternative to its pure-strategy representation $G = (I, S, \pi)$, one could sometimes more conveniently refer to its mixed-strategy extension (I, Θ, u), where Θ is the mixed-strategy space and u the combined mixed-strategy payoff function. In the special case of two-player games, one could, as noted above in the context of pure strategies, represent the game by the associated *payoff matrix pair* (A, B), where A (B) is the *payoff matrix* of player 1 (2). Hence for any pair of mixed strategies $x_1 \in \Delta_1$ and $x_2 \in \Delta_2$, we have

$$u_1(x) = \sum_{h=1}^{m_1} \sum_{k=1}^{m_2} x_{1h} a_{hk} x_{2k} = x_1 \cdot A x_2 \qquad (1.12)$$

and

$$u_2(x) = \sum_{h=1}^{m_1} \sum_{k=1}^{m_2} x_{1h} b_{hk} x_{2k} = x_1 \cdot B x_2 = x_2 \cdot B^T x_1, \qquad (1.13)$$

where the multiplication dot signifies the usual inner (scalar) product between vectors and the superscript T stands for matrix transposition. (This matrix representation brings out quite clearly the bilinearity of the players' payoff functions.) Representing a two-player game in this matrix format, player 1 chooses a row (a pure strategy) or a probability distribution over the rows (a mixed strategy), and player 2 likewise chooses a column (a pure strategy) or a probability distribution over the columns (a mixed strategy).

Example 1.2   The combined mixed-strategy payoff function $u : R^4 \to R^2$ in the Prisoner's Dilemma Game of example 1.1 is defined by equations (1.14) and (1.15) below. It is easily verified that the first player's payoff, $u_1(x)$, for any fixed strategy $x_2 \in \Delta_2$ of player 2, is maximized in Δ_1 at $x_1 = e_1^2$. Using the identity $x_{i1} + x_{i2} = 1$, one obtains $u_1(x) = (1 + 2x_{22}) x_{12} + 4x_{21}$, which is an increasing function of x_{12}.

$$u_1(x) = x_1 \cdot A x_2 = 4x_{11}x_{21} + x_{12} (5x_{21} + 3x_{22}), \qquad (1.14)$$

$$u_2(x) = x_1 \cdot B x_2 = x_{11} (4x_{21} + 5x_{22}) + 3x_{12}x_{22}. \qquad (1.15)$$

1.2   Dominance Relations and Best Replies

Noncooperative game theory uses two partial orderings of a player's (pure or mixed) strategy set, defined in terms of the payoff consequences for the player. Pure strategies being special cases of mixed strategies, we define these partial orderings on the mixed-strategy simplex Δ_i of each player i.

1.2.1   Weak, Strict, and Iterative Strict Dominance

A strategy is said to *weakly* dominate another strategy if the first strategy (1) never earns a lower payoff than the second and (2) sometimes earns a higher payoff. A strategy is called *undominated* if no strategy weakly dominates it. Formally

Definition 1.1 $y_i \in \Delta_i$ weakly dominates $x_i \in \Delta_i$ if $u_i(y_i, z_{-i}) \geq u_i(x_i, z_{-i})$ *for all* $z \in \Theta$, *with strict inequality for some* $z \in \Theta$. *A strategy* x_i *is* undominated *if no such strategy* y_i *exists.*

Likewise a strategy is said to *strictly* dominate another strategy if it always earns a higher payoff:

Definition 1.2 $y_i \in \Delta_i$ strictly dominates $x_i \in \Delta_i$ *if* $u_i(y_i, z_{-i}) > u_i(x_i, z_{-i})$ *for all* $z \in \Theta$.

For instance, the second pure strategy (*defect*) in the Prisoner's Dilemma Game of example 1.1 strictly dominates the first pure strategy (*cooperate*) for each player position $i = 1, 2$. Since these are the only pure strategies available, $x_i = e_i^2$ strictly dominates all strategies $y_i \neq x_i$. The following example illustrates the possibility that a pure strategy is strictly dominated by a mixed strategy without being dominated by any pure strategy.

Example 1.3   Consider a two-player game with payoff matrix for player 1 as in (1.16) below. Player 1 thus has three pure strategies. Her third pure strategy, $x_1 = e_1^3$, is not weakly dominated by any of her other two pure strategies. However, she always obtains a higher payoff by randomizing uniformly over the other pure strategies. Formally, let $y_1 = (\frac{1}{2}, \frac{1}{2}, 0) \in \Delta_1$. Then $1 = u_1(x_1, z_2) < u_1(y_1, z_2) = \frac{3}{2}$ for all $z_2 \in \Delta_2$, so y_1 strictly dominates x_1.

$$A = \begin{pmatrix} 3 & 0 \\ 0 & 3 \\ 1 & 1 \end{pmatrix} . \tag{1.16}$$

A basic rationality postulate in noncooperative game theory is that "rational" players never use strictly dominated strategies.[4] In this case all strictly dominated *pure* strategies may be deleted from the game without affecting the outcome. But once this is done, some remaining pure strategies may be strictly dominated in the new, reduced game. Iteratively repeated removal of strictly dominated pure strategies in a game G leads to the following definition: A pure strategy $s_i \in S_i$ is *not iteratively strictly dominated* if it is not strictly dominated in the original game G, nor in the reduced game G^1 obtained from G by deletion of (some or all) strictly dominated strategies, nor in the further reduced game G^2 obtained from G^1 by deletion of strictly dominated strategies in G^1, and so on, until no more strategies can be so eliminated (i.e., until $G^{t+1} = G^t$ for some positive integer t). Since there are finitely many players and pure strategies, this procedure of iterated elimination always stops after a finite number of rounds, and it can be shown that the remaining set of strategies (one nonempty such set for each player) is independent of the details of the elimination procedure.[5]

For any (finite normal-form) game $G = (I, S, \pi)$, let $S^D \subset S$ be its (nonempty) subset of not iteratively strictly dominated pure-strategy profiles. If this set is a singleton (has precisely one element), then the game is called *strictly dominance solvable*. For instance, the Prisoner's Dilemma Game in example 1.1 is strictly dominance solvable in this sense.

Example 1.4 The payoff matrix pair in equation (1.17) below represents another strictly dominance solvable game. Pure strategy 2 is strictly dominated by pure strategy 1 (as well as by strategy 3) for each of the two players. Once strategy 2 has been removed from each player's strategy set, strategy 1 strictly dominates strategy 3 for both players. Hence only the pure strategy profile $s = (1, 1)$ remains: $S^D = \{(1, 1)\}$,

$$A = \begin{pmatrix} 3 & 1 & 6 \\ 0 & 0 & 4 \\ 1 & 2 & 5 \end{pmatrix}, \quad B = \begin{pmatrix} 3 & 0 & 1 \\ 1 & 0 & 2 \\ 6 & 4 & 5 \end{pmatrix}. \tag{1.17}$$

---

4. Some authors even argue that "rational" players never use a weakly dominated strategy (e.g., see Kohlberg and Mertens 1986).

5. More precisely, the end result is independent of whether only some or all dominated strategies are eliminated in each round; see, for example, Fudenberg and Tirole (1991) for details.

The postulate that no player ever uses a strictly dominated strategy is a relatively weak rationality assumption. For it only requires that each player's (pure-strategy) payoff function indeed represents her preferences. In particular, no knowledge on behalf of the player about *other* players' preferences or behavior is required. In contrast, an application of the criterion of *iterative* elimination of strictly dominated strategies requires, in addition, that the players know each others' payoff functions—so that they can eliminate each others' strictly dominated strategies. Moreover this *knowledge* of preferences has to be known to all players—so that they can eliminate others' strategies which are strictly dominated in the reduced game after one round of deletion of strictly dominated strategies, and so on, up to the level t of mutual knowledge where further iteration does not eliminate any more strategies.[6]

1.2.2   Best Replies

A *pure* best reply for player i to a strategy profile $y \in \Theta$ is a pure strategy $s_i \in S_i$ such that no other pure strategy available to the player gives her a higher payoff against y. This defines the ith player's *pure-strategy best-reply correspondence* $\beta_i : \Theta \to S_i$ which maps each mixed-strategy profile $y \in \Theta$ to the nonempty (finite) set

$$\beta_i(y) = \{h \in S_i : u_i(e_i^h, y_{-i}) \geq u_i(e_i^k, y_{-i}) \ \ \forall k \in S_i\} \tag{1.18}$$

of pure best replies for player i to y. For instance, the third pure strategy in example 1.3 above is not a best reply to any strategy profile.

Since every mixed strategy $x_i \in \Delta_i$ is a convex combination of pure strategies, and $u_i(x_i, y_{-i})$ is linear in x_i, no mixed strategy $x_i \in \Delta_i$ can give a higher payoff to player i against $y \in \Theta$ than any one of her pure best replies to y. Formally, for any $y \in \Theta$, $x_i \in \Delta_i$, and $h \in \beta_i(y)$,

$$u_i(x_i, y_{-i}) = \sum_{k=1}^{m_i} u_i(e_i^k, y_{-i}) x_{ik} \leq \sum_{k=1}^{m_i} u_i(e_i^h, y_{-i}) x_{ik} = u_i(e_i^h, y_{-i}). \tag{1.19}$$

Hence

$$\beta_i(y) = \{h \in S_i : u_i(e_i^h, y_{-i}) \geq u_i(x_i, y_{-i}) \ \ \forall x_i \in \Delta_i\}. \tag{1.20}$$

---

6. It is here implicitly assumed that *knowledge* of another player's payoff function implies that this function indeed represents the other player's preferences.

A *mixed best reply* for player i to a strategy profile $y \in \Theta$ is a strategy $x_i \in \Delta_i$ such that no other mixed strategy gives a higher payoff to i against y. As noted above, every pure best reply viewed as a mixed strategy is also a mixed best reply. Moreover, by linearity of $u_i(x_i, y_{-i})$ in x_i, any convex combination of pure best replies is a mixed best reply. Accordingly the ith player's *mixed-strategy best-reply correspondence* $\tilde{\beta}_i : \Theta \to \Delta_i$ maps each mixed-strategy profile $y \in \Theta$ to the face of Δ_i which is spanned by the pure best replies to y:

$$\tilde{\beta}_i(y) = \{x_i \in \Delta_i : u_i(x_i, y_{-i}) \geq u_i(z_i, y_{-i}) \ \forall z_i \in \Delta_i\}$$
$$= \{x_i \in \Delta_i : x_{ih} = 0 \ \forall h \notin \beta_i(y)\} = \{x_i \in \Delta_i : C(x_i) \subset \beta_i(y)\} \tag{1.21}$$

Being a face of Δ_i, the best-reply set $\tilde{\beta}_i(y) \subset \Delta_i$, to a single-strategy profile $y \in \Theta$ is always nonempty, closed, and convex (ranging from a singleton in case there is only one pure best reply, for player i, to the whole simplex in case all pure strategies in S_i are best replies).

The *combined pure-strategy, best-reply correspondence* $\beta : \Theta \to S$ of the game is defined as the cartesian product of all players' pure-strategy best-reply correspondences,

$$\beta(y) = \times_{i \in I} \beta_i(y) \subset S, \tag{1.22}$$

and the combined correspondence $\tilde{\beta} : \Theta \to \Theta$ is likewise defined by

$$\tilde{\beta}(y) = \times_{i \in I} \tilde{\beta}_i(y) \subset \Theta. \tag{1.23}$$

1.2.3 Dominance versus Best Replies

A pure strategy that is a best reply to some mixed-strategy profile cannot, of course, be strictly dominated. Pearce (1984) showed that the converse holds in any *two*-player game: A pure strategy that is not strictly dominated in such a game is necessarily a best reply to some mixed-strategy profile. Likewise a pure strategy that is a best reply to some *completely* mixed-strategy profile is undominated. Pearce (1984) showed that in any *two*-player game, the converse also to this holds: An undominated pure strategy is then a best reply to some completely mixed strategy profile. Neither of these two converses are generally valid in games with more than two players.

Proposition 1.1 *Consider any two-player game. $s_i \in S_i$ is not strictly dom-inated if and only if $s_i \in \beta_i(y)$ for some $y \in \Theta$. $s_i \in S_i$ is undominated if and only if $s_i \in \beta_i(y)$ for some $y \in \mathrm{int}(\Theta)$.*

(For a proof, see Pearce 1984 or Fudenberg and Tirole 1991.)

1.3 Nash Equilibrium

One of the cornerstones of economic theory, underlying most of modern eco-nomics, is the notion of Nash equilibrium (Nash 1950a, b, 1951). In essence Nash equilibrium requires of a strategy profile $x \in \Theta$ that not only should each component strategy x_i be optimal under *some* belief on behalf of the ith player about the others' strategies, it should be optimal under the belief that x itself will be played.

1.3.1 Definition

Phrased in terms of best replies, a strategy profile $x \in \Theta$ is a *Nash equilibrium* if it is a best reply to itself, namely if it is a fixed point of the mixed-strategy best-reply correspondence $\tilde{\beta}$:

Definition 1.3 $x \in \Theta$ *is a* Nash equilibrium *if $x \in \tilde{\beta}(x)$.*

It follows from (1.21) that if $x \in \Theta$ is a Nash equilibrium, then every pure strategy in the support of each component x_i is a best reply to x: $s_i \in C(x_i) \Rightarrow s_i \in \beta_i(x)$.

Example 1.5 A (children's) game that has no Nash equilibrium in pure strategies but one in mixed strategies is the Matching Pennies Game.[7] This is a zero-sum two-player game in which each player has only two pure strategies, as given in the payoff matrices in (1.24) below. Inspection of these matri-ces shows that the game has no Nash equilibrium in pure strategies: At each pure-strategy profile exactly one of the players wants to change her strategy. However, for any player to be willing to randomize, the other player must play both his pure strategies with equal probability. Hence the unique Nash equilib-rium is x, where $x_1 = x_2 = (\frac{1}{2}, \frac{1}{2})$. Indeed this profile x is a fixed point under $\tilde{\beta}$: $x_i \in \tilde{\beta}_i(x) = \Delta$ for $i = 1, 2$ (Δ is the unit simplex in R^2).

---

7. Two children, holding a penny apiece, independently choose which side of their coin to show. Child 1 wins if both coins show the same side; otherwise, child 2 wins.

$$A = \begin{pmatrix} 1 & -1 \\ -1 & 1 \end{pmatrix}, \quad B = \begin{pmatrix} -1 & 1 \\ 1 & -1 \end{pmatrix}. \tag{1.24}$$

A Nash equilibrium $x \in \Theta$ is called *strict* if each component strategy x_i is the *unique* best reply to x, that is, if $\tilde{\beta}(x) = \{x\}$. In other words, while the Nash equilibrium criterion requires that no unilateral deviation should be profitable, strict Nash equilibrium requires that all such deviations be costly. A strict equilibrium can thus not involve any randomization at all; since then there would exist some player for whom at least two pure strategies give the same maximal payoff to her. Thus every strict equilibrium is a pure-strategy profile (a vertex of the polyhedron Θ). For instance, in the Prisoner's Dilemma Game of example 1.1, the pure-strategy profile $s = (2, 2)$ is a strict Nash equilibrium.

A Nash equilibrium strategy cannot be *strictly* dominated. However, there is nothing in the definition that prevents a Nash equilibrium strategy from being weakly dominated—there may be another best reply (to the equilibrium profile) that is never (i.e., against no other strategy profile) worse than the equilibrium strategy in question and that does better against some other strategy profile. A Nash equilibrium x is called *undominated* if every component strategy x_i is undominated.

1.3.2   Structure of the Set of Nash Equilibria

The existence of Nash equilibrium was first established by Nash (1950b). For any given game, let $\Theta^{NE} \subset \Theta$ denote its set of Nash equilibria:

Theorem 1.1   *For any finite game G: $\Theta^{NE} \neq \emptyset$.*

Proof   The polyhedron Θ is nonempty, convex, and compact. It is well known that the best-reply correspondence $\tilde{\beta} : \Theta \rightarrow \Theta$ is upper hemi-continuous, and we have seen that the image $\tilde{\beta}(x) \subset \Theta$ of every profile $x \in \Theta$ is a nonempty, convex, and closed set.[8] Hence $\tilde{\beta}$ and Θ meet the hypotheses in Kakutani's fixed-point theorem, and $x \in \tilde{\beta}(x)$ for at least one $x \in \Theta$.   ■

For certain analyses it is useful to note that the *set* of Nash equilibria can be rewritten as those mixed-strategy profiles which meet certain inequalities:

---

8. *Upper hemi-continuity* of a correspondence $\varphi : X \rightarrow Y$ at a point $x \in X$ means that for every open set V containing the image $\varphi(x) \subset Y$, there exists an open set U containing x such that $\varphi(x') \subset V$ for all $x' \in U$. $\tilde{\beta}$ has this property by virtue of the continuity of the payoff function u. Indeed this is an immediate implication of Berge's maximum theorem.

$$\Theta^{NE} = \left\{ x \in \Theta : u_i(x) - u_i(e_i^h, x_{-i}) \geq 0 \ \ \forall i \in I, \ h \in S_i \right\}. \tag{1.25}$$

Each function in the defining inequality is a polynomial, and the number of such polynomial inequalities is finite (there are m inequalities). Consider any polynomial of one variable. It is intuitively clear that the set on which it is non-negative is the union of finitely many intervals (draw a picture!). The set on the right-hand side in (1.25) is the intersection of finitely many such nonnegativity sets for polynomials in the vector variable x. It follows from a classical result in algebraic geometry that such a set consists of finitely many disjoint, closed, and connected sets. These are usually called the Nash equilibrium *components* of the game (Kohlberg and Mertens 1986):

Proposition 1.2 *The set Θ^{NE} is the finite union of disjoint, closed, and connected sets.*

Viewed as a singleton set, a strict Nash equilibrium is such a component. However, many games lack strict Nash equilibria and, indeed, singleton components. In particular, any Nash equilibrium that does not reach all the information sets in an extensive-form representation of the game is nonstrict. For a player at an unreached information set may change her local strategy there without affecting her own payoff. Hence she has multiple best replies to the profile in question. Moreover, if all payoffs at the end nodes of the extensive form differ, then sufficiently small such local unilateral deviations off the equilibrium path do not affect the best replies of the other players. Hence the equilibrium then belongs to a whole continuum of Nash equilibria, namely a nonsingleton component of Θ^{NE}. Kreps and Wilson (1982) have shown that for such generic payoffs in an extensive-form game, all players' payoff functions are constant on each component Θ^{NE}.[9]

Example 1.6 Consider the two-player *Entry Deterrence Game* given in extensive form in figure 1.4 (a). (This is equivalent to the stage game in the Chain-Store Game in Selten 1978.) Player 1 can be thought of as a potential competitor in 2's market (or territory). Player 2 (the monopolist) wants player 1 (the competitor) to stay out; then 2 earns his highest possible payoff (4). If, however, player 1 enters, then 2 has two choices: either to yield (share the market or territory) or to fight. The normal form of this game is given by the

---

9. The *extensive form* of a game was developed in Kuhn (1953). See, for example, Kreps and Wilson (1982), Fudenberg and Tirole (1991), or van Damme (1987) for formal treatments.

payoff matrix pair

$$A = \begin{pmatrix} 2 & 0 \\ 1 & 1 \end{pmatrix}, \quad B = \begin{pmatrix} 2 & 0 \\ 4 & 4 \end{pmatrix}.$$

Letting x_{11} denote the probability that the first player enters (E) and x_{21} the probability that the second player yields (Y), the set Θ^{NE} of Nash equilibria consists of two components, the singleton component $C = \{(e_1^1, e_2^1)\}$, where player 1 enters and player 2 yields, and the continuum component

$$C' = \left\{ x \in \Theta : x_{11} = 0, \ x_{21} \leq \frac{1}{2} \right\},$$

where player 1 stays out, and player 2 is more likely to fight than yield in case of entry; see figure 1.4 (b). The unique subgame perfect equilibrium of this game is that the competitor does enter, and the monopolist yields. The Nash equilibrium threat of the latter to fight is not credible; it is suboptimal for the monopolist to execute this threat in case of entry. Note also that the pure strategy "fight" is weakly dominated by the pure strategy "yield."

1.3.3   Invariance of the Set of Nash Equilibria

For the subsequent analysis it will be convenient to use certain invariance properties of the set Θ^{NE} of Nash equilibria with respect to changes in payoffs. By force of these invariance properties, computations may be considerably simplified, and apparently different games will be seen to have the same best-reply correspondences and dominance relations.

First, any two games $G = (I, S, \pi)$ and $G' = (I, S, \pi')$ that differ only by some *positive affine transformation* of each player's payoff function are clearly equivalent from this viewpoint. If, for each player $i \in I$, there exists some positive real number λ_i and real number μ_i such that $\pi_i'(s) = \lambda_i \pi_i(s) + \mu_i$ for all profiles $s \in S$, then the two games have the same best-reply correspondences and dominance relations between strategies. In particular, the set Θ^{NE} of Nash equilibria is invariant under such transformations of payoffs.

Second, best-reply sets and dominance orderings are also unaffected by addition of one and the same constant to *all* those payoffs to some player i that are associated with any *fixed* pure combination s_{-i} for the other players. To be more precise, let $i \in I$, $\bar{s}_{-i} \in \times_{j \neq i} S_j$ and $v_i \in R$; define $\pi_i' : S \rightarrow R$ by $\pi_i'(s) = \pi_i(s) + v_i$ if $s_{-i} = \bar{s}_{-i}$ and $\pi_i'(s) = \pi_i(s)$ otherwise; and let $u_i' : R^m \rightarrow R$ be the mixed-strategy payoff function associated with π_i'. Then

(a)

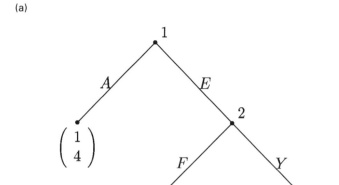

(b)

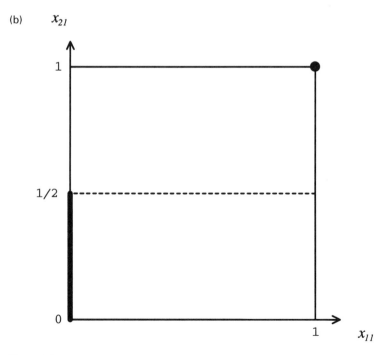

Figure 1.4
(a) The extensive form of the Entry Deterrence Game in example 1.6. (b) The two components of Θ^{NE} in this game.

$$u'_i(x_i, y_{-i}) - u'_i(z_i, y_{-i}) = u_i(x_i, y_{-i}) - u_i(z_i, y_{-i}) \qquad (1.26)$$

for all profiles $y \in \Theta$ and strategies $x_i, z_i \in \Delta_i$ for player i. Hence, whenever player i compares any two of her pure or mixed strategies, she will arrive at the same payoff *difference*, irrespective of the constant v_i and of the other players' strategies. Her pure and mixed best-reply correspondences, as well as her weak and strict dominance orderings, are unaffected by any such *local shift* v_i of her pure-strategy payoff function π_i. In particular, the set Θ^{NE} of Nash equilibria is invariant.[10]

The two types of transformation of payoff functions are particularly useful in two-player games. Let the payoff matrices of such a game be (A, B). A positive affine transformation of player 1's payoff function then simply is a substitution of matrix A by some matrix A' such that $a'_{hk} = \lambda_1 a_{hk} + \mu_1$ for some $\lambda_1 \in R_{++}$ and $\mu_1 \in R$. Player 1 being the "row player," a local shift of her payoff function corresponds to a substitution of matrix A by some matrix A' such that all entries in one column of A' differ by one and the same constant $v_1 \in R$ from the corresponding entries in the same column of A. Formally $a'_{hk*} = a_{hk*} + v_1$ for all h, and $a'_{hk} = a_{hk}$ for all h and all $k \neq k*$. Since player 2 chooses column, a local shift of his payoff function corresponds to the same kind of additive operation performed on a *row* in payoff matrix B.

Example 1.7 Reconsider the Entry Deterrence Game of example 1.6. Subtraction of 1 payoff unit from each entry in column 1 of payoff matrix A keeps 1's best-reply correspondence unchanged. Likewise subtraction of 4 payoff units in each entry in row 2 of payoff matrix B keeps 2's best-reply correspondence unchanged. These local shifts in payoffs result in payoff matrices A' and B' below. Moreover we can divide all entries in B' by 2 without affecting 2's best replies (this being a positive affine transformation) and so obtain a matrix pair (A', B'') with only zeros and ones. The set of Nash equilibria is unaffected, but calculations are simplified.[11]

$$A' = \begin{pmatrix} 1 & 0 \\ 0 & 1 \end{pmatrix}, \quad B' = \begin{pmatrix} 2 & 0 \\ 0 & 0 \end{pmatrix}, \quad B'' = \begin{pmatrix} 1 & 0 \\ 0 & 0 \end{pmatrix}.$$

---

10. The decision-theoretic irrelevance of what we here call local shifts of utilities was observed already by Savage (1954) in the context of single-person decision theory.

11. Note, however, that these transformations break the connection with the original extensive form in figure 1.4 (a).

1.4   Refinements of Nash Equilibrium

Since the late 1970s there has been a flurry of refinements of the Nash equilibrium concept, each refinement being motivated by the desire to get rid of certain implausible or fragile Nash equilibria (see van Damme 1987 for an excellent account of this research field). Here only a few normal-form refinements will be defined and briefly discussed, refinements that turn out to be related to certain evolutionary criteria.

1.4.1   Perfection

The probably most well-known noncooperative refinement is that of *"trembling hand" perfection*, due to Selten (1975). As the name suggests, this refinement discards Nash equilibria that are not robust to trembles in the players' strategies.

Let the game in question be $G = (I, \Theta, u)$, and let μ be an *error function* that to each player i and pure strategy $h \in S_i$ assigns a number $\mu_{ih} \in (0, 1)$, the probability that the strategy will be played "by mistake," where $\sum_h \mu_{ih} < 1$. Such an error function μ defines for each player $i \in I$ the subset $\Delta_i(\mu) = \{x \in \Delta_i : x_{ih} \geq \mu_{ih}\} \subset \text{int}(\Delta_i)$ of mixed strategies that the player can implement, given the error probabilities. The associated *perturbed game* is $G(\mu) = (I, \Theta(\mu), u)$, where $\Theta(\mu) = \times_{i=1}^n \Delta_i(\mu) \subset \text{int}(\Theta)$. By standard arguments every such perturbed game $G(\mu)$ has a nonempty set $\Theta^{NE}(\mu)$ of Nash equilibria. The smaller all error probabilities are, the larger is $\Theta(\mu)$, and as all error probabilities go to zero, written $\mu \to 0$, the associated perturbed game $G(\mu)$ approaches the original game.

Definition 1.4 $x \in \Theta^{NE}$ *is perfect if, for some sequence* $\{G(\mu^t)\}_{\mu^t \to 0}$ *of perturbed games there exist profiles* $x^t \in \Theta^{NE}(\mu^t)$ *such that* $x^t \to x$.

In particular, every interior Nash equilibrium is perfect. If $x \in \text{int}(\Theta)$, then for sufficiently small error probabilities μ_{ih}, $x \in \Theta(\mu)$. If moreover $x \in \Theta^{NE}$, then $x \in \Theta^{NE}(\mu)$.

Since it is sufficient that the Nash equilibrium in question be robust with respect to *some* low-probability trembles, existence is not difficult to establish even if there are no interior Nash equilibria (Selten 1975). Write Θ^{PE} for the set of perfect Nash equilibria:

Proposition 1.3   *For any (finite) game:* $\Theta^{PE} \neq \emptyset$.

Proof   For any sequence $\left\{G(\mu^t)\right\}_{\mu^t \to 0}$, let $x^t \in \Theta^{NE}(\mu^t)$ for each t. Since $\left\{x^t\right\}_{t=1}^{\infty}$ is a sequence from the compact set Θ, it has a convergent subsequence $\left\{y^s\right\}_{s=1}^{\infty}$, with limit $x^* \in \Theta$. For each s, $G(\mu^s)$ is the accompanying perturbed game. By standard continuity arguments, $x^* \in \Theta^{NE}$, and x^* is perfect since $y^s \to x^*$ and $y^s \in \Theta^{NE}(\mu^s)$ for all s. ∎

Selten (1975) shows that a Nash equilibrium profile x is perfect if and only if there in every neighborhood of x exists some *interior* strategy profile y to which x is a best reply. In other words, the players should be willing to play their equilibrium strategies x_i even if they are a bit uncertain about each other's strategies and hence ascribe (small) positive probabilities to *all* pure strategies in the game. It can also be shown that a perfect Nash equilibrium cannot be dominated, and that the converse holds if there are only two players in the game (van Damme 1987):

Proposition 1.4   *Every $x \in \Theta^{PE}$ is undominated. If $x \in \Theta^{NE}$ is undominated, in a two-player game, then $x \in \Theta^{PE}$.*

(For a proof, see van Damme 1987.)

1.4.2   Properness

The above perfection criterion requires robustness only with respect to *some* trembles, without imposing any condition that these trembles be reasonable in any sense. Myerson (1978) suggested an alternative robustness criterion that is more stringent in this respect. The idea is to require robustness with respect to some trembles that are such that more costly mistakes are less probable than less costly ones. Hence there is an element of rationality in the "mistake technology"; it is as if the players alerted themselves more against more damaging mistakes than against less damaging mistakes.

Given some $\epsilon > 0$, a strategy profile $y \in \text{int}(\Theta)$ is ϵ-proper if

$$u_i\left(e_i^h, y_{-i}\right) < u_i\left(e_i^k, y_{-i}\right) \Rightarrow y_{ih} \leq \epsilon y_{ik}. \tag{1.27}$$

Any interior Nash equilibrium $y \in \Theta^{NE}$ is clearly ϵ-proper for any $\epsilon > 0$, since then all pure strategies, for each player i, earn the same (maximal) payoff against y.

Definition 1.5 $x \in \Theta^{NE}$ is proper *if, for some sequence $\epsilon^t \to 0$, there exist ϵ^t-proper profiles $y(\epsilon^t)$ such that $y(\epsilon^t) \to x$.*

Evidently every interior Nash equilibrium x is proper; just let $y(\epsilon^t) = x$ for all t. Myerson (1978) showed that proper equilibria always exist and that every proper Nash equilibrium is perfect.

In many applications of noncooperative game theory, one may draw an extensive-form representation in which the sequence of moves and the dynamic information structure is explicit. Widely used solution concepts for extensive form games are Selten's (1975) *extensive-form (trembling hand) perfection* criterion, and, in particular, the closely related concept of _sequential equilibrium_ due to Kreps and Wilson (1982). Both solution concepts are refinements of Selten's (1965) *subgame perfection* criterion, which, in its turn, is an extensive-form refinement of the Nash equilibrium concept. As shown in van Damme (1984) and Kohlberg and Mertens (1986), any proper equilibrium in a normal-form game induces a *sequential equilibrium* in any extensive form with that normal form.

1.4.3 Strict Perfection

It may not always be clear which trembles should be deemed reasonable. What happens if one goes all the way, and asks for robustness with respect to *all* (low probability) trembles? This stringent robustness criterion was suggested by Okada (1981). In the notation of perfect equilibrium:

Definition 1.6 $x \in \Theta^{NE}$ is strictly perfect *if, for every sequence $\left\{G(\mu^t)\right\}_{\mu^t \to 0}$ of perturbed games there exist profiles $x^t \in \Theta^{NE}(\mu^t)$ such that $x^t \to x$.*

Just as in the case of perfection and properness, every interior Nash equilibrium x is strictly perfect; just let $x^t = x$ for all t sufficiently large (such that $x \in \Theta^{NE}(\mu^t)$). One can also show that every strict Nash equilibrium is strictly perfect, that a unique Nash equilibrium is strictly perfect, and that every strictly perfect equilibrium is proper (Okada 1981). The following example shows that some games have no strictly perfect equilibrium.

Example 1.8 Consider the game given by the payoff bi-matrix (A, B) below, where $\alpha, \beta > 0$. (A similar example is given in van Damme 1987.) The unique best reply for player 2, to *any* strategy used by player 1, is 2's first pure strategy. When player 2 uses this strategy (i.e., $x_{21} = 1$), player 1 is indifferent between her two pure strategies. Hence the set Θ^{NE} of Nash equilibria consists of the single component $\{x \in \Theta : x_{21} = 1\}$, see figure 1.5 below. All of these Nash equilibria are perfect. However, none is strictly perfect; any $x \in \Theta^{NE}$ is vulnerable to *some* sequence of trembles.

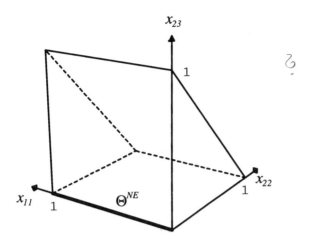

Figure 1.5
The set Θ^{NE} in the game of example 1.8.

$$A = \begin{pmatrix} 0 & \alpha & 0 \\ 0 & 0 & \alpha \end{pmatrix}, \quad B = \begin{pmatrix} \beta & 0 & 0 \\ \beta & 0 & 0 \end{pmatrix}. \qquad (1.28)$$

1.4.4   Essentiality

Apart from the weak dominance criterion, the earliest refinement of the Nash equilibrium concept seems to be the notion of an *essential* Nash equilibrium, due to Wu and Jiang (1962).[12] The idea is to discard Nash equilibria that are not robust with respect to perturbations of the players' *payoffs*. More precisely, this is done by defining "distance" between games that have the same player set I and pure-strategy space S but differing pure-strategy payoffs, and then requiring that *all* nearby games have some nearby Nash equilibrium.

Formally, let the game under scrutiny be $G = (I, S, \pi)$, and consider some game $G' = (I, S, \pi')$. Define the *payoff distance* between games G and G', as the maximal payoff difference between them: $d(G, G') = \max_{i \in I, s \in S} | \pi_i(s) - \pi_i'(s) |.$[13]

---

12. This is an application of a robustness criterion for fixed points of continuous functions, due to Fort (1950).

13. It is immaterial which metric is used here, since there are finitely many pure strategies.

Definition 1.7 $x \in \Theta^{NE}$ is essential *if for every $\varepsilon > 0$ there exists a $\delta > 0$ such that every game G' within payoff distance δ from G has a Nash equilibrium within distance ε from x.*

Unlike the other refinements, this is not met by all interior Nash equilibria. For instance, in a trivial game with all payoffs equal, *all* strategy profiles are Nash equilibria, but none is essential, since for every profile $x \in \Theta$ there exists *some* slight change in payoffs that makes no nearby profile a best reply to itself. One can show that every essential equilibrium is strictly perfect (e.g., see van Damme 1987).

1.4.5   Setwise Refinements

While some games have no equilibrium that is strictly perfect, as in example 1.8, and thus no essential equilibrium, there always exist sets of Nash equilibria that are robust, as sets, with respect to all small trembles in strategies and all small changes in payoffs, respectively.

The following setwise version of strict perfection is due to Kohlberg and Mertens (1986):

Definition 1.8 $X \subset \Theta^{NE}$ is strategically stable *if it is minimal with respect to the following property: X is nonempty and closed, and for every $\epsilon > 0$ there is some $\delta > 0$ such that every strategy-perturbed game $G(\mu) = (I, \Theta(\mu), u)$ with errors $\mu_{ih} < \delta$ has some Nash equilibrium within distance ϵ from the set X.*

Minimality here means that the set should not contain any proper subset with the stated robustness property. It can be shown that this minimality requirement implies that Nash equilibria that are not robust to *any* sequence of small trembles have to be excluded. In other words, a strategically stable set consists of perfect Nash equilibria (van Damme 1987).

Similarly one can turn the definition of essentiality set valued as follows:

Definition 1.9   *A nonempty closed set $X \subset \Theta^{NE}$ is essential if for every $\varepsilon > 0$ there exists a $\delta > 0$ such that every game G' within payoff distance δ from G has a Nash equilibrium within distance ε from X.*

Kohlberg and Mertens (1986) show that in every (finite) game, at least one of the components of the set Θ^{NE} of Nash equilibria is essential (see also Jiang 1963). Moreover such a component always contains a strategically stable subset.

Example 1.9   The set of Nash equilibria in example 1.8 was seen to be a single component. Thus the set $X = \Theta^{NE}$ is essential and contains a strategically stable subset Y. For such a subset Y to be robust against *all* trembles in strategies, Y has to contain both end points of Θ^{NE}. Indeed the union of these two points is robust in this sense, so $Y = \left\{ \left(e_1^1, e_1^2 \right), \left(e_2^1, e_1^2 \right) \right\}$ is strategically stable, the only strategically stable set in the game. Also the subset Y is essential; it is indeed a minimal set with this property (such sets are called *hyperstable* in Kohlberg and Mertens 1986).

1.5   Symmetric Two-Player Games

The subclass of symmetric two-player games provides the basic setting for much of evolutionary game theory, and indeed, many of the most important insights can be gained already in this special case.

1.5.1   Definition and Notation

More precisely, when speaking of a *symmetric two-player game $G = (I, S, \pi)$*, one assumes that there are precisely two player positions, that each position has the same number of pure strategies, and that the payoff to any strategy is independent of which player position it is applied to. Formally:

Definition 1.10   *A game $G = (I, S, \pi)$ is a* symmetric two-player game *if $I = \{1, 2\}$, $S_1 = S_2$ and $\pi_2(s_1, s_2) = \pi_1(s_2, s_1)$ for all $(s_1, s_2) \in S$.*

This symmetry requirement on the pure-strategy payoff functions is equivalent with the requirement that the second player's payoff matrix be the *transpose* of the first player's: $B = A^T$.[14] In other words, the payoff b_{ij} to player 2 when player 1 uses pure strategy i and player 2 uses pure strategy j is equal to the payoff a_{ji} to player 1 when instead player 1 uses pure strategy j and player 2 uses pure strategy i.

For instance, the Prisoner's Dilemma Game in example 1.1 is symmetric and so is the dominance solvable game in example 1.4, while neither the Matching-Pennies Game in example 1.5 nor the Entry Deterrence Game in example 1.6 is symmetric.

We will write $K = \{1, 2, \ldots, k\}$ for the common set of pure strategies, where k now is the number of pure strategies available to each of the two

---

14. In this class of games each payoff matrix is square.

player positions. The first player's mixed strategies will usually be denoted $x \in \Delta$ and those of the second player $y \in \Delta$, where Δ denotes the common mixed-strategy set, $\Delta = \{x \in R_+^k : \sum_{i \in K} x_i = 1\}$. (Hence $\Theta = \Delta^2$.) The payoff to any pure strategy $i \in K$, when played against some mixed strategy $y \in \Delta$, will be denoted $u(e^i, y) = e^i \cdot Ay$. The set of best replies to any *opponent* strategy $y \in \Delta$ will be denoted $\beta^*(y)$:

$$\beta^*(y) = \left\{ x \in \Delta : u(x, y) \ge u(x', y) \quad \forall x' \in \Delta \right\} \tag{1.29}$$

Hence, unlike the usual best-reply correspondence $\tilde{\beta}$ which maps strategy *profiles* to sets of strategy *profiles*, β^* maps strategies to sets of strategies. In any symmetric two-player game, and for any profile $(x, y) \in \Theta$: $\tilde{\beta}_1(x, y) = \beta^*(y)$ and $\tilde{\beta}_2(x, y) = \beta^*(x)$.

As a further specialized case, we will sometimes consider symmetric two-player games in which both players always fare equally well or badly. Such games are sometimes called *partnership games* (Hofbauer and Sigmund 1988). Mathematically the defining property is that the payoff matrix A is symmetric. Therefore this subclass of symmetric two-player games will be called *doubly* symmetric:

Definition 1.11   *A symmetric two-player game is* doubly symmetric *if $A^T = A$.*

Since symmetry requires $B^T = A$, a symmetric game is doubly symmetric if and only if $B = A$, or, equivalently, if $u(x, y) = u(y, x)$ for all $x, y \in \Delta$. None of the earlier examples of symmetric games are doubly symmetric.

Example 1.10   The 2×2 game given by the payoff matrices

$$A = \begin{pmatrix} 2 & 0 \\ 0 & 1 \end{pmatrix} = B = \begin{pmatrix} 2 & 0 \\ 0 & 1 \end{pmatrix}$$

is doubly symmetric. It is called a <u>*Coordination Game*</u>. Here both players (strictly) prefer the strategy profile $s = (1, 1)$, which gives payoff 2 to each player. Indeed s is a strict Nash equilibrium. However, the pure strategy profile $s' = (2, 2)$ also is a strict Nash equilibrium, resulting in payoff 1 to each player. If one player expects the other to play strategy 2 with sufficiently high probability, then her unique optimal action is to play strategy 2 as well. The game has a third Nash equilibrium, which is mixed; it is the symmetric pair $(x, x) \in \Delta^2$ where $x = (\frac{1}{3}, \frac{2}{3})$. The payoff to each player in this equilibrium is

$\frac{2}{3}$, which is lower than in each of the two strict equilibria. All Nash equilibria are clearly perfect: Two are strict, and one is interior.

1.5.2 Symmetric Nash Equilibrium

In the present context of symmetric games a strategy pair $(x, y) \in \Theta = \Delta^2$ constitutes a *Nash equilibrium*, $(x, y) \in \Theta^{NE}$, if and only if $x \in \beta^*(y)$ and $y \in \beta^*(x)$. A Nash equilibrium (x, y) is called *symmetric* if $x = y$, that is, if both players use the same (mixed or pure) strategy. The subset of strategies $x \in \Delta$ that are in Nash equilibrium with themselves will subsequently be denoted

$$\Delta^{NE} = \left\{ x \in \Delta : (x, x) \in \Theta^{NE} \right\}. \tag{1.30}$$

Geometrically this is the intersection of the set Θ^{NE} with the diagonal $D = \{(x, y) \in \Theta : x = y\}$ of Θ. Equivalently $\Delta^{NE} \subset \Delta$ is the set of fixed points of the best-reply correspondence $\beta^* : \Delta \to \Delta$.

Not all Nash equilibria of a symmetric game need to be symmetric (e.g., see example 1.11 below). However, every symmetric game has at least one symmetric Nash equilibrium. This follows from an application of Kakutani's fixed-point theorem to the correspondence β^*:

Proposition 1.5 *For any finite and symmetric two-player game:* $\Delta^{NE} \neq \emptyset$.

Proof   The set Δ is nonempty, convex, and compact and so is the subset $\beta^*(y) \subset \Delta$ for each $y \in \Delta$. By standard arguments it can be verified that β^* is upper hemi-continuous. By Kakutani's theorem there exists some $y \in \beta^*(y)$. ∎

Example 1.11   A classical example in evolutionary game theory is the Hawk-Dove Game in which each player has two pure strategies: *fight* or *yield*. Strategy 1 (fight) obtains payoff $v > 0$ when played against strategy 2 (yield), in which case strategy 2 obtains payoff 0. Each player has an equal chance of winning a fight, and the cost of losing a fight is $c > 0$. When played against itself, strategy 1 thus gives payoff v with probability $\frac{1}{2}$ and payoff $-c$ with probability $\frac{1}{2}$. Hence the expected (average) payoff of strategy 1 against itself is $(v - c)/2$. When both players yield, each gets payoff $v/2$. The resulting payoff matrix for player 1 is thus

$$A = \begin{pmatrix} (v - c)/2 & v \\ 0 & v/2 \end{pmatrix},$$

and $B = A^T$. We presume that the cost of a fight exceeds the value of a victory: $v < c$.

For such payoffs, pure strategy 2 is the unique best reply to strategy 1, and vice versa. Each of the asymmetric pure-strategy pairs $(1, 2)$ and $(2, 1)$, respectively, constitutes a strict Nash equilibrium. There is also a symmetric Nash equilibrium in mixed strategies. If player 2 plays strategy 1 with probability $\lambda = v/c$, then player 1's two pure strategies yield the same expected payoff. Therefore the mixed-strategy pair (x, x), where x assigns probability λ to strategy 1 and $1 - \lambda$ to strategy 2, constitutes a Nash equilibrium.

Example 1.12   The payoff matrix A of a symmetric 3×3 two-player game is given in (1.31) below. Note that the game is constant-sum; the sum $a_{ij} + b_{ij} = a_{ij} + a_{ji}$ of the two players' payoffs is always 2.

This is a children's game known as the *Rock-Scissors-Paper Game*: rock (strategy 1) "beats" *scissors* (strategy 2), *scissors* "beats" *paper* (strategy 3), and *paper* "beats" *rock*. It is easily verified that this game has no Nash equilibrium in pure strategies, and that it has precisely one Nash equilibrium in mixed strategies, namely the strategy pair (x, x) in which both players randomize uniformly, that is, $x = (\frac{1}{3}, \frac{1}{3}, \frac{1}{3})$:

$$A = \begin{pmatrix} 1 & 2 & 0 \\ 0 & 1 & 2 \\ 2 & 0 & 1 \end{pmatrix}. \tag{1.31}$$

1.5.3   A Classification of Symmetric 2×2 Games

We here consider symmetric two-player games in which each player has only two pure strategies. Certain similarities and differences between rationalistic and evolutionary approaches come out starkly even in this very simple setting. We will here show that for dominance relations and best replies, there exist only *three* generic categories of such games. By "generic" we mean games in which no payoffs are identical.

To see this, consider any symmetric 2×2 game with payoff matrix

$$A = \begin{pmatrix} a_{11} & a_{12} \\ a_{21} & a_{22} \end{pmatrix}. \tag{1.32}$$

Subtracting a_{21} from column 1 and a_{12} from column 2, we obtain the equivalent matrix

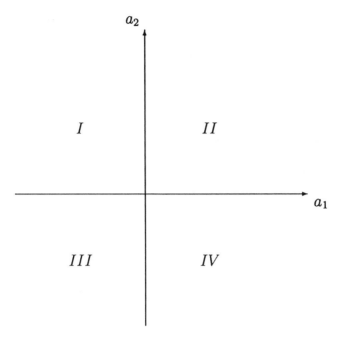

Figure 1.6
The four categories of symmetric 2×2 games.

$$A' = \begin{pmatrix} a_{11} - a_{21} & 0 \\ 0 & a_{22} - a_{12} \end{pmatrix}. \tag{1.33}$$

This new matrix is symmetric. Hence we have obtained a *doubly* symmetric game, with payoff matrix

$$A' = \begin{pmatrix} a_1 & 0 \\ 0 & a_2 \end{pmatrix}, \tag{1.34}$$

where $a_1 = a_{11} - a_{21}$ and $a_2 = a_{22} - a_{12}$.

It follows that any symmetric 2×2 game can, after this normalization, be identified with a point $a = (a_1, a_2) \in R^2$ in the *plane*. In this book we will say that symmetric 2×2 games with normalized payoff vector $a \in R^2$ in the NW orthant of 2-space belong to *category I*, those in the NE orthant to *category II*, those in the SW orthant to *category III*, and those in the SE orthant to *category IV*; see figure 1.6.

It turns out that all games in each category have the same qualitative best-reply properties and that those in category IV are just mirror images of the games in category I. Hence, from this viewpoint, there are only *three* categories of generic symmetric 2×2 games, with all four payoffs a_{ij} distinct. In such a game both a_1 and a_2 are nonzero.

Category I It is evident that strategy 2 strictly dominates strategy 1 in any game in this category ($a_1 < 0$ and $a_2 > 0$). Hence all such games are strictly *dominance solvable*: $S^D = \{(2, 2)\} \subset S$. Accordingly $\Theta^{NE} = \{(e^2, e^2)\}$ and $\Delta^{NE} = \{e^2\}$. A prototype example in this game category is the Prisoner's Dilemma Game of example 1.1. Normalization of the payoffs in matrices A and B in (1.1) gives $a_1 = -1$ and $a_2 = 3$.

Category II All games in this category ($a_1, a_2 > 0$) evidently have two symmetric strict Nash equilibria, and it is easily verified that the mixed strategy $\hat{x} = (a_2/(a_1 + a_2), a_1/(a_1 + a_2)) \in \Delta$ is in Nash equilibrium with itself. Hence we here have $S^D = S = \{1, 2\}$, $\Theta^{NE} = \{(e^1, e^1), (e^2, e^2), (\hat{x}, \hat{x})\}$, and $\Delta^{NE} = \{e^1, e^2, \hat{x}\}$. This category contains the Coordination Game of example 1.10.

Category III Also in this category ($a_1, a_2 < 0$), no strategy is dominated, $S^D = S$, but here the best reply to a pure strategy is the *other* pure strategy. Thus these games have two asymmetric strict Nash equilibria and one symmetric mixed-strategy Nash equilibrium: $\Theta^{NE} = \{(e^1, e^2), (e^2, e^1), (\hat{x}, \hat{x})\}$ and $\Delta^{NE} = \{\hat{x}\}$, where $\hat{x}$ is as in category II (now both the numerator and denominator are negative). This example contains the Hawk-Dove Game of example 1.11, where $a_1 = (v - c)/2 < 0$ and $a_2 = -v/2 < 0$.

Category IV All games in this category ($a_1 > 0$ and $a_2 < 0$) are dominance solvable: $S^D = \{(1, 1)\}$, $\Theta^{NE} = \{(e^1, e^1)\}$, and $\Delta^{NE} = \{e^1\}$. This category is hence identical, modulo relabeling of the two pure strategies, with category I and can be neglected without loss of generality.

Games in category II have caused game theorists and users of noncooperative game theory a fair amount of frustration. More specifically, it has been argued that in such Coordination Games as the one of example 1.10, rational players should be expected to play the Pareto-dominant strict Nash equilibrium (e^1, e^1). In contrast, standard tools in noncooperative game theory do not reject the two other equilibria; both (e^2, e^2) and $(\hat{x}, \hat{x})$ are perfect Nash equilibria, and (e^2, e^2) is even strict.

However, from a strictly noncooperative viewpoint there may be a trade-off between efficiency and strategic risk, a point made by Aumann (1987; see also Harsanyi and Selten 1988). Consider, for example, the symmetric ("Stag Hunt") 2×2 game with payoff matrix

$$A = \begin{pmatrix} 2 & 3 \\ 0 & 4 \end{pmatrix}. \tag{1.35}$$

Here the strict Nash equilibrium $y = (e^2, e^2)$ Pareto dominates the strict Nash equilibrium $x = (e^1, e^1)$. Should "rational" players be expected to play y? This strategy profile is more risky than x in the sense that a deviation by one's opponent results in a payoff loss of 4 payoff units versus a gain of 1, respectively. In the terminology of Harsanyi and Selten (1988), the equilibrium x *risk dominates* y.

Expressed in terms of normalized payoffs, the criterion for risk dominance is simple. Consider any symmetric 2×2 game with normalized payoffs $a_1, a_2 > 0$:

Definition 1.12 $x = (e^1, e^1) \in \Theta^{NE}$ risk dominates $y = (e^2, e^2) \in \Theta^{NE}$ if $a_1 > a_2$.

In other words, one strict Nash equilibrium risk dominates the other if, after normalization of payoffs, it strictly Pareto dominates the second. For instance, normalization of payoffs in (1.35) results in $a_1 = 2$ and $a_2 = 1$. This is the payoff matrix of the Coordination Game in example 1.10, in which $x = (e^1, e^1)$ is Pareto ranked before $y = (e^2, e^2)$, and many argue that rational players should play x rather than y!

2 Evolutionary Stability Criteria

A key concept in evolutionary game theory is that of an *evolutionarily stable strategy* (Maynard Smith and Price 1973; Maynard Smith 1974, 1982). Such a strategy is robust to evolutionary selection pressures in an exact sense. Suppose that individuals are repeatedly drawn at random from a large population to play a symmetric two-person game, and suppose that initially all individuals are genetically or otherwise "programmed" to play a certain pure or mixed strategy in this game. Now inject a small population share of individuals who are likewise programmed to play some other pure or mixed strategy. The incumbent strategy is said to be evolutionarily stable if, for each such mutant strategy, there exists a positive invasion barrier such that if the population share of individuals playing the mutant strategy falls below this barrier, then the incumbent strategy earns a higher payoff than the mutant strategy.

This approach is thus focused on symmetric pairwise interactions within a single large population. In particular, it does not deal with interactions that take place between more than two individuals at a time. Moreover the criterion of evolutionary stability refers implicitly to a close connection between the payoffs in the game and the spreading of a strategy in a population. The payoffs in the game are supposed to represent the gain in biological fitness or reproductive value from the interaction in question.[1] In this biological interpretation the evolutionary stability criterion can be said to generalize Darwin's notion of survival of the fittest from an exogenous environment to a strategic environment where the fitness of a given behavior (strategy) depends on the behaviors (strategies) of others. However, as with Nash equilibrium, the evolutionary stability property does not explain *how* a population arrives at such a strategy. Instead, it asks whether, once reached, a strategy is robust to evolutionary pressures.

When describing the evolutionary stability condition above, it was said that the population of individuals playing the game is large. What is the role of this largeness presumption? The size of the population is relevant in two distinct ways, one rather mechanical and one strategic. First, in order for the posited invasion barriers (expressed as population *shares*) to be effective against mutations, it is important that the smallest such barrier exceed $1/n$, where n is the size of the population. Second, the population needs to be large so that the

---

1. Fitness is a subtle evolutionary concept which may here be taken to simply mean the number of offspring (that survive for reproduction). See Maynard Smith (1982) for a discussion of the fitness concept in the context of evolutionary stability. A simple but exact population model in this spirit is provided in chapter 3.

effects that current individual actions may have on others' future actions can be neglected. Such repeated-game considerations are disregarded in the evolutionary stability analysis.[2] Note that evolutionary stability is a robustness test against a *single* mutation at a time. In other words, it is as if mutations are rare in the sense that the population has time to adjust back to status quo before the next mutation occurs.

Despite its biological stance, evolutionary stability also provides a relevant robustness criterion for human behaviors in a wide range of situations, including many interactions in the realm of economics. In such a social or economic environment, evolutionary stability requires that any small group of individuals who try some alternative strategy do less well than those individuals who stick to the status quo strategy. Consequently individuals who use the prevailing strategy have no incentive to change their strategy, since they do better than the experimenters, and the latter have an incentive to return to the incumbent strategy. An evolutionarily stable strategy in such a social or economic setting may be thought of as a *convention*.

The material in this chapter is organized as follows: Section 2.1 gives the formal definition of an evolutionarily stable strategy, applies this definition to a few examples, and relates it to noncooperative solution concepts. In particular, it is seen that evolutionary stability, while not based on any rationality consideration at all, requires that the strategy in question be in Nash equilibrium with itself. While we saw in section 1.4 that any interior Nash equilibrium passes all the refinements based on trembles, not all such Nash equilibrium strategies are evolutionarily stable. In this respect the criterion of evolutionary stability is more stringent than the usual refinements.

Section 2.2 provides characterizations of evolutionary stability in terms of uniform invasion barriers and local superiority, respectively. These characterizations turn out to be useful for subsequent dynamic analyses. Section 2.3 considers two weaker evolutionary stability criteria, neutral stability and robustness against equilibrium entrants. The first is closely related to evolutionary stability and is likewise characterized. The second has a rationalistic flavor, requiring robustness only against such mutations that are optimal in

---

2. In contrast, if one wants to study evolutionary stability properties of strategies in a repeated game, one may let this repeated game be the game that the randomly matched pairs from the population play when they interact. The present machinery applies without modification to any finitely repeated game, while infinitely repeated games require special considerations; for example, see Fudenberg and Maskin (1990).

the resulting postentry population; it is as if mutations are intentional and forward-looking.

Some games possess sets of strategies that, as sets, have some evolutionary stability property. Hence it is natural to investigate generalizations of evolutionary stability from being a property of individual strategies to a property of sets of strategies. Section 2.4 discusses two such setwise stability concepts, one setwise extension of evolutionary stability (Thomas 1985a), and one setwise extension of robustness against equilibrium entrants (Swinkels 1992a).

Section 2.5 focuses on doubly symmetric games, whereby both players fare equally well or badly under every strategy profile. It turns out that the discussed evolutionary stability criteria have implications for local social efficiency, defined in terms of average payoffs, in such games. Section 2.6 discusses evolutionary stability properties in *cheap-talk games*, which provide for a restricted form of costless preplay communication. Implications for global social efficiency in doubly symmetric cheap-talk games are briefly analyzed. Finally, section 2.7 sketches an extension of the present approach to pairwise interactions in which individuals can condition their strategy on their player position in the game. This extension also applies to asymmetric games.

For discussions of biological aspects of the criterion of evolutionary stability, see, for example, the pioneering work in Maynard Smith (1982) or the fine survey in Hammerstein and Selten (1993). Selten (1991) discusses important aspects of rationalistic and evolutionary paradigms in economics. For more results on connections with refinements of Nash equilibrium, see Bomze (1986) or van Damme (1987). Applications of the criterion of evolutionary stability to extensive form games are developed in Selten (1983); see also van Damme (1987). Bomze and Pötscher (1989) and Cressman (1992a) provide mathematical extensions.

2.1   Evolutionarily Stable Strategies

The analysis in this and the following two chapters is focused almost exclusively on *symmetric two-player games*. As in section 1.5 the set of pure strategies is denoted $K = \{1, 2, \ldots, k\}$ and the associated mixed-strategy set, $\Delta = \{x \in R_+^k : \sum_{i \in K} x_i = 1\}$. The polyhedron of mixed-strategy profiles is $\Theta = \Delta^2$, and the payoff to strategy $x \in \Delta$, when played against $y \in \Delta$, is written $u(x, y) = x \cdot Ay$, where A is the payoff matrix of player 1. The set of best replies $x \in \Delta$ to any strategy $y \in \Delta$ is denoted $\beta^*(y) \subset \Delta$.

2.1.1 Definition

Suppose that a small group of mutants appears in a large population of individuals, all of whom are programmed to play the same (mixed or pure) *incumbent* strategy $x \in \Delta$. Suppose also that the mutants all are programmed to play some other (pure or mixed) *mutant* strategy $y \in \Delta$. Let the share of mutants in the (postentry) population be ϵ, where $\epsilon \in (0, 1)$. Pairs of individuals in this bimorphic (two distinct strategies present) population are repeatedly drawn at random to play the game, each individual being drawn with equal probability. Hence, if an individual is drawn to play the game, then the probability that the opponent will play the mutant strategy y is ϵ, and the probability that the opponent will play the incumbent strategy x is $1 - \epsilon$. The payoff in a match in this bimorphic population is the same as in a match with an individual who plays the mixed strategy $w = \epsilon y + (1 - \epsilon)x \in \Delta$. The *postentry payoff* to the incumbent strategy is thus $u(x, w)$ and that of the mutant strategy $u(y, w)$.

Biological intuition suggests that evolutionary forces select against the mutant strategy if and only if its postentry payoff (fitness) is lower than that of the incumbent strategy,

$$u\left[x, \epsilon y + (1 - \epsilon)x\right] > u\left[y, \epsilon y + (1 - \epsilon)x\right]. \tag{2.1}$$

A strategy $x \in \Delta$ is said to be *evolutionarily stable* if this inequality holds for any "mutant" strategy $y \neq x$, granted the population share of mutants is sufficiently small (Maynard Smith and Price 1973; Maynard Smith 1974):

Definition 2.1 $x \in \Delta$ *is an* evolutionarily stable strategy (ESS) *if for every strategy $y \neq x$ there exists some $\bar{\epsilon}_y \in (0, 1)$ such that inequality (2.1) holds for all $\epsilon \in (0, \bar{\epsilon}_y)$.*

Let $\Delta^{ESS} \subset \Delta$ denote the (possibly empty) set of evolutionarily stable strategies in the game under study. It is easily verified that every ESS is necessarily optimal against itself. If a strategy x is not optimal against itself, then there exists some other strategy y that obtains a higher payoff (fitness) against x than x does. Hence, if the population share ϵ of such a mutant strategy y is small enough, then, by continuity of u it will earn more against the population mixture $w = \epsilon y + (1 - \epsilon)x$ than the incumbent strategy x will, and thus x is not evolutionarily stable. Formally,

$$\Delta^{ESS} \subset \Delta^{NE}. \tag{2.2}$$

But the criterion of evolutionary stability requires more. If x is evolutionarily stable, and y is an alternative best reply to x, then x has to be a *better* reply to y than y is to itself. To see that an ESS x has to have this second-order property, suppose, on the contrary, that an alternative best reply y to x earns at least as much against itself as x does. Then y earns at least as much as x also against the mixture $w = \epsilon y + (1 - \epsilon)x$ (irrespective of ϵ), so x is not evolutionarily stable. The converse of this also holds: If $x \in \Delta^{NE}$ and every alternative best reply y earns less against itself than x earns against it, then such mutants do worse than x in the postentry population. Since also strategies $y \neq x$ that are not best replies to x do worse than x in the postentry population, granted the population share ϵ of the mutant strategy is sufficiently small, we have established the following:

Proposition 2.1 $\Delta^{ESS} = \left\{ x \in \Delta^{NE} : u(y, y) < u(x, y) \ \ \forall y \in \beta^*(x), y \neq x \right\}.$

An equivalent way of stating this result is to say that a strategy $x \in \Delta$ is evolutionarily stable if and only if it meets these first-order and second-order best-reply conditions:

$$u(y, x) \leq u(x, x) \qquad \forall y, \tag{2.3}$$

$$u(y, x) = u(x, x) \Rightarrow u(y, y) < u(x, y) \qquad \forall y \neq x. \tag{2.4}$$

Together, the two conditions thus characterize evolutionary stability. In fact this is how evolutionary stability was originally defined (Maynard Smith and Price 1973; Maynard Smith 1974).[3]

It will turn out useful for later purposes to illustrate the equivalence between these alternative criteria for evolutionary stability as follows: For any given strategy $x \in \Delta$, the defining inequality (2.1) can be written $f(\epsilon, y) > 0$, where the *score function* $f : [0, 1] \times \Delta \to R$ is defined by $f(\epsilon, y) = u(x - y, \epsilon y + (1 - \epsilon)x)$. Evolutionary stability of x requires that its score $f(\epsilon, y)$ be positive against any $y \neq x$, for sufficiently small ϵ. In view of the bilinearity of u,

$$f(\epsilon, y) = u(x - y, x) + \epsilon u(x - y, y - x). \tag{2.5}$$

Hence, for $x, y \in \Delta$ fixed, the score $f(\epsilon, y)$ is an affine function of ϵ with (vertical) intercept $u(x - y, x)$ and slope $u(x - y, y - x)$; see figure 2.1.[4]

---

3. The present definition was first suggested in Taylor and Jonker (1978).

4. A function is *affine* if it is the sum of a linear function and a constant.

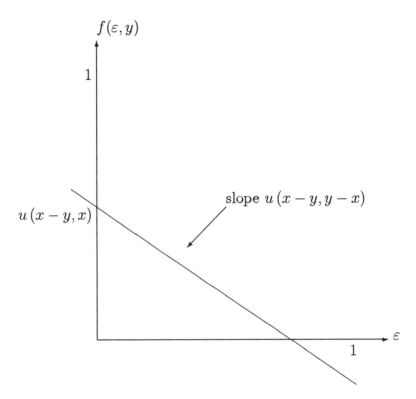

Figure 2.1
The score function f for strategy x evaluated against strategy y.

Condition (2.3) is equivalent with the requirement that this intercept be non-negative, for any $y \in \Delta$, and condition (2.4) is equivalent with the requirement that, for any $y \neq x$, the slope be positive if the intercept is zero. Hence, if these two conditions are met, there exists some $\bar{\epsilon}_y \in (0, 1)$ such that $f(\epsilon, y) > 0$ for all $\epsilon \in (0, \bar{\epsilon}_y)$; that is, $x \in \Delta^{ESS}$.

It follows immediately from proposition 2.1 that if $(x, x) \in \Theta$ is a *strict* Nash equilibrium, then x is evolutionarily stable by default—then there are *no* alternative best replies. This observation has immediate implications concerning the connection between evolutionary stability and social efficiency: Evolutionary stability does not in general imply that average population fitness $u(x, x)$ is maximized.

Example 2.1   In the Prisoner's Dilemma Game of example 1.1, $x = e^2$ is the unique best reply to any strategy $y \in \Delta$ and hence the unique ESS of the game. However, both players would obtain a higher payoff by instead playing the first pure strategy ("cooperate"). Thus evolutionary selection, as modeled by the ESS criterion, does *not* support any degree of "cooperation" in the (one-shot) Prisoner's Dilemma Game.

In the Prisoner's Dilemma Game, the social optimum is inherently unstable; it requires both players to use a strictly dominated strategy. The following example illustrates that evolutionary stability allows for social inefficiency even when the social optimum is a strict Nash equilibrium.

Example 2.2   Each of the two pure strategies in the Coordination Game of example 1.10 is an ESS, since each of these is the unique best reply to itself. In particular, evolutionary stability does not reject the socially inefficient profile (e^2, e^2). In this sense a socially inefficient convention (e.g., always use strategy 2 when meeting) may be evolutionarily stable.

So far all evolutionarily stable strategies were pure. The following example illustrates the possibility that an evolutionarily stable strategy is mixed.

Example 2.3   Consider the Hawk-Dove Game of example 1.11, with payoffs $v = 4$ and $c = 6$. The payoff matrix then is

$$A = \begin{pmatrix} -1 & 4 \\ 0 & 2 \end{pmatrix}.$$

The unique symmetric Nash equilibrium strategy is $x = (\frac{2}{3}, \frac{1}{3}) \in \Delta$. By proposition 2.1, this is the only candidate for an ESS. Since x is interior, *every* strategy $y \in \Delta$ is a best reply to x. Therefore condition (2.4) requires that $u(x - y, y) > 0$ for all $y \neq x$. For any $x, y \in \Delta$: $u(x - y, y) = (x_1 - y_1)$ $(2 - 3y_1)$. For $x = (\frac{2}{3}, \frac{1}{3})$, one obtains $u(x - y, y) = \frac{1}{3}(2 - 3y_1)^2$, a nonnegative quantity which is zero only when $y = x$, proving that $x \in \Delta^{ESS}$. Hence evolutionary stability rejects pure hawkishness and pure doveness. For instance, a population consisting of only pure hawks is vulnerable to a small invasion by, say, pure doves, since in the postentry population every individual meets virtually only pure hawks. As a result the latter earn a payoff just above -1, while pure doves earn a payoff just above 0.

There are games that have no evolutionarily stable strategy. This is the case with the Rock-Scissors-Paper Game of example 1.12. The unique symmetric

Nash equilibrium strategy in that game is $x = (\frac{1}{3}, \frac{1}{3}, \frac{1}{3})$. Being interior, *all* strategies $y \in \Delta$ are best replies to x. However, the mutant $y = e^1$ earns payoff 1 against itself, which is precisely what x earns against y. Thus x fails the second-order best-reply condition (2.4).

2.1.2   Symmetric 2×2 Games

In subsection 1.3.3 it was demonstrated that all payoff differences between any two strategies for a player, given other players' strategies, are invariant under *local shifts* of payoff functions. Since Nash equilibrium is defined in terms of such payoff differences, the set Δ^{NE} is invariant under these transformations. Also evolutionary stability is defined in terms of such individual payoff differences, and hence also the set Δ^{ESS} is invariant under local payoff shifts.

Consequently, for the purpose of evolutionary stability studies, the payoff matrix A of any 2×2 game may without loss of generality be normalized to the form

$$A = \begin{pmatrix} a_1 & 0 \\ 0 & a_2 \end{pmatrix},$$

where $a_1 = a_{11} - a_{21}$ and $a_2 = a_{22} - a_{12}$. We focus on the generic case $a_1 a_2 \neq 0$, and use the classification scheme of subsection 1.5.3.

Categories I and IV   If a_1 and a_2 are of opposite signs, then we have a game of the Prisoner's Dilemma variety, and the game has exactly one Nash equilibrium. This equilibrium is strict and symmetric. Hence such games possess exactly one ESS: $\Delta^{ESS} = \Delta^{NE} = \{e^2\}$ if $a_1 < 0$ (category I) and $\Delta^{ESS} = \Delta^{NE} = \{e^1\}$ if $a_2 < 0$ (category IV).

Category II   If both a_1 and a_2 are positive, then we have a Coordination Game, as in example 1.10, and there are three Nash equilibria, all of which are symmetric: $\Delta^{NE} = \{e^1, e^2, x\}$, where $x = \lambda e^1 + (1 - \lambda)e^2$ for $\lambda = a_2/(a_1 + a_2)$. Each of the two pure equilibria is strict, so e^1 and e^2 are evolutionarily stable. However, x is not, since all $y \in \Delta$ are best replies to x, and, for example, $y = e^1$ earns more against itself than x earns against it: $u(e^1, e^1) = a_1 > \lambda a_1 = u(x, e^1)$. In sum, $\Delta^{ESS} = \{e^1, e^2\}$.

Category III   If both a_1 and a_2 are negative, then we have a Hawk-Dove Game (as in examples 1.11 and 2.3). Such a game has two strict asymmetric Nash equilibria and one symmetric Nash equilibrium: $\Delta^{NE} = \{x\}$, where x is defined in the preceding paragraph. However, this time x *is* evolutionarily stable, since for any $y \in \Delta$,

$$u(x, y) = \lambda a_1 y_1 + (1 - \lambda)a_2 y_2 = \frac{a_1 a_2}{a_1 + a_2}$$

and for all $y \neq x$,

$$u(y, y) = a_1 y_1^2 + a_2 y_2^2 < \frac{a_1 a_2}{a_1 + a_2},$$

where the last inequality follows after a few manipulations. In sum, $\Delta^{ESS} = \{x\}$ for all games in this category.

2.1.3 Structure of the Set Δ^{ESS}

An implication of the characterization in proposition 2.1, noted by Haigh (1975), is that the support of one ESS cannot contain the support of another ESS, in fact, of any symmetric Nash equilibrium strategy. Suppose that $x \in \Delta^{ESS}$ and $C(y) \subset C(x)$ for some strategy $y \neq x$. Then $u(y, x) = u(x, x)$, since $x \in \Delta^{NE}$, and the second-order condition (2.4) implies that $u(x, y) > u(y, y)$. Hence $y \notin \Delta^{NE}$.

Proposition 2.2 *If $x \in \Delta^{ESS}$ and $C(y) \subset C(x)$ for some strategy $y \neq x$, then $y \notin \Delta^{NE}$.*

In particular, if an ESS is interior, then it is the *unique* ESS of the game. Moreover, since there are only finitely many support sets (in a finite game), the number of ESS's is always finite (possibly zero). We have established (Haigh 1975):

Corollary 2.2.1 *The set $\Delta^{ESS} \subset \Delta$ is finite. $\Delta^{ESS} = \{x\}$ if $x \in \Delta^{ESS} \cap \operatorname{int}(\Delta)$.*

More results on the number of ESS's, and on the structure of their supports, can be found in Bomze and Pötscher (1989), Cannings and Vickers (1988), and Vickers and Cannings (1988).

2.1.4 Connections with Noncooperative Criteria

No weakly dominated strategy is evolutionarily stable. Suppose that $x \in \Delta^{NE}$ is weakly dominated by $y \in \Delta$. Then y is an alternative best reply to x, and by weak dominance, $u(y, y) \geq u(x, y)$; x fails the second-order condition (2.4). Hence:

Proposition 2.3 *If $x \in \Delta$ is weakly dominated, then $x \notin \Delta^{ESS}$.*

Thus, if a strategy x is evolutionarily stable, then the profile $(x, x) \in \Theta$ constitutes an *undominated* Nash equilibrium, and since every undominated Nash equilibrium in a two-player game is perfect (proposition 1.4), we have:

Corollary 2.3.1 *If $x \in \Delta^{ESS}$, then $(x, x) \in \Theta^{PE}$.*

In fact evolutionary stability implies even more robustness than perfection requires (van Damme 1987):

Proposition 2.4 *If $x \in \Delta^{ESS}$, then $(x, x) \in \Theta^{NE}$ is a proper equilibrium.*

(For a proof, see van Damme 1987.)

Recall that while perfection requires robustness with respect to *some* low-probability mistakes, properness requires that the equilibrium be robust with respect to low-probability mistakes such that more costly mistakes are less probable than less costly mistakes (see section 1.4). Accordingly proposition 2.4 establishes that evolutionary stability requires behavior that is not only "rational" and "coordinated" in the sense of Nash equilibrium but also "cautious."

The converse of this implication is not valid, however. For instance, the unique Nash equilibrium in the Rock-Scissors-Paper Game of example 1.12 was seen above to fail the ESS criterion, and yet this is a proper equilibrium.

2.2 Characterizations of ESS

Proposition 2.1 above provides one characterization of evolutionary stability. Here two more characterizations will be given. These characterizations will turn out to be important for the subsequent setwise and dynamic analyses.

2.2.1 Invasion Barriers

First, recall that the definition of evolutionary stability of a strategy x requires that for every mutant strategy $y \neq x$ there exist an $\bar{\epsilon}_y > 0$ such that x resists an "infection" by y if it comes in a smaller dose (population share) than $\bar{\epsilon}_y$. In this sense there is an invasion barrier against each mutation. In general, this invasion barrier may depend on the mutant y (or, to continue the medical analogue, on the type of infection). In the present setting of finite games, however, evolutionary stability implies that $\bar{\epsilon}_y$ can be taken to be the same for all mutants; that is, an evolutionarily stable strategy x has a *uniform* invasion barrier.

This result, due to Vickers and Cannings (1987), justifies the large population interpretation of evolutionary stability. For an ESS x to be robust against a mutation $y \neq x$ in a (large but) *finite* population, consisting of, say, n individuals, it is necessary that the invasion barrier $\bar{\epsilon}_y$ against y exceed at least $1/n$, ⸱ where n is the population size, since any invasion consists of at least one individual. Thus, if there is no positive lower bound on invasion barriers against x, then for any finite population size n there will always exist some mutant y against which x has an invasion barrier below $1/n$.[5] In contrast, the existence of a uniform invasion barrier, established below, guarantees that an ESS x is robust against *any* single mutation y appearing simultaneously in m individuals, for all finite population of size n such that m/n is less than the uniform invasion barrier of x.[6] Formally:

Definition 2.2 $x \in \Delta$ *has a* <u>uniform invasion barrier</u> *if there is some* $\bar{\epsilon} \in (0, 1)$ *such that inequality (2.1) holds for all strategies* $y \neq x$ *and every* $\epsilon \in (0, \bar{\epsilon})$.[7]

Before establishing the claimed result, let us make the terminology more precise by defining, for any given $x \in \Delta^{ESS}$, its invasion barrier $b(y)$ against any other strategy y as the highest possible value for $\bar{\epsilon}_y$ in the defining inequality (2.1). Formally,

$$b(y) = \sup \{\delta \in [0, 1] : f(\epsilon, y) > 0 \ \ \forall \epsilon \in (0, \delta)\} . \tag{2.6}$$

Since $x \in \Delta^{ESS}$ by hypothesis, $b(y) > 0$ for all $y \neq x$. Moreover x has a uniform invasion barrier if and only if there exists some $\beta > 0$ such that $b(y) \geq \beta$ for all $y \neq x$.

Proposition 2.5 $x \in \Delta^{ESS}$ *if and only if x has a uniform invasion barrier.* ⸱

---

5. See Maynard Smith (1988), Riley (1979), and Shaffer (1988) for discussions of the ESS criterion in the case of a finite population.

6. Note, however, that the condition for immunity against a mutation in a single individual, $m = 1$, is technically different since a single mutant individual never meets itself. In this case the counterpart to inequality (2.1) is $u(x, x(n-1)/n + y/n) > u(y, x)$.

7. Bomze and Pötscher (1989) call such a strategy x *uninvadable*.

Proof The "if" part follows immediately from the definition of an ESS by choosing $\bar{\epsilon}_y = \bar{\epsilon}$ for every strategy $y \neq x$. For the "only if" part, suppose that $x \in \Delta^{ESS}$, and let $Z_x \subset bd(\Delta)$ be the union of all boundary faces of Δ that do *not* contain x; that is, $Z_x = \{z \in \Delta : z_i = 0 \text{ for some } i \in C(x)\}$. Suppose that $x \in \Delta^{ESS}$, and let the barrier function $b : Z_x \to [0, 1]$ be defined by (2.6) above.

Fix $y \in Z_x$, and consider the score function $f(\cdot, y)$ defined in equation (2.5). Since $x \in \Delta^{ESS}$, $f(\epsilon, y) = 0$ for at most one ϵ, which we here denote ϵ_o. If $\epsilon_o \in (0, 1)$, then $u(x - y, x - y) \neq 0$ and $b(y) = \epsilon_o = u(x - y, x)/u(x - y, x - y)$; otherwise, $b(y) = 1$ (see figure 2.1). It is not difficult to verify from these observations that b is a continuous function. Since b is positive and the set Z_x compact, $\min_{y \in Z_x} b(y) > 0$.

Having established the claim for all $y \in Z_x$, now suppose that $y \in \Delta$ and that $y \neq x$. Then there exists some $z \in Z_x$ and $\lambda \in (0, 1]$ such that $y = \lambda z + (1 - \lambda)x$. But this implies that $b(y) \geq b(z)$. For

$$f(\epsilon, y) = u(x - y, (1 - \epsilon\lambda)x + \epsilon\lambda z) = f(\epsilon\lambda, z).$$

Hence $b(y) = \min\{b(z)/\lambda, 1\} \geq b(z)$. ∎

Contrary to what one might first believe, the above characterization does *not* imply that an ESS is necessarily resistant against simultaneous *multiple* mutations. Suppose, for the sake of illustration, that $x \in \Delta$ is evolutionarily stable with uniform invasion barrier $\bar{\epsilon}$, and suppose that two distinct strategies y and z appear in positive population shares α and β such that $\alpha + \beta < \bar{\epsilon}$. The resulting population mixture

$$w = (1 - \alpha - \beta)x + \alpha y + \beta z \in \Delta \tag{2.7}$$

is formally equivalent with the population mixture $(1 - \epsilon)x + \epsilon y' \in \Delta$, where $y' = \alpha y/(\alpha + \beta) + \beta z/(\alpha + \beta)$ and $\epsilon = \alpha + \beta < \bar{\epsilon}$. Hence, x earns, by definition of the uniform invasion barrier $\bar{\epsilon}$, a higher postentry payoff than the equivalent but fictitious single mutant strategy y'. By linearity of the payoff function, at least one of the two constituent mutant strategies y and z does worse than x. However, it is not necessarily the case that both do.

Example 2.4 Reconsider the Hawk-Dove Game of example 2.3. Let x be its unique ESS, $x = \frac{2}{3}e^1 + \frac{1}{3}e^2$, and let $y = e^1$ and $z = e^2$. Suppose that the two mutants y and z enter the population simultaneously, in (postentry) shares $\frac{1}{2}\epsilon$

and $\frac{1}{2}\epsilon$, respectively, for some small $\epsilon > 0$. The equivalent fictitious mutant is thus $y' = \frac{1}{2}e^1 + \frac{1}{2}e^2$, and the postentry population mix is $w = (1 - \epsilon)x + \epsilon y'$. Since $w_1 < \frac{2}{3}$, $y = e^1$ is its unique best reply, and $u(x, w) < u(y, w)$. In other words, the mutant y earns a higher postentry payoff than the incumbent ESS x.

2.2.2 Local Superiority

The second characterization of evolutionary stability is related to the earlier observation that an *interior* ESS necessarily earns a higher payoff against all mutants than these earn against *themselves* (subsection 2.1.3). More precisely, it turns out that one can generalize this global superiority of an interior ESS to the claim that *any* ESS is locally superior in the sense of earning a higher payoff against all *nearby* mutants than these earn against themselves. This characterization of evolutionary stability is due to Hofbauer, Schuster, and Sigmund (1979).

Definition 2.3 $x \in \Delta$ *is locally superior if it has a neighborhood U such that* $u(x, y) > u(y, y)$ *for all* $y \neq x$ *in U.*

Proposition 2.6 $x \in \Delta^{ESS}$ *if and only if x is locally superior.*

Proof   To first prove the "if" part, suppose that $U \subset R^k$ is a neighborhood of x such that $u(x, y) > u(y, y)$ for all $y \neq x$, $y \in \Delta \cap U$. For any $z \neq x$, $z \in \Delta$, there then exists some $\bar{\epsilon}_z \in (0, 1)$ such that for all $\epsilon \in (0, \bar{\epsilon}_z)$, $w = \epsilon z + (1 - \epsilon)x \in U$. By hypothesis, we thus have $u(x, w) > u(w, w)$. Bilinearity of u gives

$$u(w, w) = \epsilon u(z, w) + (1 - \epsilon)u(x, w),$$

so $u(x, w) > u(w, w) \Leftrightarrow 0 > u(z, w) - u(x, w)$. Hence $x \in \Delta^{ESS}$.

Second, to prove the "only if" part, suppose $x \in \Delta^{ESS}$, let $\bar{\epsilon} \in (0, 1)$ be its uniform invasion barrier, and let $Z_x \subset \mathrm{bd}(\Delta)$ be as in the proof of proposition 2.5. Let

$$V = \{y \in \Delta : y = \epsilon z + (1 - \epsilon)x \text{ for some } z \in Z_x \text{ and } \epsilon \in [0, \bar{\epsilon})\}.$$

Since Z_x is a closed set not containing x, there exists a neighborhood $U \subset R^k$ of x such that $U \cap \Delta \subset V$. Suppose that $y \neq x$, $y \in \Delta \cap U$. Then $y \in V$, and

$u(z, y) < u(x, y)$, where z is as in the definition of V, by proposition 2.5. By
bilinearity of u this inequality is equivalent with $u(y, y) < u(x, y)$. ∎

2.3 Weaker Evolutionary Stability Criteria

We here consider two weakenings of the criterion of evolutionary stability. Instead of requiring, as does evolutionary stability, that all mutants earn less than
the incumbent strategy, *neutral stability* (Maynard Smith 1982) requires that
no mutant earn more than the incumbent, and *robustness against equilibrium
entrants* (Swinkels 1992a) requires that no mutant earn the maximal payoff
possible (in the postentry population mix).

2.3.1 Neutral Stability

Definition 2.4 $x \in \Delta$ *is* neutrally stable (an NSS) *if for every strategy* $y \in \Delta$
there exists some $\bar{\epsilon}_y \in (0, 1)$ *such that the inequality*

$$u\left[x, \epsilon y + (1 - \epsilon)x\right] \geq u\left[y, \epsilon y + (1 - \epsilon)x\right] \qquad (2.8)$$

holds for all $\epsilon \in (0, \bar{\epsilon}_y)$.

In other words, while evolutionary stability requires that no mutant strategy
persist in the sense of earning an equal or higher payoff (fitness), neutral
stability requires that no mutant thrive in the sense of earning a higher payoff
(fitness) than the incumbent strategy.

Let $\Delta^{NSS} \subset \Delta$ denote the (possibly empty) set of neutrally stable strategies
in the game under study. It is easily verified that a strategy x is neutrally
stable if and only if it meets the first-order best-reply condition (2.3) and the
following *weak* second-order best-reply condition:

$$u(y, x) = u(x, x) \Rightarrow u(y, y) \leq u(x, y) \qquad \forall y . \qquad (2.9)$$

In fact this is how neutral stability was originally defined (Maynard Smith
1982). While being less stringent than evolutionary stability, neutral stability
is thus still a refinement of symmetric Nash equilibrium:

$$\Delta^{ESS} \subset \Delta^{NSS} \subset \Delta^{NE}. \qquad (2.10)$$

Example 2.5 The unique symmetric Nash equilibrium strategy x of the Rock-Scissors-Paper Game of example 1.12 was seen to fail the strict second-order condition (2.4) for evolutionary stability against the mutant $y = e^1$. However, this mutant does not violate the weak second-order condition (2.9). In fact no mutant y violates this condition, so $x \in \Delta^{NSS}$. To see this, note that $u(x, y) = 1 = u(y, y)$ holds for all $y \in \Delta$. The first equality is easily verified, and the second follows from the following computation:

$$u(y, y) = y \cdot Ay = (y_1 + y_2 + y_3)^2 = 1.$$

Similar characterizations as for evolutionary stability can be established for neutral stability. Since the only difference between the two definitions is the weak instead of strict inequality, it may not appear surprising that the characterizations of neutral stability differ only in this respect. However, with neutral stability there is a slight mathematical difficulty that is absent in the case of evolutionary stability, namely that the corresponding weak invasion barrier is not necessarily continuous. Such a discontinuity arises if a strategy x is neutrally but not evolutionarily stable strategy and y is some alternative best reply such that the associated score $f(\epsilon, y)$, defined in (2.5), is zero for *all* ϵ (see figure 2.1). In such a case the weak invasion barrier may jump down when y is slightly perturbed. However, it can be shown that it cannot jump down to zero (Bomze and Weibull 1994).

Example 2.6 Consider the symmetric two-player game (Bomze and Weibull 1994) with payoff matrix

$$A = \begin{pmatrix} 1 & 0 & 1 \\ 1 & 0 & 0 \\ 0 & 1 & 2 \end{pmatrix}.$$

Here $x = \left(\frac{2}{3}, \frac{1}{3}, 0\right) \in \Delta^{NSS}$. For $x \in \beta^*(x) = \{y \in \Delta : y_3 = 0\}$, and for any $y \in \beta^*(x)$: $u(y, y) = y_1 = u(x, y)$. Define the *weak* invasion barrier $b^*(y)$ of x against any strategy $y \neq x$ by

$$b^*(y) = \sup \{\delta \in [0, 1] : f(\epsilon, y) \geq 0 \ \ \forall \epsilon \in (0, \delta)\}.$$

We have $f(\epsilon, e^2) = u\left(x - e^2, (1 - \epsilon)x + \epsilon e^2\right) = 0$ for all $\epsilon \in [0, 1]$, so $b^*(e^2) = 1$. However, for $y^\lambda = (\lambda, 1 - 2\lambda, \lambda)$, where $\lambda \in (0, \frac{1}{2})$, we obtain $f(\epsilon, y^\lambda)$

$= (1 - 2\epsilon)\frac{\lambda}{3}$, so $b^*(y^\lambda) = \frac{1}{2}$ for all $\lambda \in (0, \frac{1}{2})$. Since $y^\lambda \to e^2$ as $\lambda \to 0$, b^* is discontinuous at $y = e^2$.

To state the characterizations of neutral stability formally, we say that a strategy $x \in \Delta$ has a *uniform weak invasion barrier* if there exists some $\bar{\epsilon} \in (0, 1)$ such that the defining weak inequality (2.8) holds for all $y \in \Delta$ and $\epsilon \in (0, \bar{\epsilon})$. Likewise a strategy $x \in \Delta$ will be called *locally weakly superior* if $u(x, y) \geq u(y, y)$ for all nearby strategies $y \neq x$. The following result is partly due to Thomas (1985a) and partly to Bomze and Weibull (1994):

Proposition 2.7 *For any $x \in \Delta$, the following three statements are equivalent:*

a. $x \in \Delta^{NSS}$.

b. *x has a uniform weak invasion barrier.*

c. *x is locally weakly superior.*

There are games that have no NSS. This is, for instance, the case in the following modification of the Rock-Scissors-Paper Game of example 1.12.

Example 2.7 Consider the symmetric two-player game given by the payoff matrix A in (2.11) below. The Nash equilibria of this game are all symmetric: Each of the three pure strategies is in Nash equilibrium with itself and so is the uniformly randomized strategy $p = (\frac{1}{3}, \frac{1}{3}, \frac{1}{3}) \in \Delta$. Hence $\Delta^{NE} = \{e^1, e^2, e^3, p\}$. However, none of these strategies is neutrally stable. For instance, $x = e^1$ is vulnerable to invasions by the alternative best reply $y = e^3$: x earns payoff 0 when meeting this mutant y, while y earns payoff 1 when meeting itself. Hence p is the only remaining candidate for an NSS. However, all strategies $y \in \Delta$ are best replies to p, and any pure-strategy mutant $y = e^i$ earns payoff 1 against itself, while $u(p, e^i) = \frac{2}{3}$. Therefore p is not neutrally stable.

$$A = \begin{pmatrix} 1 & 1 & 0 \\ 0 & 1 & 1 \\ 1 & 0 & 1 \end{pmatrix}. \tag{2.11}$$

2.3.2 Robustness against Equilibrium Entrants

Evolutionary stability makes no restrictions on the mutant strategies. In an economic environment where mutations may be due to experimentation by small groups of individuals (or firms), Swinkels (1992a) argues that it may be reasonable to require robustness only against such mutant strategies that are optimal in the postentry population, so-called equilibrium entrants. Hence, while evolutionary stability requires no rationality from individuals who adopt a differing strategy (entrants), Swinkels endows them with the capacity and foresight to choose a strategy which is optimal in the postentry environment, and requires robustness only against such mutants.

More precisely, if the incumbent strategy is $x \in \Delta$, the mutant strategy is $y \in \Delta$, and the population share of mutants is ϵ, then the postentry mixed strategy is $w = \epsilon y + (1 - \epsilon)x \in \Delta$, and y is called an *equilibrium entrant* if it is a best reply to w (Swinkels 1992a).

Definition 2.5 *A strategy $x \in \Delta$ is* robust against equilibrium entrants (REE) *if there exists some $\bar{\epsilon} \in (0, 1)$ such that condition (2.12) below holds for all $y \neq x$ and $\epsilon \in (0, \bar{\epsilon})$:*

$$y \notin \beta^* \left[\epsilon y + (1 - \epsilon)x \right] . \tag{2.12}$$

By proposition 2.5, the invasion barrier against an ESS may be taken to be uniform (it is required to be uniform in the definition of an REE), so it follows that every ESS is robust against equilibrium entrants. A neutrally stable strategy, however, does not need to be robust against equilibrium entrants. In a game in which all payoffs are the same, every strategy is an NSS while no strategy is an REE.

We will write Δ^{REE} for the (possibly empty) set of REE strategies in the game under consideration. Then $\Delta^{ESS} \subset \Delta^{REE} \subset \Delta$. As shown in Swinkels (1992a), if a strategy is robust against equilibrium entrants, then it has to be a best reply to itself. Thus we have:

Proposition 2.8 $\quad \Delta^{ESS} \subset \Delta^{REE} \subset \Delta^{NE}$.

Proof The first inclusion was already shown above. Suppose that $x \in \Delta^{REE}$. Let $\epsilon \in (0, \bar{\epsilon})$, where $\bar{\epsilon}$ is as in the definition of an REE. Define the correspondence $\alpha : \Delta \to \Delta$ by $\alpha(y) = \beta^*((1 - \epsilon)x + \epsilon y)$. Then $\alpha(y) \subset \Delta$ is nonempty, closed, and convex for every $y \in \Delta$. Since β^* is upper hemicontinuous, so is α. Hence, by Kakutani's fixed-point theorem, there exists some y such that $y \in \alpha(y)$. Since x is robust against equilibrium entrants, $y = x$. But then $x \in \alpha(x) = \beta^*(x)$, so $x \in \Delta^{NE}$. ∎

Swinkels establishes the remarkably stronger result that just as evolutionary stability, the present weak form of evolutionary stability implies properness

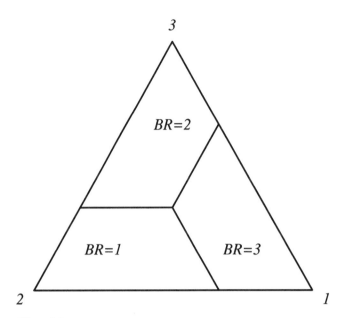

Figure 2.2
Best-reply regions in the Rock-Scissors-Paper Game of examples 2.5 and 2.8.

(see proposition 2.4). In a sense evolutionary stability with respect to "rational" mutations is sufficient for robustness with respect to "rational" trembles:

Proposition 2.9   *If $x \in \Delta$ is robust against equilibrium entrants, then $(x, x) \in$
Θ^{NE} is proper.*

The following example illustrates the possibility that a non-ESS strategy
may be an REE.

Example 2.8   Reconsider the Rock-Scissors-Paper Game of example 2.5. We
saw that the unique Nash equilibrium strategy, $x = (\frac{1}{3}, \frac{1}{3}, \frac{1}{3})$ is not an ESS.
Figure 2.2 shows the three best-reply regions to any strategy $z \in \Delta$. For instance, if z is in the region near the vertex e^1 for pure strategy 1, then its best
reply is pure strategy 3, and so on. It follows that x is robust against any mutant
y in this region, since the postentry population w belongs to the same region.
The same is true for each of the three regions, including their boundaries, so x
is robust against equilibrium entrants.

2.4   Setwise Evolutionary Stability Criteria

We here consider setwise generalizations of the criteria of evolutionary stability and robustness against equilibrium entrants, respectively.

2.4.1   Evolutionarily Stable Sets

Thomas (1985a) suggests that a closed *set* of symmetric Nash equilibrium strategies be called evolutionarily stable if each strategy in the set earns at least the same payoff against any nearby alternative best reply as these earn against themselves, with equal payoffs only in case also the mutant belongs to the set. Formally,

Definition 2.6 $X \subset \Delta^{NE}$ *is an* evolutionarily stable (ES) *set if it is nonempty and closed, and each $x \in X$ has some neighborhood U such that $u(x, y) \geq u(y, y)$ for all $y \in U \cap \beta^*(x)$, with strict inequality if $y \notin X$.*

Thomas shows that the definition is unchanged if the intersection with the best-reply set $\beta^*(x)$ is left out. If this is done, it follows that evolutionarily stable sets consist of neutrally stable strategies. Suppose that $x \in X$. Then x has a neighborhood U such that $u(x, y) \geq u(y, y)$ for all strategies y in U, and hence $x \in \Delta^{NSS}$ by proposition 2.7. In sum, if $X \subset \Delta$ is an ES set, then $X \subset \Delta^{NSS}$. Consequently, since there are games that lack neutrally stable states (as in example 2.7), there are games which have no ES set. Moreover we derived the inclusion $X \subset \Delta^{NSS}$ without invoking the Nash equilibrium requirement in the definition of an ES set. That requirement is redundant (since $\Delta^{NSS} \subset \Delta^{NE}$). Hence:

Proposition 2.10 $X \subset \Delta$ *is an ES set if and only if it is nonempty and closed and each $x \in X$ has some neighborhood U such that $u(x, y) \geq u(y, y)$ for all $y \in U$, with strict inequality if $y \notin X$.*

In a game where all payoffs are the same, no strategy is evolutionarily stable, but all strategies are neutrally stable and $X = \Delta$ is an ES set. The following example provides a nontrivial game that has no evolutionarily stable strategy but possesses a whole continuum of neutrally stable strategies that together constitute an evolutionarily stable set.

Example 2.9   Consider the symmetric two-player game given by the payoff matrix A in equation (2.13) below (equivalent to an example in Cressman

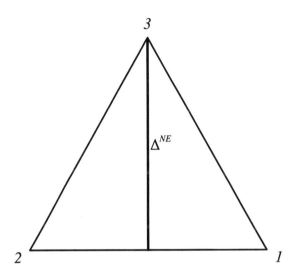

Figure 2.3
The set Δ^{NE} in the game of example 2.9.

1992a). It is easily verified that Δ^{NE} contains two points on the boundary of Δ, namely $p = (\frac{1}{2}, \frac{1}{2}, 0)$ and $q = e^3$. Also every $x \in \Delta^{NE} \cap \text{int}(\Delta)$ has to assign equal probability to the first two pure strategies in the game. Hence $\Delta^{NE} = \{x \in \Delta : x_1 = x_2\}$; see figure 2.3. For any $x \in \Delta^{NE}$ and $y \in \Delta$, we have $u(x, y) - u(y, y) = (y_1 - y_2)^2$. Thus $u(x, y) \geq u(y, y)$ for all $y \in \Delta$, with equality if and only if $y \in \Delta^{NE}$. Hence $\Delta^{EES} = \emptyset$, but $X = \Delta^{NE} = \Delta^{NSS}$ is an ES set.

$$A = \begin{pmatrix} 0 & 2 & 0 \\ 2 & 0 & 0 \\ 1 & 1 & 0 \end{pmatrix}. \tag{2.13}$$

The second part of the characterization of an ES set in proposition 2.10 guarantees that each strategy in the set "behaves" like an evolutionarily stable strategy against nearby mutants *outside* the set: Every $x \in X$ earns a higher payoff against all nearby mutants $y \notin X$ than these earn against themselves. Consequently a singleton set $X = \{x\}$ is an ES set if and only if its unique strategy x is an ESS. Moreover (Thomas 1985a):

Proposition 2.11   *(a) If $X \subset \Delta^{ESS}$, then X is an ES set. (b) The union of ES sets is an ES set. (c) If an ES set is the finite union of disjoint closed sets, then each such set is an ES set.*

Proof (a) By proposition 2.2, the set Δ^{ESS} is finite, and so is $X \subset \Delta^{ESS}$. Thus each $x \in X$ has a neighborhood U_x such that $U_x \cap X = \{x\}$. For each $x \in X$, let U be the intersection of U_x with the neighborhood in the definition of local superiority, establishing that X is an ES set. (b) If $Y \subset \Delta$ is the union of ES sets $X \subset \Delta$, then every $x \in Y$ belongs to at least one ES set X, and hence there exists a neighborhood U of x such that $u(x, y) \geq u(y, y)$ for all strategies $y \in U$, and $u(x, y) > u(y, y)$ for all strategies $y \in U \cap \sim Y \subset U \cap \sim X$. (c) If an ES set $X \subset \Delta$ is the union of disjoint closed sets $X_1, \ldots, X_t$, then there are disjoint neighborhoods V_s of each component X_s. For each $x \in X_s$, let $U_s = U \cap V_s$, where U is as in the definition of the ES property for X. This proves that each set X_s is an ES set. ∎

Cressman (1992b) shows that every ES set is the finite union of disjoint closed and connected sets, each such subset being itself an ES set.[8] While existence of ES sets is not guaranteed in general, every doubly symmetric two-player game possesses at least one ES set (see section 2.5). A weaker form of setwise evolutionary stability is considered in subsection 3.5.4, a criterion that is met by at least one set in every symmetric two-player game.

2.4.2 Equilibrium Evolutionarily Stable Sets

The following set-valued version of *robustness against equilibrium entrants* (subsection 2.3.2) is suggested in Swinkels (1992a):[9]

Definition 2.7 $X \subset \Delta$ *is an* equilibrium evolutionarily stable (EES) *set if it is minimal with respect to the following property: X is a nonempty and closed subset of Δ^{NE} for which there is some $\bar{\epsilon} \in (0, 1)$ such that if $x \in X$, $y \in \Delta$, $\epsilon \in (0, \bar{\epsilon})$ and $y \in \beta^*((1 - \epsilon)x + \epsilon y)$, then $(1 - \epsilon)x + \epsilon y \in X$.*

In other words, an EES set X is a minimal closed set of symmetric Nash equilibrium strategies such that no small-scale invasion of equilibrium entrants can lead the population out of X. In the special case of a singleton set $X = \{x\}$, this set-valued stability criterion coincides with the point-valued criterion of robustness against equilibrium entrants. For instance, in the Rock-Scissors-Paper Game of example 2.8, $X = \Delta^{NE} = \{(\frac{1}{3}, \frac{1}{3}, \frac{1}{3})\}$ is an EES set.

---

8. In fact, it is not difficult to show that each component ES set coincides with a component of the set Δ^{NE}, a fact which also follows from the results in subsection 2.4.2.

9. Swinkels (1992a) develops this concept also for multipopulation interactions in arbitrary (finite) normal-form games; see chapter 5.

We noted in chapter 1 that the set $\Theta^{NE} \subset \Theta$ of Nash equilibria of a (finite n-player) game is the finite union of disjoint, connected, and closed sets, the *components* of Θ^{NE}. Likewise, in any symmetric two-player game, the set $\Delta^{NE} \subset \Delta$ is the finite union of disjoint, connected, and closed sets, the *components of Δ^{NE}*.[10] Swinkels (1992a) shows that these components are the only candidates for EES sets:

Proposition 2.12   *Every EES set $X \subset \Delta^{NE}$ is a component of Δ^{NE}.*

Proof   First, we show that every EES set $X \subset \Delta^{NE}$ is contained in some open set U such that $\Delta^{NE} \cap U = X$. Suppose that this is not the case for some EES set X. Then there exist some $x \in X$, sequence $y^t \in \Delta$, and accompanying sequence $\epsilon^t \to 0$ such that $w^t = \epsilon^t y^t + (1 - \epsilon^t)x \in \Delta^{NE} \cap \sim X$ for all t sufficiently large, say $t \geq T$. Since each support $C(y^t)$ is contained in the associated support $C(w^t)$, and $w^t \in \Delta^{NE}$ for $t \geq T$, y^t is a best reply to w^t, for all $t \geq T$. Hence $w^t \in X$ for all $t \geq T$ such that $\epsilon^t < \bar{\epsilon}$, where $\bar{\epsilon}$ is the entry barrier in the definition of X as an EES set, a contradiction.

Hence X is either one of the components of Δ^{NE}, or the union of two or more such components. The latter possibility is excluded by minimality: If X has the property requested in the definition of an EES, then so does each of its components.   ∎

There are games that have no EES set. However, every ES set contains some EES set. For the EES criterion requires robustness with respect to a smaller set of mutants than the ES criterion—it is sufficient to consider mutants which are (postentry) optimal. Hence any ES set meets this criterion, and contains a minimal set meeting this weaker entry criterion—an EES set. One difficulty remains with this line of argument, however: It neglects that ES sets are defined in terms of neighborhoods adapted to individual points in the set while EES sets are defined in terms of a uniform bound $\bar{\epsilon}$ on postentry mutation shares. Nevertheless, Balkenborg and Schlag (1994) show that for every ES set X there exists some $\hat{\epsilon} \in (0, 1)$ such that $u(x, w) \geq u(w, w)$ for all $x \in X$, $y \in \Delta$, and $\epsilon \in (0, \hat{\epsilon})$, where $w = (1 - \epsilon)x + \epsilon y$. In force of proposition 2.12, we also have that every connected ES set is an EES set:[11]

---

10. This follows from the observation that $\Delta^{NE} = \left\{ x \in \Delta : u(x - e^i, x) \geq 0 \; \forall i \in K \right\}$, the set of points x where a finite number of polynomials in x are nonnegative (see subsection 1.3.2).

11. I am grateful to Karl Schlag for providing this latter observation.

Proposition 2.13   *Every ES set contains some EES set. Any connected ES set is an EES set.*

Proof   Suppose that $X \subset \Delta^{NE}$ is an ES set, and let $x \in X$. Suppose that $y \in \Delta$, and let $w = \epsilon y + (1 - \epsilon)x$ for some $\epsilon \in (0, 1)$. If y is a best reply to w, then $u(y, w) \geq u(x, w)$. By bilinearity of u, $u(w, w) \geq u(x, w)$. This implies that $w \in X$ for all ϵ sufficiently small, since X is an ES set. Hence X has the property stated in the definition of an EES set. But X is closed and nonempty, and it contains some minimal set Y with the stated property, by Zorn's lemma. If X is connected, then the only EES set Y contained in $X \subset \Delta^{NE}$ is X itself, by proposition 2.12. ∎

Example 2.10   Consider a Coordination Game with payoffs $a_1, a_2 > 0$. Each of the two singleton sets $X = \{e^1\}$ and $Y = \{e^2\}$ is an ES and EES set, and $X \cup Y$ is an ES set but not an EES set (rejected by the minimality requirement). What about the singleton $Z = \{z\}$, where $(z, z) \in \Theta$ is the unique mixed-strategy Nash equilibrium? Since z is not an ESS (see subsection 2.1.2), Z is not an ES set. Z is also not an EES set. For each of the two pure strategies is an equilibrium entrant against z, since the postentry population is closer to the entrant (pure) strategy than z is, and hence the entrant is a best reply to the postentry mix.

Combining the above-mentioned observation in Cressman (1992b), concerning the structure of ES sets, with propositions 2.12 and 2.13, we have established that every ES set is the finite union of components of the set Δ^{NE}, each such component subset being a minimal ES set and also an EES set.

2.5   Social Efficiency in Doubly Symmetric Games

In section 1.5 we defined a symmetric two-player game as *doubly* symmetric if the payoff matrix A to player 1 is symmetric: $A^T = A$. Since the payoff matrix to player 2 in any symmetric game is $B = A^T$, we have $B = A$ in a doubly symmetric game. In other words, each player then always earns the same payoff as the other player.

2.5.1   Definitions

The setup for the evolutionary stability criteria developed above was that of a large population in which *all* individuals play the same pure or mixed strategy

$x \in \Delta$. Evolutionary stability properties were defined in terms of how the pay-off to strategy x is affected when a few individuals in the population switch to some other strategy $y \in \Delta$. Here we instead consider the payoff to any strategy x when played by all individuals in the population, and compare it with the payoff to some other strategy y if all individuals were to switch to y. Social efficiency of a strategy x is defined in terms of such payoff comparisons. Accordingly a strategy x is called *locally socially efficient* if there is no nearby strategy y that will give a higher payoff if all individuals shift to it, and x is called *globally socially efficient* if there is no such strategy $y \in \Delta$ at all. More exactly:

Definition 2.8   *A strategy $x \in \Delta$ is*

a. locally strictly efficient *if it has a neighborhood U such that $u(x, x) > u(y, y)$ for all strategies $y \neq x$ in U.*

b. locally weakly efficient *if it has a neighborhood U such that $u(x, x) \geq u(y, y)$ for all strategies y in U.*

c. globally efficient *if $u(x, x) \geq u(y, y)$ for all strategies y in Δ.*

Since the payoff function u is continuous and the strategy set Δ compact, there always exists at least one globally efficient strategy (in any finite and symmetric, not necessarily doubly symmetric, game). Let the set of globally efficient strategies be denoted

$$\Delta^* = \arg \max_{x \in \Delta} u(x, x) = \{x \in \Delta : u(x, x) \geq u(y, y) \quad \forall y \in \Delta\} . \qquad (2.14)$$

By continuity of u, this set is closed, and each strategy x in Δ^* is locally weakly efficient.

2.5.2   Local Strict Efficiency and Δ^{ESS}

It turns out that evolutionary stability in doubly symmetric games is equivalent with local strict efficiency (Hofbauer and Sigmund 1988; see also Schlag 1993a; Wärneryd 1994). This equivalence follows from the characterization of evolutionary stability in terms of local superiority, in proposition 2.6, combined with the symmetry of the payoff function.

Proposition 2.14 $x \in \Delta^{ESS}$ *if and only if x is locally strictly efficient.*

Proof   Suppose that $A^T = A$, and let $x \in \Delta$. For any $y \neq x$ and $z = \frac{1}{2}x + \frac{1}{2}y$, we have, by bilinearity of u,

$$u(y, y) = u(x, x) - 2u(x, z) - 2u(z, x) + 4u(z, z) .$$

Hence, by symmetry of u,

$$u(x, x) - u(y, y) = 4 \left[u(x, z) - u(z, z) \right] .$$

The equivalence between local strict efficiency and local superiority of x follows from the observation that $y \neq x$ is within distance ϵ from x if and only if $z \neq x$ is within distance $\epsilon/2$ from x. By proposition 2.6, local superiority is equivalent with evolutionary stability. ∎

2.5.3 Local Weak Efficiency and Δ^{NSS}

Replacing strict inequalities with weak, and using the characterization of neutral stability in proposition 2.7, one obtains that neutral stability in doubly symmetric games is equivalent with local weak efficiency:

Proposition 2.15 $x \in \Delta^{NSS}$ if and only if x is locally weakly efficient.

A consequence of this result is that all globally efficient strategies in a doubly symmetric game are neutrally stable: $\Delta^* \subset \Delta^{NSS}$. In particular, since the set Δ^* is nonempty, existence of neutrally stable strategies is guaranteed in doubly symmetric games.

2.5.4 Locally Efficient Sets and Evolutionarily Stable Sets

As shown in Schlag (1993a), a set of locally socially efficient strategies in a doubly symmetric game constitutes an ES set.

Definition 2.9 A nonempty closed set $X \subset \Delta$ is locally efficient if it is contained in some open set U such that

$$X = \arg \max_{x \in \Delta \cap U} u(x, x) = \{ x \in \Delta : u(x, x) \geq u(y, y) \ \forall y \in \Delta \cap U \} .$$

There are locally efficient sets that are not connected, such as the set $X \cup Y$ in example 2.10 with $a_1 = a_2$. However, a locally efficient set is always the finite union of disjoint closed and connected sets, the *components* of X. To see this, suppose that $X \subset \Delta$ is locally efficient with neighborhood U. Then there exists some $\alpha \in R$ such that $u(x, x) = \alpha$ for all $x \in X$ and $u(y, y) < \alpha$ for all $y \in \Delta \cap U \cap \sim X$. In other words, X is the set of points $x \in U$ where average payoff $u(x, x)$ achieves its maximum value α in U. Since u is a polynomial function, X is the finite union of disjoint, closed, and connected subsets of U, the *components* of X. Within a suitable neighborhood each component of X is, by itself, a connected locally efficient set. Recall that an ES set is the finite union of connected ES sets.

Proposition 2.16   *Any locally efficient set $X \subset \Delta$ is an ES set. Any connected ES set $X \subset \Delta$ is locally efficient.*

Proof   To establish the first claim, assume that $X \subset \Delta$ is locally efficient with neighborhood U. By proposition 2.15, $X \subset \Delta^{NSS}$. By the characterization of neutral stability in proposition 2.7, each $x \in X$ has some neighborhood V_x such that $u(x, y) \geq u(y, y)$ for all $y \in V_x$. Hence $u(x, y) \geq u(y, y)$ for all $y \in U \cap V_x \cap \beta^*(x)$, and by definition of an ES set, it remains to show that this inequality is strict if $y \notin X$. But then $u(y, y) < u(x, x)$, so $u(x, y) = u(y, x) = u(x, x) > u(y, y)$. For a proof of the second claim, see Schlag (1993a).   ∎

2.6   Preplay Communication

Consider a symmetric 2×2 coordination game with payoff matrix

$$A = \begin{pmatrix} a_1 & 0 \\ 0 & a_2 \end{pmatrix}, \tag{2.15}$$

for some $a_1 > a_2 > 0$. The game has three Nash equilibria, two of which are strict. While intuition might suggest that evolution will lead players to play the Pareto-efficient strict equilibrium (e^1, e^1), the Pareto-dominated Nash equilibrium (e^2, e^2) is strict and hence evolutionarily stable. Indeed this equilibrium also meets the usual refinements of the Nash equilibrium concept.[12]

This conflict between intuition and formal analysis has spurred some recent research efforts among game theorists. One research approach argues that if the players can communicate with each other before play of the game, they will agree to play the efficient Nash equilibrium (e^1, e^1).[13] Costless such preplay communication is called *cheap talk*. We will here briefly outline a formal

---

12. The third, mixed, Nash equilibrium, which gives even lower payoffs, meets the refinement criteria in chapter 1 but is not evolutionarily stable, as was seen in example 2.2.

13. An assumption underlying the notion of *renegotiation proofness* (e.g., see Fudenberg and Tirole 1991).

model of cheap talk and examine some connections between evolutionary stability criteria and Pareto efficiency.

For this purpose let us first informally reconsider the coordination game with payoff matrix (2.15). Suppose that a monomorphic population is currently playing the inefficient strategy $e^2 \in \Delta^{ESS}$, but suddenly a new *kind* of mutation arises in the population. Namely clever mutants appear who (1) have the capacity to recognize their own kind when matched and (2) always play the first (good) pure strategy when meeting each other and the second (bad) strategy when meeting an individual in the original population, a "native." The natives, on the other hand, continue playing the second (bad) strategy 2 at every matching. Using a term coined by Robson (1990), it is as if the mutants use a "secret handshake" when meeting each other.

In such a bimorphic population each native still earns the low payoff a_2 in every interaction, while each mutant earns a_2 when meeting a native and a_1 when meeting another mutant. Hence mutants do better than the natives in the postentry population, suggesting that the inefficient payoff outcome may be evolutionarily unstable in the presence of such communicating mutants.

2.6.1 Definitions

More generally, consider any symmetric two-person game G with pure-strategy set $K = \{1, \ldots, k\}$ and pure-strategy payoff function π. As usual, let the associated mixed-strategy simplex be $\Delta \subset R^k$ and the mixed-strategy payoff function be denoted u. When proceeding to define a cheap-talk game G_M based on such a game G, we will call the latter the *base game* and refer to its (pure and mixed) strategies as *actions*.

Suppose that every individual can send some preplay signal or message to her opponent when matched to play the base game G and that every individual may condition her choice of action G on these two preplay messages. Formally, let M be a finite set of preplay *messages*, available to each of the two players. We here focus on the case when each individual sends exactly one message, and the two messages are sent simultaneously (without knowledge of the other message). Hence the communication or "talking" in these models takes quite a rudimentary form—no involved discussions here![14] (The option

---

14. Interesting alternative settings are when the two players have different message sets (e.g., one being empty or a singleton) and/or when messages are sent sequentially (e.g., see Blume, Kim, and Sobel 1993).

not to send any message can be formally included by letting one element of M represent "no message.")

When both players' messages have been sent, each player can costlessly and without error observe both messages.[15] Hence at the end of the preplay communication stage both players face a message-pair $(\mu, \nu) \in M^2$, upon which they may condition their choice of action in the base game G. Formally, let F be the set of functions $f : M^2 \to K$ from message-pairs to pure actions in G. Each function $f \in F$ thus represents a deterministic decision rule, which for each possible message-pair (μ, ν) assigns a pure strategy $h = f(\mu, \nu) \in K$.

A *pure strategy* in the associated cheap-talk game G_M is a pair $(\mu, f) \in M \times F$. Since the sets K and M are finite, so is the set K_M of pure strategies in G_M. The payoff to a player using pure strategy (μ, f) against an opponent who uses pure strategy (ν, g) is

$$\pi_M [(\mu, f), (\nu, g)] = \pi [f(\mu, \nu), g(\mu, \nu)]. \tag{2.16}$$

A *mixed strategy* in the cheap-talk game G_M is simply a probability distribution p over the (finite) pure-strategy set $K_M = M \times F$, and we will write Δ_M for the unit simplex of mixed strategies in G_M.

A message $\mu' \in M$ is said to be *unused* in $p \in \Delta_M$ if p assigns zero probability to all pure strategies (μ, f) that have $\mu = \mu'$.

The associated mixed-strategy payoff function $u_M : \Delta_M^2 \to R$ specifies the expected payoff $u_M(p, q)$ of the mixed cheap-talk strategy $p \in \Delta_M$ when used against the mixed cheap-talk strategy $q \in \Delta_M$:

$$u_M(p, q) = \sum_{(\mu, f) \in K_M} \sum_{(\nu, g) \in K_M} p[(\mu, f)] \pi_M [(\mu, f), (\nu, g)] q[(\nu, g)]. \tag{2.17}$$

It is evident that if G is a finite and symmetric two-player game, then so is any cheap-talk game G_M defined above (for any finite set M). Consequently all concepts and results discussed in this chapter apply also to G_M.

The notation for such a two-player cheap-talk game can be somewhat simplified. Without loss of generality, one may assume that each player conditions her base-game action only on the *other* player's message. Formally, a pure strategy may be taken to be a pair $(\mu, f) \in M \times F$, where F now is the set of functions $f : M \to K$. This can be done because, for any pure strategy

---

15. Bhaskar (1991) develops an evolutionary model of noisy cheap talk.

$(\mu, f) \in M \times F$ as originally defined, $f : M^2 \to K$ needs only to be applied to message-pairs where the player's own message is μ. Thus there is a function $f' : M \to K$ such that $f'(\nu) = f(\mu, \nu)$ for all messages $\nu \in M$ that the opponent player may send. This simplified notation will be used henceforth.

Note that no meaning has been exogenously attached to the elements of the set M; their meaning may be endogenously defined by the associated equilibrium actions. This is the case if a particular message-pair is always followed by the same base-game action pair. It is as if the message-pair means the accompanying action pair. In this sense language can be endogenously created in equilibrium.[16] Moreover, since in the evolutionary setting cheap-talk strategies are programmed, one may alternatively interpret messages as inherited (distinct and easily observable) physical traits. A pure strategy in the cheap-talk game is then such a physical trait combined with a rule that assigns a behavior (base-game action) to one's opponent's physical trait.

Note finally that in terms of the Nash equilibrium criterion, communication does not help players to coordinate on socially efficient outcomes: For each Nash equilibrium strategy $x \in \Delta^{NE}$ in the base game there exist Nash equilibrium strategies $p \in \Delta_M^{NE}$ in the associated cheap-talk game such that play of p results in the randomization x over the base-game actions. Such a Nash equilibrium strategy p is obtained if all messages are sent with equal probability, and for each base-game action $i \in K$ the constant decision rule $f_i : M \to K$, which assigns action $i \in K$ to all messages μ, is used with probability x_i.[17] It turns out, however, that if one uses the discussed criteria for evolutionary stability, then a certain selection in favor of efficiency takes place.

2.6.2 Evolution, Communication, and Efficiency in Doubly Symmetric Games

Does such preplay communication allow evolutionary forces to lead play away from such Pareto-inefficient equilibria as (e^2, e^2) in the above coordination game? Indeed there is now a technical possibility for this, since a strict equilibrium s in the base game G need not correspond to a strict equilibrium in the associated cheap-talk game G_M. In particular, if there is another symmetric Nash equilibrium in G which Pareto dominates s, then mutants may use the

---

16. This appears to be in accordance with the view of Ludwig Wittgenstein as expressed in his *Philosophical Investigations*.

17. Technically for each message $\mu \in M$ and constant decision rule f_i, let p select the cheap-talk pure strategy $h = (\mu, f_i)$ with probability x_i/m, where m is the number of elements in M.

communication stage to coordinate on this better equilibrium when matched with each other. Hence in the presence of cheap talk there is some scope for evolutionary drift away from inefficient strict equilibrium outcomes. A critical element for such destabilization is that some message is unused in the cheap-talk equilibrium, a message that can be used as a secret handshake between mutants.

Some fairly strong efficiency implications from neutral stability and setwise evolutionary stability have been established for doubly symmetric two-player games, although the efficiency implications from these criteria generally do not appear to be strong. We here state only one result, without proof, and provide a few simple examples to illustrate the techniques.

The following proposition is due to Schlag (1993a). Closely related results can be found in Wärneryd (1991), Kim and Sobel (1991), and Blume, Kim, and Sobel (1993). In accordance with our earlier terminology for doubly symmetric games, we will call a cheap-talk strategy $p \in \Delta_M$ *globally efficient* if $u_M(p, p) \geq u_M(q, q)$ for all $q \in \Delta_M$.

Proposition 2.17   *Let G be a doubly symmetric two-player game, M a finite message set, G_M the associated cheap-talk game, and $p \in \Delta_M$ a strategy that does not use all messages in M. Then p belongs to an ES set $P \subset \Delta_M$ if and only if p is globally efficient.*

Our first example formalizes the above heuristic secret handshake story.

Example 2.11   Consider any 2×2 game with payoff matrix A as in (2.15) above, and let M be any preplay message set with at least two elements. One formalization of the intuitive story given above is to suppose that all natives use some pure cheap-talk strategy (α, f^*), where $\alpha \in M$ and f^* is the decision rule which assigns the "bad" action (base-game strategy 2) to all messages: $f^*(\nu) = 2$ for all $\nu \in M$. Clearly (α, f^*) is in Nash equilibrium with itself, $(\alpha, f^*) \in \Delta_M^{NE}$. The clever mutants, on the other hand, use the pure cheap-talk strategy (β, g), where $\beta \neq \alpha$ and g is the decision rule which assigns the "good" action (base-game strategy 1) when faced with message β, and otherwise the "bad" action: $g(\nu) = 1$ if $\nu = \beta$, otherwise $g(\nu) = 2$. Clearly (β, g) is a best reply to (α, f^*) in G_M:

$$\pi_M\left[(\beta, g), (\alpha, f^*)\right] = \pi(2, 2) = a_2 = \pi_M\left[(\alpha, f^*), (\alpha, f^*)\right].$$

Moreover (β, g) is a better reply to itself than (α, f^*):

$$\pi_M\left[(\beta, g), (\beta, g)\right] = a_1 > a_2 = \pi_M\left[(\alpha, f^*), (\beta, g)\right].$$

Hence (α, f^*) is not even neutrally stable in the cheap-talk game G_M (see subsection 2.3.1).

Note, however, that had the natives instead used *all* messages in M (i.e., had their strategy been some $p \in \Delta_M$, which places positive probability on every pure strategy $(\mu, f) \in K_M$ for which $f = f^*$), then every best reply to p has to play base-game strategy 2, and hence $p \in \Delta_M^{NSS}$. More generally, neutral stability rules out the inefficient outcome a_2 if and only if there is some unused message in the associated cheap-talk equilibrium (an observation due to Wärneryd 1991).

The next example illustrates the possibility that an inefficient outcome that is not even compatible with Nash equilibrium in the base game may be compatible with evolutionary stability in a cheap-talk extension of the game.

Example 2.12   Consider again any 2×2 game with payoff matrix A as in (2.15) above, and let M be any preplay message set with exactly two elements, $M = \{\mu, \nu\}$. The inefficient non-Nash payoff outcome $b = (a_1 + a_2)/2$ is then compatible with evolutionary stability in the cheap-talk game G_M (an observation due to Kim and Sobel 1991). Let the cheap-talk strategy $p \in \Delta_M$ mix uniformly over the two pure strategies (μ, f) and (ν, g), where $f(\mu) = 2$ and $f(\nu) = 1$, and $g(\mu) = 1$ and $g(\nu) = 2$. Hence, in any matching, the "bad" base-game strategy 2 is played if the messages are the same and otherwise the "good" base-game strategy 1 is played. When meeting itself, p clearly earns payoff b, and p is a best reply to itself. Indeed any best reply to p has to use the above decision rule f. Suppose that p' is another best reply to p, where p' randomizes between the two messages with a nonuniform probability distribution σ'. Then p' earns less than b when meeting itself, since the two messages are identical more than half of the time (and $a_1 < b$). However, p earns b when meeting p', so $p \in \Delta_M^{ESS}$, and accordingly $\{p\} \subset \Delta_M$ is a socially inefficient ES set (using all messages in M).

If there are more than two strict Nash equilibria in a doubly symmetric two-player game, then an inefficient outcome may be *neutrally* stable even when there is an unused message (an observation due to Wärneryd 1991):

Example 2.13   Consider a symmetric 3×3 coordination game with zeros off the diagonal, and payoffs $a_1 > a_2 > a_3 > 0$ on the diagonal. Suppose that M contains two messages. Then the cheap-talk strategy $p \in \Delta_M$—which sends one of the messages, say, $\mu \in M$, plays the "mediocre" base-game strategy 2 when faced with this message μ, and otherwise plays the "bad" base-game strategy 3—is neutrally stable. However, mutants can arise who do not punish the other message, and, once these mutants have a strong enough foothold, new mutants with a secret handshake, leading to the good payoff, can arise. And indeed, according to proposition 2.17, p does not belong to any ES set.

2.7   Role-Conditioned Behaviors

A key assumption behind the analytical framework presented in this chapter is that individuals who are engaged in some pairwise strategic interaction represented as a symmetric two-player game in normal form, do not condition their strategy on their player position or *role* in the game.

It is true that the payoff to an individual's strategy $x \in \Delta$, when used against any strategy $y \in \Delta$, is the same, $u(x, y)$, irrespective of whether the individual is assigned player position 1 (the row player) or player position 2 (the column player). However, if other individuals in the population condition their strategy on their player position, then the same strategy $x \in \Delta$ may obtain different payoffs when used in the two player positions. That is, if others use $y^1 \in \Delta$ when they find themselves in player position 1 (and hence their opponent in player position 2) and $y^2 \in \Delta$ when they are in player position 2 (and their opponent in player position 1), then strategy $x \in \Delta$ earns payoff $u(x, y^2)$ when used in player position 1 and $u(x, y^1)$ in player position 2, where one may well have $u(x, y^2) \neq u(x, y^1)$.

Whether it is reasonable to assume, in a given application, that individuals can identify their player position in a game is a matter of modeling judgment; it will not be discussed here.[18]

The subsequent model is a special case of a general framework developed in Selten (1980), in which individuals may condition their strategy on a wide range of information available to them (see also Maynard Smith 1982; Selten 1983; van Damme 1987; Hammerstein and Selten 1993). As will be seen, even the present special case of this general approach can be applied to asymmetric games, and it has striking implications.

---

18. There are interesting modeling subtleties here; see Selten (1980), van Damme (1987), and Hammerstein and Selten (1993) for discussions.

2.7.1 Definitions

Formally, suppose that the interaction takes the form of a finite (but not necessarily symmetric) two-player base game $G = (I, S, \pi)$ with a mixed-strategy extension (I, Θ, u). Pairs of individuals are still drawn at random from a large population to play the game, but now each individual can observe her player position ($i = 1$ or 2) in G, and condition her strategy on this observation. In every random matching, exactly one individual is allocated to each player position, and all individuals are equally likely to be allocated to any of the two positions in the game.

By a *behavior strategy* in this setting is meant a strategy pair $\bar{x} = (x^1, x^2) \in \Theta = \Delta_1 \times \Delta_2$, where $x^1 \in \Delta_1$ is used in player position 1 and $x^2 \in \Delta_2$ in position 2; see figure 2.4.[19] In this extensive-form representation, nature (player 0) has a first move, allocating the two individuals to one player position each. The underlying game is represented as a 2×2 simultaneous-move game with payoff bi-matrix (A, B).

For any underlying game G, let Γ denote the associated extensive-form game in which the interacting individuals are allocated player positions as described above. In Γ the expected payoff to behavior strategy $\bar{x} = (x^1, x^2) \in \Theta$, when played against behavior strategy $\bar{y} = (y^1, y^2) \in \Theta$, is

$$u^*(\bar{x}, \bar{y}) = \frac{1}{2}\left[u_1(x^1, y^2) + u_2(y^1, x^2) \right].$$ (2.18)

In bi-matrix representation (A, B), this becomes

$$u^*(\bar{x}, \bar{y}) = \frac{1}{2}\left[x^1 A y^2 + y^1 B x^2 \right].$$ (2.19)

We may now imagine a large monomorphic population in which all individuals are programmed to a certain behavior strategy $\bar{x} = (x^1, x^2)$ in Γ. Such a behavior strategy $\bar{x}$ is called *evolutionarily stable* in Γ if it is a best reply to itself, $u^*(\bar{x}, \bar{x}) \geq u^*(\bar{y}, \bar{x})$ for all $\bar{y} \in \Theta$, and any alternative best reply $\bar{y} \in \Theta$ earns less against itself than $\bar{x}$ earns, namely if $u^*(\bar{y}, \bar{x}) = u^*(\bar{x}, \bar{x})$ for some $\bar{y} \neq \bar{x}$, then $u^*(\bar{x}, \bar{y}) > u^*(\bar{y}, \bar{y})$. The intuition is the same as in the standard formulation; an evolutionarily stable behavior strategy $\bar{x}$ is "immune" against

---

19. In view of the preceding analysis of evolutionary stability, it might appear natural to also here consider mixed strategies. However, as noted in Selten (1983), behavior strategies constitute a more satisfactory representation when it comes to evolutionary stability considerations; see also van Damme (1987) and Hammerstein and Selten (1993).

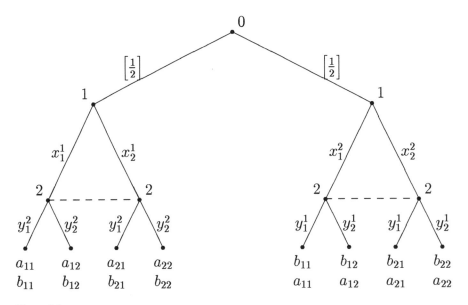

Figure 2.4
The extensive form of the population game in which individuals are randomly assigned player roles by nature (player 0).

a small invasion of any mutant behavior strategy $\bar{y} \neq \bar{x}$ in the sense that the latter earns a lower postentry payoff than the former if the mutant population share is small enough.

2.7.2 Characterization

Selten (1980) establishes a general result with the striking implication for the present special case that *every* evolutionarily stable behavior strategy $\bar{x} = (x^1, x^2) \in \Theta$ in Γ constitutes a strict Nash equilibrium of the underlying game G. The intuition behind this result is that if $\bar{x} = (x^1, x^2)$ is *not* a strict Nash equilibrium, then at least one of its two component strategies, x^1 and x^2, has an alternative best reply. A mutation of $\bar{x}$ in one such component to an alternative best reply to the other component will do just as well as $\bar{x}$ in the postentry population, since the mutant component will never meet itself. Formally:[20]

---

20. A similar result is established for a multipopulation version of evolutionary stability in subsection 5.1.1.

Proposition 2.18 *A behavior strategy $\bar{x}$ in Γ is evolutionarily stable if and only if $\bar{x}$ is a strict Nash equilibrium of G.*

Proof   First, suppose that $\bar{x} = (x^1, x^2) \in \Theta$ is a strict Nash equilibrium of G. Then

$$u^*(\bar{x}, \bar{x}) = \frac{1}{2}\left[u_1(x^1, x^2) + u_2(x^1, x^2)\right] > \frac{1}{2}\left[u_1(y^1, x^2) + u_2(x^1, y^2)\right]$$

for all $\bar{y} = \left(y^1, y^2\right) \neq \bar{x}$, so $\bar{x}$ is an evolutionarily stable strategy in Γ.

Second, suppose that $\bar{x} = (x^1, x^2) \in \Theta$ is *not* a strict Nash equilibrium of G. Suppose that $u_1(y^1, x^2) = u_1(x^1, x^2)$ for some $y^1 \neq x^1$, and let $\bar{z} = (y^1, x^2)$. Then $u^*(\bar{z}, \bar{x}) = u^*(\bar{x}, \bar{x})$, and

$$u^*(\bar{z}, \bar{z}) = \frac{1}{2}\left[u_1(y^1, x^2) + u_2(y^1, x^2)\right]$$

$$= \frac{1}{2}\left[u_1(x^1, x^2) + u_2(y^1, x^2)\right]$$

$$= u^*(\bar{x}, \bar{z}).$$

Hence $\bar{x}$ is not an evolutionarily stable behavior strategy in Γ. The same conclusion is reached if $u_2(x^1, y^2) = u_2(x^1, x^2)$ for some $y^2 \neq x^2$. ∎

The following example illustrates how a base-game ESS can be destabilized in an environment where individuals can condition on their player position in the game, and how an asymmetric base game strategy profile can emerge as an evolutionarily stable behavior strategy in the associated role-conditioned game Γ.

Example 2.14   Reconsider the (symmetric) Hawk-Dove Game in example 2.3, but now with payoffs $v = 2$ and $c = 4$. Normalizing these payoffs as in subsection 1.5.3, we obtain $A = B$ and $a_1 = a_2 = -1$. This game has three Nash equilibria: two asymmetric strict equilibria, in which one player "fights" and the other "yields," and one symmetric mixed equilibrium in which both players randomize uniformly. We found that the latter was an ESS in the standard setup of unconditioned behaviors. However, if individuals can condition their strategy on their player position, as modeled in the present section, then this equilibrium, viewed as a behavior strategy in the associated expanded game Γ, is not evolutionarily stable. The reason is that a monomorphic population in which all individuals randomize uniformly over both strategies, irrespective of their player position, is vulnerable to mutants who fight in one position, say position 1, and yield in the other. These individuals earn the same payoff, $-\frac{1}{2}$, as the incumbents when meeting an incumbent (since the incumbent strategy profile is an interior Nash equilibrium), and they earn more, 0, when meeting each other. This can be formally seen as follows: First, for any pair of behavior strategies $(\bar{x}, \bar{y})$, we have

$$u^*(\bar{x}, \bar{y}) = \frac{1}{2}\left[x^1 \begin{pmatrix} -1 & 0 \\ 0 & -1 \end{pmatrix} y^2 + y^1 \begin{pmatrix} -1 & 0 \\ 0 & -1 \end{pmatrix} x^2 \right]$$

$$= -\frac{1}{2}\left[x_1^1 y_1^2 + x_2^1 y_2^2 + x_1^2 y_1^1 + x_2^2 y_2^1 \right]$$

Hence, if $\hat{x} \in \Theta$ denotes the unique symmetric Nash equilibrium of the base game, $\hat{x} = ((\frac{1}{2}, \frac{1}{2}), (\frac{1}{2}, \frac{1}{2}))$, then $u^*(\bar{y}, \hat{x}) = u^*(\hat{x}, \bar{y}) = u^*(\hat{x}, \hat{x}) = -\frac{1}{2}$ for all behavior strategies $\bar{y} \in \Theta$. Moreover, for $\bar{y} = (e^1, e^2)$, we have $u^*(\bar{y}, \bar{y}) = 0 > u^*(\hat{x}, \bar{y}) = -\frac{1}{2}$, so $\hat{x}$ is not an evolutionarily stable strategy in Γ.

The only evolutionarily stable behavior strategies in Γ correspond to the two strict (and asymmetric) equilibria of the underlying game G. Intuitively this is evident. If the incumbent behavior strategy is to fight in position 1 and yield in position 2, namely $\bar{x} = (e^1, e^2)$, then the unique best reply, in terms of behavior strategies, is $\bar{x}$ itself.

The next example illustrates how the present machinery can be applied to asymmetric games.

Example 2.15 Reconsider the (asymmetric) Entry Deterrence Game in example 1.6, and now imagine that an individual can condition her strategy choice on her role. We saw that the game has a unique strict Nash equilibrium strategy profile, where the intruder (player 1) enters and the incumbent (player 2) yields. The associated behavior strategy is indeed evolutionarily stable: All mutants fare poorly in a population where all individuals enter when they are playing the role of intruder and yield when playing the role of incumbent.

3 The Replicator Dynamics

In general, an evolutionary process combines two basic elements: a *mutation mechanism* that provides variety and a *selection mechanism* that favors some varieties over others. While the criterion of evolutionary stability highlights the role of mutations, the replicator dynamics highlights the role of selection. In its standard formulation to which this chapter is devoted, the replicator dynamics is formalized as a system of ordinary differential equations that do not include any mutation mechanism at all. Instead robustness against mutations is indirectly taken care of by the way of dynamic stability criteria.

In the setup for the evolutionary stability criteria discussed in chapter 2, individuals were imagined to be programmed to pure *or mixed* strategies. In contrast, the usual replicator dynamics presumes that individuals can only be programmed to pure strategies.[1] Hence, instead of interpreting a mixed strategy as a particular randomization, performed by each and every individual in the population, one here interprets a mixed strategy x as a *population state*, each component x_i representing the *population share* of individuals who are programmed to the corresponding pure strategy i. However, one still imagines random pairwise matchings in a large population where payoffs represent fitness, measured as the number of offspring, and each offspring inherits its single parent's strategy (strategies breed true).

If reproduction takes place continuously over time, then this results in a certain population dynamics in continuous time—the *replicator dynamics* (Taylor and Jonker 1978). The *replicators* are here the pure strategies; these can be copied without error from parent to child, the individuals in the population being their hosts.[2] As the population state changes, so do the payoffs to the pure strategies and also their fitness.

As mentioned above, this dynamics and subsequent other selection dynamics (in chapters 4 and 5) are modeled as a system of ordinary differential equations. For the reader's convenience many concepts and techniques for such representations of dynamics are introduced in chapter 6. The discussion of the replicator dynamics in the present chapter is, however, intended

---

1. Mixed-strategist replicator dynamics are discussed, for example, by Zeeman (1981), Akin (1982), Thomas (1985b), and Bomze (1991); see also the discussion in subsection 3.5.2.

2. The term *replicator* appears to have been coined by the British biologist Richard Dawkins (1976). These are entities that can get copied. The probability of being copied may depend on the performance and environment of the replicator, and a copy of a replicator is an identical replicator that may be copied ad infinitum.

to be largely self-explanatory, so an occasional glance in chapter 6 may be sufficient.[3]

The rest of this chapter is organized as follows: Section 3.1 provides a derivation of the replicator dynamics and discusses some of its basic properties. The qualitative dynamic behavior in generic 2×2 games is analyzed, and an application to a certain class of generalized Rock-Scissors-Paper games is given. Section 3.2 studies the long-run survival of weakly, strictly, and iteratively strictly dominated strategies. In section 3.3 implications for Nash equilibrium behavior are studied. It is found that among the stationary population states in the replicator dynamics are those that correspond to aggregate Nash equilibrium behavior. Moreover those stationary states that are dynamically unstable in this dynamics do not correspond to aggregate Nash equilibrium behavior. Hence dynamic stability in the replicator dynamics, while derived without any rationality assumption, implies aggregate behavior that is "rational" and "coordinated" in the sense of Nash equilibrium. While any interior Nash equilibrium passes all the refinement criteria based on trembles in strategies, some of these Nash equilibria are dynamically unstable in the replicator dynamics. In this sense dynamic evolutionary selection may be more demanding than the usual refinements. Section 3.4 establishes that the stringent dynamic stability criterion of asymptotic stability implies perfect Nash equilibrium.

Having established these and other connections with noncooperative solution criteria, we turn in section 3.5 to connections with the static criteria of evolutionary and neutral stability. It is shown how a certain entropy function from information theory provides a key link between static and dynamic evolutionary approaches. In particular, this function can be used to show that evolutionary stability of a strategy $x \in \Delta$ implies that the corresponding population state x is asymptotically stable in the replicator dynamics. By the same token, it is shown that the weaker criterion of neutral stability implies the likewise weaker dynamic stability property of Lyapunov stability. The section is concluded with some results for setwise asymptotic stability.

Section 3.6 focuses on the special case of *doubly* symmetric games—games in which the two players' payoffs always coincide—and establishes the so-called fundamental theorem of natural selection for this class. This result states

---

3. For an excellent textbook introduction to ordinary differential equations, see Hirsch and Smale (1974).

that the population's *average* fitness increases monotonically over time in the replicator dynamics. Evolutionary stability of strategies and sets, respectively, are shown to be equivalent with asymptotic stability in the replicator dynamics in this class of games.

In some applications it is of interest to know which pure strategies survive in the long run. We know from the results in section 3.2 that if initially all pure strategies are present, then the set of surviving pure strategies is a subset of those that are iteratively strictly undominated. However, the subset of survivors may be smaller, depending on initial conditions. Building on the multipopulation model in Ritzberger and Weibull (1993) (to be discussed in chapter 5), section 3.7 provides a sufficient condition for a subset of pure strategies to be a long-run survivor set in the sense that the subset is minimal with the property that if initially virtually no other strategies are present in the population, then all pure strategies outside this subset will vanish over time. The condition in question is simple and based solely on the payoff matrix A of the game.

For more results on the replicator dynamics, the interested reader is advised to consult the excellent book by Hofbauer and Sigmund (1988). Chapter 4 discusses several related topics, including generalizations of the above results to fairly wide classes of selection dynamics, to discrete-time replicator models, and to cheap-talk games.

3.1 Preliminaries

Consider a large but finite population of individuals who are programmed to pure strategies $i \in K$ in a symmetric two-player game with mixed-strategy simplex Δ and payoff function u.[4] At any point t in time, let $p_i(t) \geq 0$ be the *number* of individuals who are currently programmed to pure strategy $i \in K$, and let $p(t) = \sum_{i \in K} p_i(t) > 0$ be the total population. The associated *population state* is defined as the vector $x(t) = (x_1(t), \ldots, x_k(t))$, where each component $x_i(t)$ is the population share programmed to pure strategy i at time

---

4. The same machinery as is developed below can be used also for mixed-strategist replicator dynamics, granted there are only finitely many mixed strategies to which an individual can be programmed. Formally, let this finite subset of mixed strategies be $\{z^r\}_{r=1}^m \subset \Delta$, and consider the associated finite and symmetric two-player game G' which has pure strategy set $K' = \{1, \ldots, m\}$ and pure-strategy payoffs $\pi(r, s) = u(z^r, z^s), r, s \in K'$. See also subsection 3.5.2 for a brief discussion.

t: $x_i(t) = p_i(t)/p(t)$. Thus $x(t) \in \Delta$; in other words, a population state is formally identical with a mixed strategy.

The expected payoff to any pure strategy i at a random match, when the population is in state $x \in \Delta$, is accordingly $u(e^i, x)$. Indeed it is immaterial for an individual whether she interacts with an individual drawn at random from such a polymorphic population or, as in the setup for evolutionary stability, an individual playing the mixed strategy x. The associated *population average payoff*, in other words, the payoff to an individual drawn at random from the population, is

$$u(x, x) = \sum_{i=1}^{k} x_i u(e^i, x), \tag{3.1}$$

the same payoff as the mixed *strategy* x earns when played against itself.

3.1.1 Derivation

Suppose that payoffs represent the incremental effect from playing the game in question, on an individual's *fitness*, measured as the number of offspring per time unit. Suppose also that each offspring inherits its single parent's strategy—strategies breed true. If reproduction takes place continuously over time, then the *birthrate* at any time t, of individuals programmed to pure strategy i, is $\beta + u[e^i, x(t)]$, where $\beta \geq 0$ is the background fitness of individuals in the population (independent of the outcomes in the game under study). Let the death rate $\delta \geq 0$ be the same for all individuals. With dots for time derivatives and suppressing time arguments, this results in the following population dynamics:[5]

$$\dot{p}_i = \left[\beta + u(e^i, x) - \delta \right] p_i. \tag{3.2}$$

The corresponding dynamics for the population shares x_i becomes

$$\dot{x}_i = \left[u(e^i, x) - u(x, x) \right] x_i. \tag{3.3}$$

To see this, take the time derivative of both sides of the identity $p(t)x_i(t) = p_i(t)$:

---

5. By the law of large numbers, the average number of offspring to individuals playing strategy i is close to the expected payoff value $u(e^i, x)$ when n_i is large. For a critical analysis of deterministic approximations of random matching models, see Boylan (1992).

$$p\dot{x}_i = \dot{p}_i - \dot{p}x_i = \left[\beta + u(e^i, x) - \delta\right]p_i - \left[\beta + u(x, x) - \delta\right]px_i. \qquad (3.4)$$

Division of both sides by p gives (3.3).

In other words, the *growth rate* $\dot{x}_i/x_i$ of the population share using strategy i equals the difference between the strategy's current payoff (fitness) and the current average payoff (fitness) in the population. This growth rate is independent of the background birthrates and deathrates β and δ, since these are the same for all subpopulations (pure strategies). Equation (3.3) gives the *replicator dynamics* (Taylor and Jonker 1978). Exploiting the linearity of the payoff $u(x, y)$ in x, one may write this dynamics more concisely as

$$\dot{x}_i = u(e^i - x, x)x_i. \qquad\qquad e^i Ax - xAx = (e^i - x)Ax \qquad\qquad (3.5)$$

Hence those subpopulations that are associated with better-than-average strategies grow, while those associated with worse-than-average strategies decline. The subpopulations associated with pure *best* replies to the current population state $x \in \Delta$ have the highest growth rate.

Note also that the ratio between any two population shares $x_i > 0$ and $x_j > 0$ increases (decreases) over time if strategy i earns a higher (lower) payoff than strategy j:

$$\frac{d}{dt}\left[\frac{x_i}{x_j}\right] = \frac{\dot{x}_i}{x_j} - \frac{x_i}{x_j}\frac{\dot{x}_j}{x_j} = [u(e^i, x) - u(e^j, x)]\frac{x_i}{x_j}. \qquad (3.6)$$

3.1.2 Invariance under Payoff Transformations

The replicator dynamics (3.5) is invariant under positive affine transformations of payoffs, modulo a change of time scale. For if the payoff function u is replaced by a function $\bar{u} = \lambda u + \mu$, for some positive real number λ and real number μ, then the replicator dynamics becomes

$$\dot{x}_i = \bar{u}(e^i - x, x)x_i = \lambda u(e^i - x, x)x_i. \qquad (3.7)$$

The effect of such a payoff transformation is thus equivalent to a change of time scale by the factor $\lambda > 0$ in the replicator dynamics (3.5). In particular, all solution orbits are the same for both dynamics; only the *velocity* at which the population state moves along these orbits differs, by the factor λ.

Similarly local shifts of payoff functions (subsection 1.3.3) do not affect the replicator dynamics at all. If some constant $v \in R$ is added to all entries in some column j of the payoff matrix A, then the payoff $u(e^i, x)$ to any pure strategy i is replaced by $\bar{u}(e^i, x) = u(e^i, x) + vx_j$, resulting in $\bar{u}(x, x) = u(x, x) + vx_j$, with no change at all in the replicator dynamics (3.5).

3.1.3   The Induced Solution Mapping

The right-hand side of (3.5) defines the associated *vector field* $\varphi : R^k \to R^k$, where

$$\varphi_i(x) = u(e^i - x, x)x_i \, .$$

Since this vector field is a polynomial in the population shares, the system of differential equations (3.5) has a unique *solution* through any initial state $x^o \in R^k$, by the Picard-Lindelöf theorem (theorem 6.1). Furthermore the simplex $\Delta \subset R^k$ can be shown to be *invariant* in this dynamics. That is the solution orbit to (3.5) through any initial state in Δ is contained in Δ. Intuitively this is clear, since, by (3.5), the sum of all population shares necessarily remains equal to one ($\sum \dot{x}_i = 0$) and no population share can ever turn negative ($x_i = 0 \Rightarrow \dot{x}_i = 0$).

More precisely, the system of differential equations (3.5) defines a continuous *solution mapping* $\xi : R \times \Delta \to \Delta$ which to each initial state $x^o \in \Delta$ and time $t \in R$ assigns the population state $\xi(t, x^o) \in \Delta$ at time t. Since the unit simplex Δ is invariant, so is its interior and boundary. In other words, if all pure strategies are present in the population at any time, then they have always been and always will be present, and likewise, if a pure strategy is absent from the population at any time, then it has always been and always will be absent. Of course it is not precluded that an interior solution trajectory converges to the boundary of the simplex as time goes to infinity; at any time the population state will then be interior, but its distance to the boundary goes to zero, and so in the limit some pure strategies may become extinct. (For formal statements and proofs of these claims, see propositions 6.1 and 6.2 and the appendix at the end of this chapter.)

3.1.4   Symmetric 2×2 Games

In this section we apply the replicator dynamics (3.5) to the special case of generic symmetric two-player games with only two pure strategies. It turns out that in such games a population state is *asymptotically stable* in the replicator dynamics if and only if the corresponding mixed strategy is evolutionarily stable (see subsection 2.1.2).[6]

Since the replicator dynamics (3.5) is invariant under a local shift of payoffs, we may, without loss of generality, presume that the payoff matrix has the following form:

$$A = \begin{pmatrix} a_1 & 0 \\ 0 & a_2 \end{pmatrix}. \tag{3.8}$$

We focus on the generic case when $a_1 a_2 \neq 0$. The replicator dynamics in these normalized payoffs becomes

$$\dot{x}_1 = [a_1 x_1 - a_2 x_2] x_1 x_2, \tag{3.9}$$

where $\dot{x}_2 = -\dot{x}_1$ (the two shares always sum to one). In the classification of subsection 1.5.3:

Categories I and IV   If $a_1 a_2 < 0$, then the population share x_1 either always declines (when $a_1 < 0$ and $a_2 > 0$) or always grows (when $a_1 > 0$ and $a_2 < 0$). Hence, starting from any interior initial position, the population state converges over time to the unique ESS of such a game; see figures 3.1 (a) and (d) for categories I and IV, respectively.

Categories II and III   If $a_1 a_2 > 0$, then the growth rate of x_1 changes sign when $a_1 x_1 = a_2 x_2$, which occurs precisely at the mixed-strategy Nash equilibrium value $x_1 = \lambda = a_2/(a_1 + a_2)$. Suppose, first, that both payoffs are positive (category II). Then x_1 decreases toward 0 from any initial value $x_1^o < \lambda$, and, conversely, increases toward 1 from any initial value $x_1^o > \lambda$; see figure 3.1 (b). In other words, starting from any interior initial position, the population state converges to one of the two ESS's of such a game. The "basins of attraction" of these meet precisely at the mixed-strategy Nash equilibrium point $x_1 = \lambda$. Second, suppose that both payoffs are negative (category III). Then the population share x_1 increases toward λ from any lower (interior) initial value and decreases toward λ from any higher (interior) initial value; see figure 3.1 (c). Hence the population state converges over time to the unique ESS of any such game, from any interior initial state.

---

6. See section 6.4 for formal definitions of Lyapunov and asymptotic stability. Intuitively, a state $x \in \Delta$ is *Lyapunov stable* if no small change in the population composition can lead it away, and x is *asymptotically stable* if moreover any sufficiently small such change results in a movement back toward x.

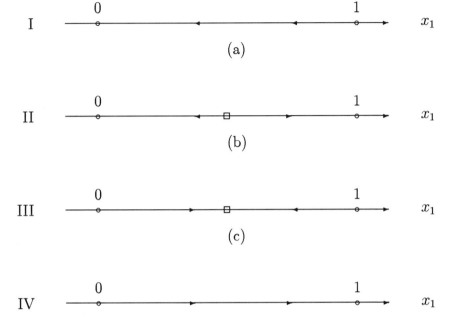

Figure 3.1
The replicator dynamics in symmetric 2×2 games: (a) Category I, (b) category II, (c) category III, (d) category IV.

Example 3.1 To obtain the replicator dynamics for the Prisoner's Dilemma Game of example 1.1, first note that $a_1 = -1$ and $a_2 = 3$. Using the identity $x_1 + x_2 = 1$ in equation (3.9), we get

$$\dot{x}_1 = (2x_1 - 3)(1 - x_1)x_1$$

(and $\dot{x}_2 = -\dot{x}_1$). Likewise, for the Coordination Game of example 1.10, we obtain

$$\dot{x}_1 = (3x_1 - 1)(1 - x_1)x_1 ,$$

and, for the Hawk-Dove Game of example 2.3, we have $a_1 = -1$ and $a_2 = -2$, and hence

$$\dot{x}_1 = (2 - 3x_1)(1 - x_1)x_1 .$$

3.1.5   Generalized Rock-Scissors-Paper Games

Consider the following generalization of the Rock-Scissors-Paper Game of example 1.12:

$$A = \begin{pmatrix} 1 & 2+a & 0 \\ 0 & 1 & 2+a \\ 2+a & 0 & 1 \end{pmatrix}, \tag{3.10}$$

where $a \in R$. The original RSP Game now is the special case $a = 0$. and the game of example 2.7 corresponds to the case $a = -1$. For any a the game has a unique interior Nash equilibrium strategy, $x^* = (\frac{1}{3}, \frac{1}{3}, \frac{1}{3})$.[7]

While section 3.5 provides the general principle, it will be shown below that the product $x_1 x_2 x_3$ increases (decreases, is constant) along any interior solution path of the replicator dynamics if a is positive (negative, zero). To see this, first note that the replicator dynamics (3.5) becomes

$$\dot{x}_1 = [x_1 + (2+a)x_2 - x \cdot Ax]x_1, \tag{3.11}$$

$$\dot{x}_2 = [x_2 + (2+a)x_3 - x \cdot Ax]x_2, \tag{3.12}$$

$$\dot{x}_3 = [x_3 + (2+a)x_1 - x \cdot Ax]x_3. \tag{3.13}$$

Hence the time derivative of $h(x) = log(x_1 x_2 x_3)$ is

$$\begin{aligned} \dot{h}(x) &= \dot{x}_1 x_2 x_3 / x_1 + x_1 \dot{x}_2 x_3 / x_2 + x_1 x_2 \dot{x}_3 / x_3 \\ &= (x_1 + x_2 + x_3) + (2+a)(x_1 + x_2 + x_3) - 3x \cdot Ax \\ &= 3 + a - 3x \cdot Ax. \end{aligned} \tag{3.14}$$

By the identity

$$1 = (x_1 + x_2 + x_3)^2 = \|x\|^2 + 2(x_1 x_2 + x_2 x_3 + x_1 x_3), \tag{3.15}$$

where $\|x\|^2 = x_1^2 + x_2^2 + x_3^2$, the average payoff $x \cdot Ax$ can be written

$$x \cdot Ax = 1 + a(x_1 x_2 + x_2 x_3 + x_1 x_3) = 1 + \frac{a}{2}(1 - \|x\|^2), \tag{3.16}$$

and hence

---

7. See Weissing (1991) for a comprehensive analysis of continuous-time and discrete-time replicator dynamics in a class of 3×3 games including these games.

$$\dot{h}(x) = \frac{a}{2}(3\|x\|^2 - 1). \tag{3.17}$$

Note that the squared norm $\|x\|^2$ is maximal at each of the three vertices of the unit simplex Δ, where it achieves the value 1, and is minimal at its center point x^*, where it achieves the value $\frac{1}{3}$. Hence the factor $(3\|x\|^2 - 1)$ in the right-hand side of (3.17) is zero at $x = x^*$ and positive elsewhere on Δ.

It follows that, in the original Rock-Scissors-Paper Game ($a = 0$), all solution paths are *cycles* on Δ. More exactly, for any initial state $x^o \in \text{int}(\Delta)$, the solution $\xi(t, x^o)$ moves perpetually along the closed curve on which $x_1 x_2 x_3$ is constantly equal to $\gamma = x_1^o x_2^o x_3^o$. (Recall that x^* is the only interior stationary state.) Geometrically such a curve is the intersection of the hyperbola in R^3 given by the equation $x_1 x_2 x_3 = \gamma$ with the unit simplex Δ; see figure 3.2 (a). If $x^o = x^*$, then this intersection reduces to the single point x^* itself, while for any other $x^o \in \text{int}(\Delta)$, the intersection is a smooth closed curve in $\text{int}(\Delta)$. Hence all interior solution trajectories to the replicator dynamics are periodic when $a = 0$.

In contrast, if $a < 0$, then the dynamic paths induced on Δ move *outward*, toward hyperbolas with lower γ, from all interior initial states except $x^o = x^*$; see figure 3.2 (b) for an orbit when $-1 < a < 0$. Conversely, if $a > 0$, then all trajectories move *inward*, toward hyperbolas with higher γ; see figure 3.2 (c).

Hence, for any $a > 0$, the unique Nash equilibrium strategy x^* in this game is asymptotically stable and attracts the whole interior of the state space. When $a = 0$, x^* is Lyapunov stable but not asymptotically stable, and when $a < 0$, x^* is unstable (not Lyapunov stable).

Phrased in terms of *sets* of population states, we have found that, when a is positive (negative), all upper (lower) contour sets of the function $h(x) = x_1 x_2 x_3$ are asymptotically stable. In the second case ($a < 0$), also the boundary of Δ is asymptotically stable. In the knife-edge case when a is zero, the full space Δ is the only asymptotically stable set.[8]

The dynamic stability properties of x^* fit well with how x^* meets the criteria of evolutionary and neutral stability. It is easily verified, from the above computations, that for any $x \in \Delta$, $u(x^*, x) - u(x, x) = a(\|x\|^2 - \frac{1}{3})/2$. Hence x^* is evolutionarily stable when $a > 0$, neutrally but not evolutionarily stable when $a = 0$, and not even neutrally stable when $a < 0$.

---

8. The definition of asymptotic stability of a set is a straightforward extension of asymptotic stability of a point; see section 6.4 for details.

3.2 Dominated Strategies

The population share of individuals programmed to a certain pure strategy grows in the replicator dynamics (3.5) if and only if the strategy earns a payoff above the current population average. Since even a strictly dominated strategy may earn more than average, it is not clear a priori whether such strategies necessarily get wiped out in the replicator dynamics. Indeed Dekel and Scotchmer (1992) provide a game in which a strategy for this reason does *not* become extinct in a *discrete-time* version of the replicator dynamics (see section 4.1). It turns out, however, that in the continuous-time replicator dynamics (3.5), strictly dominated strategies do vanish in the long run. The same is true for all iteratively strictly dominated strategies, but not for all weakly dominated strategies.

Recall that ξ denotes the solution mapping for the replicator dynamics (3.5). Hence $\xi(t, x^o) \in \Delta$ is the population state at time $t \in R$ if the initial state is $x^o \in \Delta$.

3.2.1 Strict and Iterated Strict Dominance

The following result, due to Akin (1980; see also Samuelson and Zhang 1992), establishes that the replicator dynamics wipes out all strictly dominated pure strategies from the population, granted all pure strategies in the game are initially present:

Proposition 3.1 *If a pure strategy i is strictly dominated, then $\xi_i(t, x^o)_{t \to \infty} \to 0$, for any $x^o \in \text{int}(\Delta)$.*

Proof Suppose that $i \in K$ is strictly dominated by $y \in \Delta$, and let

$$\epsilon = \min_{x \in \Delta} u(y - e^i, x).$$

By continuity of u and compactness of Δ, $\epsilon > 0$. Define the function v_i: $\text{int}(\Delta) \to R$ by

$$v_i(x) = \log(x_i) - \sum_{j=1}^{k} y_j \log(x_j)$$

Clearly v_i is differentiable, and its time derivative along any interior solution path to (3.5) is, at any point $x = \xi(t, x^o)$,

(a)

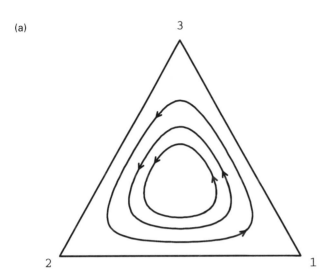

(b)

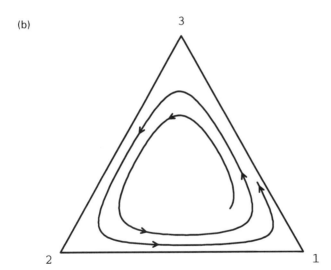

(c)

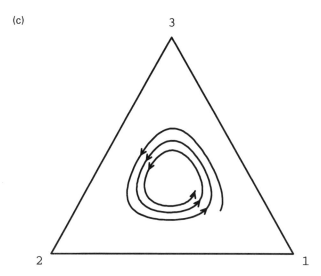

Figure 3.2
The replicator dynamics in generalized Rock-Scissors-Paper games: (a) $a = 0$, (b) $a < 0$,
(c) $a > 0$.

$$\dot{v}_i(x) = \left[\frac{dv_i(\xi(t, x^o))}{dt}\right]_{\xi(t,x^o)=x}$$

$$= \sum_{j=1}^{k} \frac{\partial v_i(x)}{\partial x_j} \dot{x}_j$$

$$= \frac{\dot{x}_i}{x_i} - \sum_{j=1}^{k} \frac{y_j \dot{x}_j}{x_j} = u(e^i - x, x) - \sum_{j=1}^{k} y_j u(e^j - x, x)$$

$$= u(e^i - y, x) \le -\epsilon < 0.$$

Hence $v_i(\xi(t, x^o))$ decreases toward minus infinity as $t \to \infty$. By definition of v_i, this implies that $\xi_i(t, x^o) \to 0$. ∎

By proposition 1.1, a strategy is strictly undominated in a two-player game if and only if it is a best reply to some (pure or mixed) strategy. Hence one may rephrase the above result as saying that evolution selects against behavior which is *irrational* in the sense of being suboptimal under *any* probabilistic belief about the opponent's strategy. This selection takes place irrespective of whether the evolutionary solution path converges or not, so in the long run (virtually) no individual will behave irrationally in this sense even if aggregate behavior fluctuates forever.

Note the importance of the hypothesis that all pure strategies in the game are initially present. For instance, if some strategy i is strictly dominated but no other pure strategy is initially present, then clearly $\xi_i(t, x^o) = 1$ at all times t. Or, more generally, if some strategy i is not strictly dominated when some other pure strategy j is removed from the game, then we need not have $\xi_i(t, x^o) \to 0$ if strategy j is initially absent.

By a somewhat more involved argument, Samuelson and Zhang (1992) have shown that the replicator dynamics wipes out all *iteratively* strictly dominated pure strategies from the population. Intuitively this extension is not surprising. Proposition 3.1 tells that after a sufficiently long time the population state will be and forever remain arbitrarily near the face of the mixed-strategy simplex Δ which is spanned by the subset $K^1 \subset K$ of pure strategies that are not strictly dominated. By continuity, those pure strategies that are strictly dominated in the reduced game G^1 (with pure strategy set K^1) vanish, according to proposition 3.1 as applied to the reduced game G^1, and so on, until no more pure strategies can be so eliminated. Samuelson and Zhang give a formal proof of this result, for a class of evolutionary selection dynamics including (3.5):[9]

Theorem 3.1 *If a pure strategy i is iteratively strictly dominated, then $\xi_i(t, x^o)_{t \to \infty} \to 0$, for any $x^o \in \text{int}(\Delta)$.*

In two-player games it is as if evolution not only selects against behaviors that are irrational in the sense of being suboptimal under every probabilistic belief concerning one's opponent's strategy, it also selects against all behaviors that are optimal under probabilistic beliefs that presume that one's opponent is irrational in this sense, ad infinitum, along a hierarchy of mutual beliefs.

Example 3.2 Reconsider the strictly dominance solvable game of example 1.4. If all pure strategies are initially present, then all pure strategies but strategy 1 get wiped out in the replicator dynamics (3.5), by theorem 3.1. In other words, every interior solution path converges to the vertex e^1 of Δ. This is also the unique ESS of the game, so both evolutionary approaches agree with noncooperative game theory in this example.

---

9. Their result concerns the interaction between two distinct populations; it is stated in chapter 5, where the connection between multipopulation and single-population dynamics is discussed.

3.2.2 Weak Dominance

While the replicator dynamics has been seen to wipe out all strictly dominated strategies, this is not generally the case with weakly dominated strategies. This issue is addressed in Samuelson (1993), where it is found that, in a number of alternative evolutionary selection dynamics, including the replicator dynamics, such strategies are not necessarily eliminated.

However, one can show that if a pure strategy i is weakly dominated by some strategy $y \in \Delta$, and the subpopulation programmed to strategy i does *not* vanish over time, then all those pure strategies j against which y is better than i vanish from the population. This result follows from a modification of the above proof of proposition 3.1:[10]

Proposition 3.2 *Suppose that a pure strategy i is weakly dominated by some strategy $y \in \Delta$. If $u(y - e^i, e^j) > 0$, then $\xi_i(t, x^o)_{t \to \infty} \to 0$ or $\xi_j(t, x^o)_{t \to \infty} \to 0$ (or both) for any $x^o \in int(\Delta)$.*

Proof Let $v_i : int(\Delta) \to R$ be as in the proof of proposition 3.1, where now $y \in \Delta$ *weakly* dominates e^i. Then

$$\frac{d}{dt} v_i \left(\xi(t, x^o) \right) = u \left(e^i - y, \xi(t, x^o) \right) \leq 0$$

at all times $t \geq 0$. Suppose that $j \in K$ is such that $u(y - e^i, e^j) = \varepsilon > 0$. Since y weakly dominates e^i,

$$u(y - e^i, x) = \sum_h u(y - e^i, e^h) x_h \geq u(y - e^i, e^j) x_j \geq \varepsilon x_j$$

for any $x \in \Delta$. Hence at all times $t \geq 0$,

$$\frac{d}{dt} v_i \left(\xi(t, x^o) \right) \leq -\varepsilon \xi_j(t, x^o) \leq 0 .$$

Integration with respect to t gives $v_i[\xi(t, x^o)] \leq v_i(x^o) - \epsilon \int_0^t \xi_j(\tau, x^o) d\tau$. The integral is increasing in t and thus either tends to $+\infty$ or to some $\beta \in R_+$, as $t \to +\infty$. In the first case $v_i(\xi(t, x^o)) \to -\infty$, and hence $\xi_i(t, x^o) \to 0$ by definition of v_i. In the second case $\xi_j(t, x^o) \to 0$ by uniform continuity of $\xi(t, x^o)$ in t: By (3.5), $|\frac{d}{dt} \xi_j(t, x^o)| \leq \gamma$ for all t, where $\gamma = \max_{x \in \Delta} |u(e^j - x, x)| \in R_+$. (If $\xi_j(t, x^o)$ did not converge to 0, then there would exist some

---

10. I am grateful to Josef Hofbauer and Larry Samuelson for helpful comments.

$\delta > 0$ and an increasing and unbounded sequence of times $t_k > 0$ such that $\xi_j(t_k, x^o) > \delta$ for all k. Without loss of generality we may assume that $t_{k+1} - t_k > 2\delta/\gamma$ for all k, and then the integral $\int_0^\infty \xi_j(\tau, x^o)d\tau = \beta$ would represent an area containing infinitely many nonoverlapping triangles, each with height δ and base $2\delta/gamma$, a contradiction.) ∎

By proposition 1.1, a pure strategy is undominated if and only if it is a best reply to some completely mixed strategy. Hence one may rephrase the above result as saying that evolution selects weakly against behavior that is suboptimal under any probabilistic belief about one's opponent's strategy that assigns positive probability to *all* his pure strategies. The selection is weak in the sense that such behavior need not vanish if, in the long run, those pure strategies j against which i is suboptimal vanish.

The following simple example illustrates how this result can be used to show that, in certain games, a weakly dominated strategy does vanish along any interior solution path.

Example 3.3   Consider the 2×2 game with payoff matrix

$$A = \begin{pmatrix} 0 & 1 \\ 0 & 0 \end{pmatrix}.$$

The second pure strategy, $i = 2$, is weakly dominated by the first pure strategy, $y = e^1$, and y outperforms i against $j = 2$. Hence $\xi_2(t, x^o) \to 0$, for any $x^o \in \text{int}(\Delta)$. Indeed in this game equation (3.9) becomes $\dot{x}_1 = (1 - x_1)^2 x_1$ and $\dot{x}_2 = -\dot{x}_1$, showing that x_1 increases monotonically toward 1 from any initial state with $x_1^o > 0$.

In the following example a weakly dominated strategy survives in the long run, in fact in any positive population share that one may wish.

Example 3.4   Consider the 3×3 game with payoff matrix

$$A = \begin{pmatrix} 1 & 1 & 1 \\ 1 & 1 & 0 \\ 0 & 0 & 0 \end{pmatrix}.$$

The second pure strategy, $i = 2$, is weakly dominated by the first pure strategy, $y = e^1$, and y outperforms i against $j = 3$. Hence $\xi_2(t, x^o) \to 0$ or $\xi_3(t, x^o) \to 0$ for any $x^o \in \text{int}(\Delta)$. Strategy 3 is strictly dominated by strategy 1, so we do have $\xi_3(t, x^o) \to 0$, allowing for the possibility that strategy 2 does not

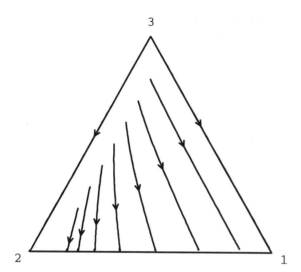

Figure 3.3
Replicator solution orbits in the game of example 3.4.

vanish. Indeed in this game equation (3.6) becomes $d(x_1/x_2)/dt = x_1 x_3/x_2 > 0$. Hence in the interior of the simplex subpopulation 1 does grow faster than subpopulation 2, but as subpopulation 3 converges to zero, the difference in growth rates goes to zero. All interior solution paths are convergent; they all end up on the boundary face where strategy 3 is extinct, and in the limit, x_2 may take any value between zero and one, depending on the initial population state. See figure 3.3 for a few solution orbits.

3.3 Nash Equilibrium Strategies

For any finite and symmetric two-player game under study, let $\Delta^{NE} \subset \Delta$ as before denote its (nonempty) subset of strategies which are in Nash equilibrium with themselves. It turns out to be convenient for the subsequent dynamic analysis to use the fact that a strategy x belongs to Δ^{NE} if and only if all those pure strategies to which x assigns positive probability earn the maximal payoff that can be obtained against x. Formally,

$$\Delta^{NE} = \left\{ x \in \Delta : u(e^i, x) = \max_{z \in \Delta} u(z, x) \;\; \forall i \in C(x) \right\} . \tag{3.18}$$

We proceed to study relationships between this set and the sets of stationary, Lyapunov stable, and limit states, respectively, under the replicator dynamics (3.5). We also briefly examine two connections with time averages over solution trajectories.

3.3.1 Stationary States and Δ^{NE}

By definition, a population state $x \in \Delta$ is stationary in (3.5) if and only if the product $u(e^i - x, x)x_i$ is zero for all pure strategies $i \in K$, or equivalently, if and only if all pure strategies i which are present in population state x earn precisely the same payoff. Let $\Delta^o \subset \Delta$ denote the set of stationary states in (3.5):

$$\Delta^o = \left\{ x \in \Delta : u(e^i, x) = u(x, x) \;\; \forall i \in C(x) \right\} . \tag{3.19}$$

The condition for stationarity is trivially met by each vertex $x = e^i$ of the simplex, since in such a population state x all individuals use the same pure strategy i and earn the same payoff. Hence the finite set $\left\{ e^1, \ldots, e^k \right\}$ of vertices is a subset of Δ^o. In a sense the stationarity of these points is an artifact of the replicator dynamics; since the replicator dynamics does not involve any mutations (strategies breed true), there is nothing in the model that can get evolution started from such an extreme population state.

A comparison between (3.18) and (3.19) immediately reveals that also the (nonempty and closed) set Δ^{NE} is a subset of Δ^o: If all pure strategies in the support of a strategy x earn the same maximal payoff against x, then they all earn the population average payoff,

$$u(x, x) = \sum_{j=1}^{k} u(e^j, x)x_j = \sum_{j \in C(x)} u(e^j, x)x_j . \tag{3.20}$$

For interior population states x, also the converse is true: If $x \in \text{int}(\Delta)$ is stationary in (3.5), then $u(e^i, x) = u(x, x)$ for all pure strategies i in the game, by (3.19), and so all pure strategies are best replies to the mixed strategy x, and consequently $x \in \Delta^{NE}$. Letting Δ^{oo} denote the (possibly empty) set of interior stationary states, $\Delta^{oo} = \Delta^o \cap \text{int}(\Delta)$, we have just shown that Δ^{oo} is a subset of Δ^{NE}. Since all Nash equilibria are stationary, we actually have $\Delta^{oo} = \Delta^{NE} \cap \text{int}(\Delta)$. Moreover, as noted by Zeeman (1981), the set Δ^{oo} is necessarily convex. In fact any linear combination $z = \alpha x + \beta y \in \Delta$ of states

x, y in Δ^{oo} is again a stationary state, indeed belongs to the subset Δ^{NE} of stationary states. In sum:

Proposition 3.3 $\{e^1, \ldots, e^k\} \cup \Delta^{NE} \subset \Delta^o$, $\Delta^{oo} = \Delta^{NE} \cap \text{int}(\Delta)$, *and* Δ^{oo} *is a convex set such that any linear combination* $z \in \Delta$ *of states in* Δ^{oo} *belongs to* Δ^{NE}.

Proof It only remains to prove the last claim. For this purpose suppose that $x, y \in \Delta^{oo}$, and let $\alpha, \beta \in R$ be such that $z = \alpha x + \beta y \in \Delta$. For any pure strategy $i \in K$ we have

$$u(e^i, z) = \alpha u(e^i, x) + \beta u(e^i, y) = \alpha u(x, x) + \beta u(y, y)$$

by bilinearity of u, stationarity of x and y, and the hypothesis that these two states are interior. Hence, ~~since~~ all pure strategies i earn the same pay-off against z, $z \in \Delta^o$. If $z \in \Delta^{oo}$, then $z \in \Delta^{NE}$. Otherwise, z is a boundary point of $\Delta^{oo} = \Delta^{NE} \cap \text{int}(\Delta)$, and hence $z \in \Delta^{NE}$, since Δ^{NE} is a closed set. Moreover, since Δ is convex and $z \in \Delta^{oo}$ for all $\alpha, \beta \geq 0$ with $\alpha + \beta = 1$, Δ^{oo} is convex. ∎

This proposition has strong implications for the geometric nature of the set $\Delta^o \subset \Delta$ of stationary states in the replicator dynamics. For instance, in 2×2 games the set Δ^{oo} is empty, a singleton, or the whole interior of the (one-dimensional) simplex; see figure 1.1 (a). Likewise in 3×3 games the set Δ^{oo} contains no state at all, exactly one state x, or all states on some straight line through $\text{int}(\Delta)$, or else all of $\text{int}(\Delta)$; see figure 1.1 (b). In the first case Δ^{NE} contains no interior point but, by proposition 1.5, at least one point x on the boundary of Δ. In the second case the unique interior stationary point x belongs to Δ^{NE}, while no other interior point does. In the third case all points on the line segment through Δ, including its two intersections with the boundary of the simplex, are stationary states and belong to Δ^{NE}. In the fourth (degenerate) case every state is stationary and in Nash equilibrium with itself. Note also the implications for the geometry of the set of stationary states on the edges (boundary faces) of the simplex in these games: Such stationary states are either isolated points, in which case there is at most one on the relative interior of each edge, or they constitute a whole edge. This follows from an application of the above proposition to each edge in isolation: Each such edge is invariant in the replicator dynamics (3.5) and may thus be treated as the mixed-strategy space of the associated 2×2 game, and so on.

Example 3.5   Reconsider the game in example 2.9. By proposition 3.3, the set Δ^o of stationary points in the replicator dynamics contains the three vertices and the whole continuum $\Delta^{NE} = \{x \in \Delta : x_1 = x_2\}$ but no other point in the interior of the simplex. It is easily verified that no other boundary point is stationary.

3.3.2   Lyapunov Stable States and Δ^{NE}

It was earlier noted that the replicator dynamics does not account for the evolutionarily relevant possibility of mutations. In the present setup the replicators are the pure strategies of the game, so a mutation can only take the form of a shift from one pure strategy to another. Suppose that the population initially is in some stationary state $x \in \Delta$, and suddenly such mutations take place in a small fraction ϵ of the population (perhaps mutations to different pure strategies in different individuals). For instance, if all pure strategies are equally prone to mutate, and y_i is the probability that a mutation results in any pure strategy $i \in K$, then this amounts to a shift from the initial population state x to the population state $x' = (1 - \epsilon)x + \epsilon y \in \Delta$. Stationary states that are not robust to this type of perturbation of the population state thus appear less interesting from an evolutionary viewpoint. It turns out that *all* stationary states that are not in Δ^{NE} can be rejected on these grounds: Dynamic stability in (3.5) requires (symmetric) Nash equilibrium, just as evolutionary and neutral stability was seen to do in chapter 2.

More precisely, stationary states that are not Nash equilibria fail even the weak dynamic stability criterion of *Lyapunov* stability. The reason why a stationary state x not in Δ^{NE} is dynamically unstable is simply that then there exists some pure strategy i that is unused in the population state ($x_i = 0$) but that earns a higher payoff against x than those pure strategies used in state x; all of the latter have to earn the same payoff by stationarity. Hence, if some arbitrarily small but positive fraction of the population starts using such a profitable but in x absent strategy i, then these mutating individuals earn a higher payoff, and thus their population share grows, leading the population state to leave x. This result is due to Bomze (1986).

Proposition 3.4   *If $x \in \Delta$ is Lyapunov stable in (3.5), then $x \in \Delta^{NE}$.*

Proof   Suppose that $x \in \Delta^o$ and $x \notin \Delta^{NE}$. Then all pure strategies in the support $C(x)$ earn the same suboptimal payoff against x. Hence there exists some $i \notin C(x)$ such that $u(e^i - x, x) > 0$. By continuity of u, there is a $\delta > 0$

and a neighborhood U of x such that $u(e^i - y, y) \geq \delta$ for all $y \in U \cap \Delta$. But then $\xi_i(t, x^o) \geq x_i^o \exp(\delta t)$ for any $x^o \in U \cap \Delta$ and all times $t > 0$ such that $\xi(t, x^o) \in U \cap \Delta$. Thus $\xi_i(t, x^o)$ initially increases exponentially from any $x^o \in U \cap \text{int}(\Delta)$, and yet $x_i = 0$, so x is not Lyapunov stable. ∎

Like the evolutionary stability criteria in chapter 2, Lyapunov stability in the replicator dynamics goes beyond Nash equilibrium. For instance, the unique interior Nash equilibrium in the generalized Rock-Scissors-Paper games in subsection 3.1.5 is symmetric and completely mixed, and the corresponding strategy $x \in \Delta^{NE}$ is seen to be Lyapunov stable if and only if $a \geq 0$. In contrast, this Nash equilibrium passes all the trembles-based noncooperative refinements in section 1.4 for any value of a. Likewise in subsection 3.1.4 we found that the mixed-strategy Nash equilibrium in Coordination games (category II) is dynamically unstable, while, again, this equilibrium satisfies all the refinement criteria. In contrast, the mixed-strategy Nash equilibrium in Hawk-Dove games (category III), which also passes the refinement tests, was seen to be asymptotically stable in the replicator dynamics, so for this particular equilibrium the rationalistic and evolutionary paradigms agree.

3.3.3 Limit States and Δ^{NE}

It was shown in section 3.2 that even if an interior solution trajectory to the replicator dynamics does not converge over time, long-run aggregate behavior is nevertheless rational in the sense that iteratively strictly dominated strategies are abandoned. It is not difficult to show that if such a solution trajectory does converge over time, then long-run aggregate behavior is not only rational in this sense but even coordinated in the sense of Nash equilibrium. It is as if (virtually) all individuals in the population knew the long-run population distribution of pure strategies and maximized their own payoff against this distribution.

When proving this result, one may first make the general observation that if a state is the limit of a solution trajectory (to a system of autonomous ordinary differential equations), then the state is necessarily stationary (see proposition 6.3). In particular, if a solution trajectory to the replicator dynamics happens to converge to some *interior* population state, then this limit state belongs to Δ^{oo} and hence also to Δ^{NE}, by proposition 3.3. The following result extends this result to limit states that are on the boundary of the simplex (Nachbar 1990):

Proposition 3.5   *If $x^o \in \text{int}(\Delta)$ and $\xi(t, x^o)_{t \to \infty} \to x$, then $x \in \Delta^{NE}$.*

Proof   Suppose that $x^o \in \text{int}(\Delta)$, $\xi(t, x^o)_{t \to \infty} \to x$ but $x \notin \Delta^{NE}$. Then there exists some strategy $i \in K$ such that $u(e^i - x, x) = \epsilon$ for some $\epsilon > 0$. Since $\xi(t, x^o) \to x$ and u is continuous, there exists some $T \in R$ such that $u\left(e^i - \xi(t, x^o), \xi(t, x^o)\right) > \epsilon/2 \ \forall t \geq T$. By (3.5), $\dot{x}_i > x_i \epsilon/2 \ \forall t \geq T$, and hence $\xi_i(t, x^o) > \xi_i(T, x^o) \exp(\epsilon(t - T)/2) \ \forall t \geq T$, implying that $\xi_i(t, x^o) \to \infty$ (since $\xi_i(T, x^o) > 0$), a contradiction. Hence $x \in \Delta^{NE}$. ■

This result may be rephrased as follows. One may call a state $x \in \Delta$ *reachable* if there exists *some* interior state from which the solution trajectory converges to x. By proposition 3.1, any interior Nash equilibrium strategy $x \in \Delta^{NE}$ is reachable in this sense: Just let the initial state be x itself (much in the same spirit as with refinements based on perturbations of the strategy space). The result then says that every reachable population state $x \in \Delta$ belongs to the subset Δ^{NE}.

The following example illustrates the possibility that a state $x \in \Delta^{NE}$ is the limit point to *all* interior solution trajectories to (3.5), and yet x is not even Lyapunov stable. The reason for its special dynamic properties is that this state x (pure strategy 1) is vulnerable to a pure-strategy mutant (strategy 3) which initially does well in the postentry population, but as its population share grows, it opens the door for a second mutant (pure strategy 2) that exploits the first mutant. Once the second mutant is prevalent in the population and the first has somewhat diminished, the second mutant starts to fare badly against the incumbent strategy. Hence in the long run only the incumbent strategy prevails.

Example 3.6   Consider the symmetric two-player game given by the payoff matrix

$$A = \begin{pmatrix} 0 & 1 & 0 \\ 0 & 0 & 2 \\ 0 & 0 & 1 \end{pmatrix}$$

(Ritzberger and Weibull 1993; see Nachbar 1990 for a similar example). Let $x = e^1$. Clearly $x \in \Delta^{NE}$. However, x is not Lyapunov stable, since solution trajectories along the edge to vertex e^3 lead away from x. Strategy 3, however, is weakly dominated by strategy 2. Moreover strategy 3 does worse than strategy 2 against strategy 3, so by proposition 3.2, strategy 3 is wiped out in the long run, along any interior solution orbit. By continuity of $\xi(t, x^o)$ with re-

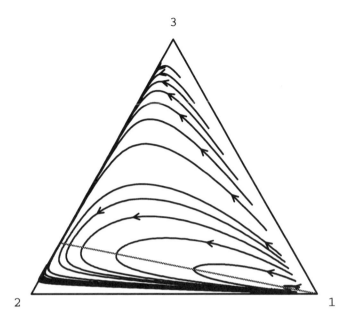

Figure 3.4
Replicator solution orbits in the game of example 3.6.

spect to the initial state x^o, there are interior solution orbits that start near $x = e^1$ and pass arbitrarily near the vertex e^3. By (3.6), the ratio $\xi_2(t, x^o)/\xi_3(t, x^o)$ increases monotonically with time t, and when $\xi(t, x^o)$ is near the edge between $x = e^1$ and e^2, $\xi_1(t, x^o)$ increases monotonically toward 1, since on that edge, $x = e^1$ earns a higher payoff than e^2. See figure 3.4.

3.3.4   Time Averages and $\triangle^{NE}$

We have established two positive results for the evolutionary foundations of Nash equilibrium: Dynamic stability and interior convergence, respectively, imply aggregate Nash equilibrium behavior. There is a third such positive result. It is less general, since it applies only to games that have a unique interior stationary state x, or equivalently, a unique interior symmetric Nash equilibrium (proposition 3.3). However, the result requires neither stability nor convergent solution trajectories. Instead the hypothesis is that the solution trajectory $\xi(\cdot, x^o)$ be bounded away from the boundary of the simplex. A precise mathematical statement of the latter requirement is that the closure of the forward orbit $\gamma^+(x^o)$ be contained in the interior of the simplex.[11]

Under these hypotheses the time average $\bar{\xi}(T, x^o) \in \Delta$, defined by

$$\bar{\xi}_i(T, x^o) = \frac{1}{T} \int_{t=0}^{T} \xi_i(t, x^o)\, dt \qquad \forall i \in K, \tag{3.21}$$

converges toward the interior Nash equilibrium strategy as T goes to infinity. Hence, even if a solution trajectory to the replicator dynamics fluctuates forever, the population's long-run aggregate behavior, observed as a time average rather than as a population average, may constitute a Nash equilibrium. This is, for instance, the case for any *periodic* solution trajectory in int(Δ).

This result is due to Schuster, Sigmund, Hofbauer, and Wolff (1981a):

Proposition 3.6 *Suppose that* $\Delta^{NE} \cap$ int(Δ) $= \{x\}$, $x^o \in$ int(Δ) *and that* $\overline{\gamma^+(x^o)} \subset$ int(Δ). *Then*

$$\lim_{T \to \infty} \bar{\xi}(T, x^o) = x. \tag{3.22}$$

(For a proof, see Schuster, Sigmund, Hofbauer, and Wolff 1981a or Hofbauer and Sigmund 1988.)

Example 3.7 We showed in subsection 3.1.3 that all interior solution orbits to the replicator dynamics in a generalized Rock-Scissors-Paper Game are bounded away from the boundary of the simplex if and only if $a \geq 0$. Hence for these parameter values the time average along any solution trajectory converges to the unique Nash equilibrium (also when $a = 0$ and the trajectories are periodic).

As a partial complement to this result, it can be shown that if Δ^{NE} contains no interior state, then every solution path to the replicator dynamics converges to the boundary (Hofbauer 1981):

Proposition 3.7 *Suppose that* $\Delta^{NE} \cap$ int(Δ) $= \emptyset$. *Then* $\xi(t, x^o)_{t \to \infty} \to$ bd(Δ), *for all* $x^o \in \Delta$.

(For a proof, see Hofbauer 1981 or Hofbauer and Sigmund 1988.)

The replicator dynamics (3.5) is said to be *permanent* if no pure strategy gets extinct in the long run or, more precisely, if there exists some interior

---

11. The *forward orbit* $\gamma^+(x^o) \subset \Delta$ through a state $x^o \in \Delta$ is the set of all those population states reached at some time in the future, along the solution through x^o. See chapter 6 for details.

compact set to which all interior solution paths converge. It has been shown that if the replicator dynamics is permanent in this sense, then the game has precisely one interior symmetric Nash equilibrium (Hofbauer and Sigmund 1988). By proposition 3.6, the time average of *every* interior solution trajectory then converges to this unique interior strategy. In general, it may not be so easy to verify whether the replicator dynamics indeed is permanent in a given game. However, there is a fairly transparent sufficient condition for permanence, due to Jansen (1986), namely that there exists some interior strategy z which is superior to all stationary states y on the boundary in the sense $u(z, y) > u(y, y)$. In sum:

Proposition 3.8 *If there is some $z \in \text{int}(\Delta)$ such that $u(z, y) > u(y, y)$ for all $y \in \Delta^o \cap \text{bd}(\Delta)$, then (3.5) is permanent. If (3.5) is permanent, then $\Delta^{NE} \cap \text{int}(\Delta)$ is a singleton, and the time average $\bar{\xi}(T, x^o)$ converges to this singleton as $T \to \infty$, from any $x^o \in \text{int}(\Delta)$.*

3.4 Perfect Equilibrium Strategies

For the purpose of making dynamic predictions, asymptotic stability is a more reliable property than Lyapunov stability. For Lyapunov stability does not protect against unmodeled evolutionary drift; occasional small perturbations of the population state may pass unchecked by the dynamics at such a population state (e.g., for a discussion of such drift, see Gale, Binmore, and Samuelson 1993; Binmore and Samuelson 1994). Hence a sequence of such shocks may carry the population to a state from where the replicator dynamics leads it far away. Asymptotic stability, in contrast, guarantees a pull back to status quo after any small perturbation of the population state. Hence robust evolutionary predictions call for asymptotic stability.

We know from proposition 3.4 that already the weaker criterion of Lyapunov stability implies Nash equilibrium behavior. Thus, if we look for population states that are asymptotically stable in the replicator dynamics (3.5), only states x in the subset Δ^{NE} are candidates. As shown in Bomze (1986), Nash equilibria that are not perfect (see subsection 1.4.1) are not asymptotically stable in this dynamics. In other words, it is necessary that the associated strategy profile $(x, x) \in \Theta^{NE}$ be robust against some sequence of small trembles. This is not sufficient for asymptotic stability, however. For instance, the unique interior Nash equilibrium of the generalized Rock-Scissors-Paper

Game in subsection 3.1.5 is perfect (being interior) but was seen to be dynamically unstable for all payoff parameter values $a < 0$. Also asymptotic stability of a strategy $x \in \Delta^{NE}$ clearly requires that it be *isolated* in the sense that $\{x\}$ has to be a *component* of the set Δ^{NE} (see subsection 2.4.2). Otherwise, there are arbitrarily nearby strategies $y \in \Delta^{NE}$, all of which are stationary (and thus we do not have, as required by asymptotic stability, $\xi(t, y)_{t \to \infty} \to x$).

Proposition 3.9   *If $x \in \Delta$ is asymptotically stable in (3.5), then $(x, x) \in \Theta^{NE}$ is perfect, and x is isolated.*

Proof   Suppose that $x \in \Delta$ is asymptotically stable in (3.5). Then x is Lyapunov stable, and so $x \in \Delta^{NE}$, by proposition 3.4. Suppose that (x, x) is not perfect. Then x is weakly dominated by some strategy $y \in \Delta$, by proposition 1.4. Consequently $u(y - x, z) \geq 0$ for all $z \in \Delta$.

For $x, y \in \Delta$ fixed, define the function $v : \Delta \to R$ by

$$v(z) = \sum_{i \in C(z)} (y_i - x_i) \log(z_i) .$$

By the same calculations as in the proof of proposition 3.1, we obtain that v is nondecreasing along all interior solution trajectories to (3.5). Formally, at any state $z \in \text{int}(\Delta)$,

$$\dot{v}(z) = \sum_{i \in K} (y_i - x_i) u(e^i - z, z) = u(y - x, z) \geq 0 .$$

By hypothesis, x is asymptotically stable, so x has a neighborhood U such that $\xi(t, x^o) \to x$ for all $x^o \in U \cap \Delta$. Combined with the above observation that v is nondecreasing along all interior solution trajectories, this implies that $v(x) \geq v(z)$ for all $z \in U \cap \text{int}(\Delta)$. However, there exist $z \in U \cap \text{int}(\Delta)$ for which $v(z) > v(x)$. Such a strategy z is obtained by taking any $\delta \in (0, 1)$, $w \in \text{int}(\Delta)$, and $\varepsilon > 0$ sufficiently small, as follows:

$$z = (1 - \varepsilon)\left[(1 - \delta)x + \delta y\right] + \varepsilon w .$$

For $\varepsilon > 0$ sufficiently small, $y_i \gtrless x_i$ implies that $z_i \gtrless x_i$. Moreover

$$v(z) - v(x) = \sum_{i \in K} (y_i - x_i) \log(z_i) - \sum_{i \in C(x)} (y_i - x_i) \log(x_i)$$

$$= \sum_{i \in C(x)} (y_i - x_i)\left[\log(z_i) - \log(x_i)\right] + \sum_{i \notin C(x)} y_i \log(z_i) .$$

It can be shown that the second term is zero. Hence $v(z) > v(x)$, contradicting the above implication that $v(z) \leq v(x)$, so $(x, x) \in \Theta^{PE}$.

To prove that the second term is zero, it is sufficient to establish $C(y) \subset C(x)$. For this purpose, suppose that $j \in C(y)$ but that $j \notin C(x)$. By asymptotic stability of x, $\xi(t, x^o) \to x$ for all $x^o \in U \cap \text{int}(\Delta)$. In particular, $v(\xi(t, x^o))$ is nondecreasing over time t. However, $\xi_j(t, x^o) \to x_j = 0$ while $y_j > 0$, so for some constant γ we have $v(\xi(t, x^o)) \leq \gamma + y_j \log(\xi_j(t, x^o))$ $\to -\infty$, a contradiction. ∎

3.5 Evolutionarily and Neutrally Stable Strategies and Sets

We here address the question how stability in the replicator dynamics is related to the criteria of evolutionary and neutral stability of the associated mixed strategy. It turns out that every population state in the subset Δ^{ESS} is asymptotically stable in the replicator dynamics, and every population state in Δ^{NSS} is Lyapunov stable. In this sense evolutionary stability implies asymptotic stability, and neutral stability implies Lyapunov stability. Moreover every ES set is asymptotically stable. However, the converse of these implications does not generally hold.

These results can be established formally by means of a suitable chosen so-called *Lyapunov function* (see chapter 6). The particular function to be used for this purpose is a well-known relative entropy function in information theory and statistical mechanics. Its connection with the mentioned evolutionary stability criteria goes via propositions 2.6 and 2.7, which establish that an evolutionarily stable strategy is locally superior and that a neutrally stable strategy is locally weakly superior, respectively. The first characterization can be used to extend the asymptotic stability of ESS's to that of ES sets.

3.5.1 The Relative-Entropy Function

For any mixed strategy $x \in \Delta$, let $Q_x \subset \Delta$ be the set of those mixed strategies $y \in \Delta$ that assign positive probabilities to *all* pure strategies with positive probabilities assigned by x:

$$Q_x = \{y \in \Delta : C(x) \subset C(y)\}. \tag{3.23}$$

Clearly x itself belongs to Q_x, as do all points y in the interior of the simplex Δ. In fact Q_x is the union of $\text{int}(\Delta)$ and the minimal boundary face containing x, namely the subsimplex spanned by the carrier $C(x) \subset K$ of x. Hence Q_x constitutes a *neighborhood* of x *relative* to Δ (formally, $Q_x = \Delta \cap U$ for some

(a)

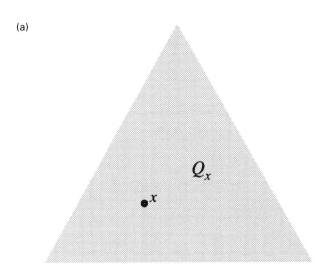

open set $U \subset R^k$ containing x); see figure 3.5 for illustrations in the case of three pure strategies $(k = 3)$.

The mentioned key function for stability analysis is defined with respect to a given mixed strategy $x \in \Delta$, the candidate asymptotically stable state, and has the (relative) neighborhood Q_x as its domain. It is usually called the *(Kullback-Leibler) relative-entropy measure* $H_x : Q_x \to R$, and it is defined by

$$H_x(y) = \sum_{i \in C(x)} x_i \log \left(\frac{x_i}{y_i} \right). \tag{3.24}$$

This is an information-theoretic measure of distance in probability space between the distributions x and y.[12] Clearly $H_x(x) = 0$, and it has been shown in information theory that the number $H_x(y)$ always exceeds $\|x - y\|^2$, the square of the euclidean distance between x and y (see Reiss 1989; Bomze 1991).[13] Hence, if for any fixed $x \in \Delta$ the value $H_x(y)$ decreases toward zero as $y \in Q_x$ changes, then y must approach x. Indeed, for any fixed strategy $x \in \Delta$, the associated entropy function H_x is convex; see figure 3.6 for illustrations in the case $k = 3$.

---

12. In information theory one usually thinks of $H_x(y)$ as a measure of the entropy of the distribution x relative to the distribution y; see Kullback (1959).

13. However, H_x does not define a metric because it is not symmetric.

(b)

(c)

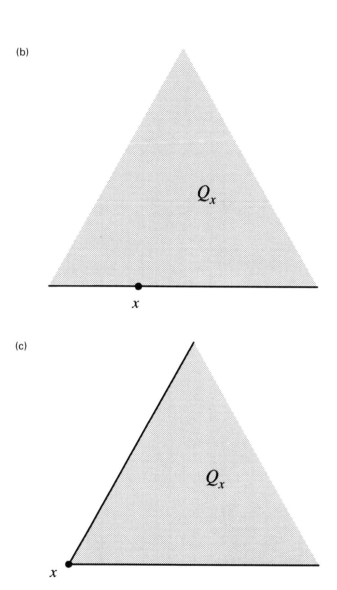

Figure 3.5
The domain Q_x of the relative-entropy function H_x: (a) x is interior, (b) x belongs to an edge of the simplex, (c) x is a vertex of the simplex.

A direct proof that the function H_x achieves its global minimum at $y = x$ can be established by means of Jensen's inequality. Moreover this function has the remarkable dynamic property that its time derivative in the replicator dynamics, evaluated at any point y in its domain Q_x, equals the payoff difference between strategies y and x when played against y. Formally, for any fixed $x \in \Delta$, the *time derivative* of the function value $H_x(y)$ at some point $y \in Q_x$, is defined as the rate of change in $H_x(y)$ as the state y changes according to equation (3.5):

$$\dot{H}_x(y) = \frac{d}{dt} \left[H_x(\xi(t, y)) \right]_{t=0} = \sum_{i=1}^{k} \frac{\partial H_x(y)}{\partial y_i} \dot{y}_i . \tag{3.25}$$

Lemma 3.1 *Suppose that $x \in \Delta$ and $y \in Q_x$. Then $H_x(y) \geq 0$, with equality if and only if $y = x$. Moreover $\dot{H}_x(y) = -u(x - y, y)$.*

Proof   First note that $H_x(x) = 0$ and that, for any $y \in Q_x$,

$$H_x(y) = - \sum_{i \in C(x)} x_i \log \left(\frac{y_i}{x_i} \right)$$

$$\geq - \log \left(\sum_{i \in C(x)} \frac{x_i y_i}{x_i} \right)$$

$$\geq - \log \left(\sum_{i=1}^{k} y_i \right) = - \log(1) = 0.$$

(a) $H_x(y)$

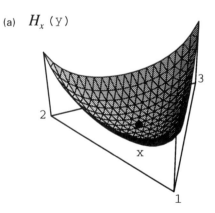

(b)

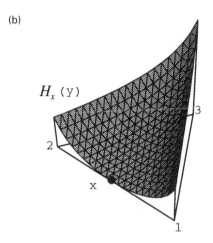

(c)

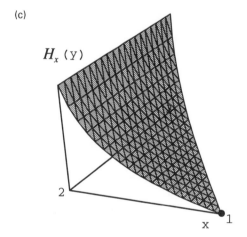

Figure 3.6
The graph of the relative-entropy function H_x in the three cases (a–c) of figure 3.5.

Suppose that $y \neq x$, and recall that $C(x) \subset C(y)$. If $C(x) = C(y)$, then the first weak inequality is strict. If $C(x) \neq C(y)$, then the second inequality is strict. Hence in both cases $H_x(y) > 0$.

Next at any point $y \in Q_x$,

$$\dot{H}_x(y) = - \sum_{i \in C(y)} \frac{x_i}{y_i} \left[u(e^i, y) - u(y, y) \right] y_i$$

$$= - \sum_{i \in C(x)} x_i \left[u(e^i, y) - u(y, y) \right] = - \left[u(x, y) - u(y, y) \right] . \quad \blacksquare$$

Suppose that the population state y is in the domain Q_x of some strategy $x \in \Delta$ such that x earns a higher payoff against strategy $y \in Q_x$ than y earns against itself. Then the replicator dynamics (3.5) induces a movement into lower and lower contour sets of H_x, and unless the population state $\xi(t, y)$ in the meantime leaves the domain Q_x, it will converge to x as time $t \to \infty$. This application of what is called *Lyapunov's direct method* (see chapter 6), combined with the characterizations of evolutionary and neutral stability in section 2.2, is the key whereby some of the static evolutionary stability criteria in chapter 2 can be connected with asymptotic and Lyapunov stability in the replicator dynamics.

3.5.2 Asymptotically Stable States and Δ^{ESS}

Lemma 3.1, together with the characterization of evolutionary stability in proposition 2.6 and Lyapunov's direct method can be used to establish the claim that every ESS is an asymptotically stable state in the replicator dynamics. This route was suggested by Taylor and Jonker (1978); see also Hofbauer, Schuster, and Sigmund (1979):[14]

Proposition 3.10 *Every $x \in \Delta^{ESS}$ is asymptotically stable in the replicator dynamics (3.5).*

Proof Suppose that $x \in \Delta^{ESS}$. By proposition 2.6, there is a neighborhood U of x such that $u(x - y, y) > 0$ for all $y \neq x$ in $\Delta \cap U$. As noted above, the domain Q_x of the function H_x is a relative neighborhood of x, so H_x is a so-called strict local Lyapunov function for the replicator dynamics on the (relative) neighborhood $V = U \cap Q_x$, by lemma 3.1. More precisely, $H_x : V \to R_+$

---

14. The result in Taylor and Jonker (1978) is slightly weaker. They also show by counterexample that their result does not carry over to the discrete-time version of the replicator dynamics in which every time period represents a generation; see section 4.1.

is continuously differentiable, $H_x(y) = 0$ if and only if $y = x$, and $\dot{H}_x(y) < 0$ $\forall y \in V$. By theorem 6.4, this implies that x is asymptotically stable.[15] ∎

Recall that an interior ESS is necessarily unique (proposition 2.2). Hence one may conjecture that such a strategy is globally stable in the sense of attracting *all* interior initial states. This conjecture is easily proved (Hofbauer and Sigmund 1988):

Proposition 3.11 *If $x \in \text{int}(\Delta) \cap \Delta^{ESS}$, then $\xi(t, x^o)_{t \to \infty} \to x$, for any $x^o \in \text{int}(\Delta)$.*

unique S, ESS

Proof If $x \in \text{int}(\Delta)$, then $Q_x = \text{int}(\Delta)$. If moreover $x \in \Delta^{ESS}$, then all strategies $y \in \Delta$ are best replies to x, and thus $u(x - y, y) > 0$ for *all* $y \neq x$ (proposition 2.1). By lemma 3.1, we then have $\dot{H}_x(y) < 0$ for all $y \neq x$. The subset $\text{int}(\Delta)$ is positively invariant in (3.5), and $\dot{H}_x(y) < 0$ means that the replicator vector field $\varphi(y)$ points (strictly) into every contour set of H_x, so $\xi(t, x^o) \to x$, for any $x^o \in \text{int}(\Delta)$. ∎

Example 3.8 Reconsider the generalized Rock-Scissors-Paper games in subsection 3.1.5 in the light of propositions 3.10 and 3.11. The unique Nash equilibrium strategy of such a game is $x = (\frac{1}{3}, \frac{1}{3}, \frac{1}{3})$, for any $a > -1$. In subsection 3.1.5 we showed that x is *not* asymptotically stable in the replicator dynamics when $a \leq 0$. Hence $x \notin \Delta^{ESS}$ by proposition 3.10. In fact x gives payoff $1 + \frac{a}{3}$ when played against any of the three pure strategies of the game, while each pure strategy obtains payoff 1 when played against itself. Hence, for $a \leq 0$, x is not evolutionarily stable. What if $a > 0$? Since x is interior, it is an ESS if and only if $u(x, y) > u(y, y)$ for all $y \neq x$ by proposition 2.6. As shown in subsection 3.1.5, $u(y, y) = 1 + a(1 - \|y\|^2)/2$, for any $y \in \Delta$. As noted above, $u(x, y) = 1 + a/3$, again for any $y \in \Delta$. When $a > 0$, $u(y, y)$ is maximal for $\|y\|$ minimal, which on Δ occurs at $y = x$. We get $u(x, x) = 1 + a/3$, so $x \in \Delta^{ESS}$, by proposition 2.6. It follows from proposition 3.11 that x then attracts the whole interior, something we showed directly in subsection 3.1.5. Indeed in this class of games $H_x(y) = c - h(y)/3$.

Taylor and Jonker (1978) and Zeeman (1981) give examples of games in which a non-ESS strategy constitutes an asymptotically stable population state (

---

15. The partial converse also holds: If H_x is a strict local Lyapunov function, then lemma 3.1 implies that $u(x - y, y) > 0$ for all $y \neq x$ in some neighborhood of x, and so $x \in \Delta^{ESS}$ by proposition 2.6.

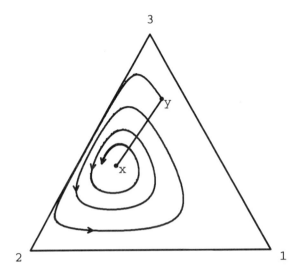

Figure 3.7
The replicator dynamics in a game with an asymptotically but not neutrally stable strategy; see example 3.9.

in the replicator dynamics (3.5). The following example illustrates this possibility. In fact the strategy in question, $x \in \text{int}(\Delta)$, is not even neutrally stable, and yet x, viewed as a population state in the replicator dynamics, attracts all interior solution trajectories to (3.5). Here x is vulnerable to mutations to a particular pure strategy, $y = e^3$, in the sense that y is an alternative best reply to x and y does better against itself than x does against y. However, there is another pure strategy, $z = e^2$, that does even better against y, and so forth, resulting in a spiraling movement in the replicator dynamics around the point x, a spiral which occasionally drifts away from x, when intersecting the straight-line segment between x and y, and yet approaches x in the long run (see figure 3.7).

Example 3.9 Consider the symmetric two-player game with payoff matrix

$$A = \begin{pmatrix} 1 & 5 & 0 \\ 0 & 1 & 5 \\ 5 & 0 & 4 \end{pmatrix}.$$

Apart from the payoff that the third pure strategy earns against itself, this matrix is the same as in the generalized Rock-Scissors-Paper Game with $a = 3$ (subsection 3.1.5). In this new game, $x = (3/18, 8/18, 7/18)$ is the unique interior stationary population state in the replicator dynamics, and hence the unique interior point in the set Δ^{NE}. In fact $\Delta^{NE} = \{x\}$. Since x is interior, all strategies $y \in \Delta$ are best replies to x. Moreover the alternative best reply $y = e^3$ earns payoff 4 against itself, while x only earns payoff $68/18 < 4$ when meeting this pure-strategy mutant y. Hence $x \notin \Delta^{NSS}$. However, x does very well against the two other pure-strategy mutants, e^1 and e^2: Each of these earns only payoff 1 against itself, while $u(x, e^1) = 38/18$ and $u(x, e^2) = 23/18$.

As in the generalized Rock-Scissors-Paper Game with $a > 0$ (figure 3.2c), the solution orbits to the replicator dynamics spiral inward; see figure 3.7.

The replicators in the dynamics (3.5) are the pure strategies of the game in question. However, the same dynamic machinery can be applied also when mixed strategies are replicators, as long as the total number of replicators is finite. Suppose that the (pure and/or mixed) strategies in some finite subset $Z = \{z^1, z^2, \ldots, z^m\} \subset \Delta$ are the replicators. The pure-strategy replicator dynamics (3.5) then corresponds to the special case when $m = k$ and $z^r = e^r$ for all replicators r. Given such an arbitrary finite set $Z \subset \Delta$ of replicators, let p_r be the population share programmed to strategy $z^r \in Z$. Just as in the derivation of the pure-strategy replicator dynamics in section 3.1, the growth rate of p_r is $u(z^r - z, z)$, where $z = \sum_r p_r z^r \in \Delta$.

Consider now any strategy $x \in \Delta$, and let an arbitrary finite collection Z of mixed strategies be given as replicators, such that x is a convex combination of the strategies in Z, namely such that $x = \sum_r p_r z^r$ for some population shares $p_r \geq 0$ adding up to one. For instance, this is always the case if Z consists of all the n pure strategies e^i of the game, as in the usual replicator dynamics. Thomas (1985b), as well as Cressman (1990) and Weissing (1991), show that a strategy $x \in \Delta$ is evolutionarily stable if and only if the corresponding population state x is asymptotically stable (modulo certain behavioral equivalencies) in *all* such replicator dynamics (see also Bomze and van Damme 1992; Hammerstein and Selten 1993).

In particular, there exists some such replicator dynamics in which the non-NSS strategy (hence non-ESS) x in example 3.9 is *not* asymptotically stable. Such a collection of replicators is easy to find. Just let $z^1 = x$ and $z^2 = e^3$; that is, z^2 is the mutant strategy against which x was seen to be vulnerable. In the associated one-dimensional replicator dynamics, the growth rate of z^1 is seen to be negative whenever $p_1 < 1$, showing that the population state $x = z^1$ is unstable in this particular replicator dynamics.

3.5.3   Lyapunov Stable States and Δ^{NSS}

We used lemma 3.1 together with the characterization of evolutionary stability in proposition 2.6 to show that evolutionary stability implies asymptotic stability in the pure-strategy replicator dynamics (3.5). Likewise the characterization of neutral stability in proposition 2.7 can be used to establish that this weaker form of evolutionary stability implies the weaker form of dynamic stability known as Lyapunov stability (Thomas 1985a; Bomze and Weibull 1994):

Proposition 3.12   *Every $x \in \Delta^{NSS}$ is Lyapunov stable in the replicator dynamics (3.5).*

Proof   Suppose that $x \in \Delta^{NSS}$. By proposition 2.7, there is a neighborhood U of x such that $u(x - y, y) \geq 0$ for all $y \in U$. The domain Q_x of H_x being a relative neighborhood of x, H_x is a so-called weak local Lyapunov function for the replicator dynamics on the (relative) neighborhood $V = U \cap Q_x$, by lemma 3.1. More precisely, $H_x : V \to R_+$ is continuously differentiable, $H_x(y) = 0$ if and only if $y = x$, and $\dot{H}_x(y) \leq 0$ for all $y \in V$. By theorem 6.4, this implies that x is Lyapunov stable.[16]   ∎

This result, combined with proposition 3.6 concerning time averages, has the further implication that if a (symmetric two-player) game has a *unique* interior strategy $x \in \Delta^{NE}$, and this strategy is neutrally stable, then there is a neighborhood of x such that the *time average* over any solution trajectory starting in this neighborhood converges to x, even if the state $\xi(t, x^o)$ itself does not converge. The game in example 3.9 shows that the converse of proposition 3.12 is not generally valid.

3.5.4   Asymptotically Stable Sets and ES*Sets

Since evolutionarily stable states are asymptotically stable in the replicator dynamics, it seems fair to guess that also evolutionarily stable sets of strategies, so-called ES sets (subsection 2.4.2) are, as sets, asymptotically stable. In essence a closed *set $X \subset \Delta$ is *evolutionarily stable* (an *ES set*) if every strategy x in the set does weakly better than *all* nearby strategies y do against

---

16. The partial converse also holds that if H_x is a weak local Lyapunov function, then lemma 3.1 implies that $u(x - y, y) \geq 0$ for all y in some neighborhood of x, and so $x \in \Delta^{NSS}$ by proposition 2.7.

themselves, and strictly better than all nearby strategies y that are *not* in the set X.

In fact dynamic stability properties of a set of strategies do not depend on how strategies in the set perform against each other. These properties depend only on how strategies in the set perform against strategies *outside* the set. One weakening of the ES criterion in this spirit is to only require that every strategy in the set be locally superior to strategies y outside the set in question:

Definition 3.1   *A set $X \subset \Delta$ is* evolutionarily stable* (an ES* set) *if it is nonempty and closed, and each $x \in X$ has a neighborhood U such that $u(x, y) > u(y, y)$ for all strategies $y \in U \cap \sim X$.*

Clearly every ES set is an ES* set, and by proposition 2.6, a singleton $X = \{x\}$ is an evolutionarily stable* set if and only if $x \in \Delta^{ESS}$. Hence the ES* criterion is another, weaker, setwise generalization of the ESS concept. The full strategy space $X = \Delta$ is an ES* set by default; by definition there are no outside strategies. Hence existence of ES* sets is trivially guaranteed. Moreover one can show, by Zorn's lemma, that every finite and symmetric game possesses at least one *minimal* ES* set, that is, an ES* set that does not properly contain another ES* set.[17]

Since an evolutionarily stable strategy, viewed as a singleton set, is a special case of an ES* set, the following result has proposition 3.10 as a corollary:

Proposition 3.13   *Every ES* set $X \subset \Delta$ is asymptotically stable in (3.5).*

Proof   Suppose that $X \subset \Delta$ is an ES* set. For each $x \in X$, let U_x be a neighborhood of x such that $u(x, y) > u(y, y)$ for all strategies $y \in U_x \cap \sim X$. Let $Q_x \subset \Delta$ be as in equation (3.23). Then $V_x = U_x \cap Q_x$ is a (relative) neighborhood of x on which the entropy function H_x is defined. Next, we identify a neighborhood P of X which is a basin of attraction for X. For this purpose note that for each $x \in \Delta$ there exists some $\alpha_x > 0$ such that the lower contour set $P_x = \{y \in Q_x : H_x(y) < \alpha_x\}$ is contained in the above neighborhood V_x. Let P be the union of all P_x. Then $P \subset \Delta$ is a neighborhood of X (relative to Δ). Moreover, if $y \in P \cap \sim X$, then $y \in P_x$ for some $x \in X$, and $\dot{H}_x(y) < 0$ for each such x, by lemma 3.1.

---

17. Note that in the definition of an ES* set X it is sufficient to check superiority at boundary points of X: A closed set $X \subset \Delta$ is an ES* set if and only if each $x \in bd(X)$ has a neighborhood U such that $u(x, y) > u(y, y)$ for all $y \in U \cap \sim X$.

For each $y \in P$, let $X(y) = \{x \in X : C(x) \subset C(y)\}$, and define the function $H : P \to R_+$ by

$$H(y) = \min_{x \in X(y)} H_x(y).$$

By Berge's maximum theorem, H is continuous. Moreover $H(y) \geq 0$ for all $y \in P$, with equality if and only if $y \in X$. If $y \in P \cap \sim X$, then $\xi(t, x^o) \in P$ and $H[\xi(t, x^o)] < H(x^o)$ for all $t > 0$. Consequently X is asymptotically stable by theorem 6.3.[18] ∎

The following example provides a whole family of nested ES* sets, only one of which (their intersection) is an ES set:

Example 3.10 Reconsider the Coordination Game of example 1.10. The unique mixed-strategy Nash equilibrium value for x_1 is $\lambda = \frac{1}{3}$. Moreover, for any $\alpha \in (\lambda, 1]$, the set $X_\alpha = \{x \in \Delta : x_1 \geq \alpha\}$ is an ES* set, since for any $x \in X_\alpha$ and $y \in \Delta$ with $y \notin X_\alpha$, $u(x - y, x) = (x_1 - y_1)(3x_1 - 1) > 0$. We saw in example 3.1 that the population share x_1 converges monotonically to 1 from any initial value above λ, so X_α is indeed asymptotically stable. However, only for $\alpha = 1$ is X_α an ES set.

Example 3.11 Reconsider the set $X = \Delta^{NE}$ in the game of example 2.9. It was shown that $X = \Delta^{NSS}$ is an ES set. Hence X is an ES* set. Each $x \in X$ is Lyapunov stable, but not asymptotically stable, and the full set X is asymptotically stable in the replicator dynamics; see figure 3.8 for some solution orbits.

Example 3.9 shows that the converse of proposition 3.13 is not generally valid.

Example 3.12 Consider the symmetric two-player game given by the payoff matrix

$$A = \begin{pmatrix} 0 & 2 & 0 \\ 2 & 0 & 2 \\ 1 & 1 & 1 \end{pmatrix}.$$

It is easily verified that Δ^{NE} contains two points on the boundary of Δ, namely $p = \left(\frac{1}{2}, \frac{1}{2}, 0\right)$ and $q = \left(0, \frac{1}{2}, \frac{1}{2}\right)$. It is clear from the third row of A

---

18. I thank Klaus Ritzberger for helpful suggestions.

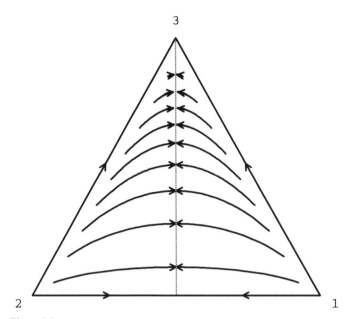

Figure 3.8
Replicator solution orbits in the game of example 3.11.

that every interior strategy $x \in \Delta^{NE}$ has to earn payoff 1, which, in view of row 1, implies that $x_2 = \frac{1}{2}$. From row 3 it is clear that every interior strategy x meeting this condition belongs to Δ^{NE}. Hence $\Delta^{NE} = \left\{ x \in \Delta : x_2 = \frac{1}{2} \right\}$; see figure 3.9 (a). For any $x \in \Delta^{NE}$ and $y \in \Delta$, we have

$$u(x, y) - u(y, y) = (1 - 2y_2)(y_1 - y_2 + \frac{1}{2} - x_1).$$

For each $x \in \Delta^{NE}$, this quantity is negative for some nearby $y \notin \Delta^{NE}$; see figure 3.9 (b). Hence the game has no neutrally stable strategy, and Δ^{NE} is not an ES* set.[19]

However, Δ^{NE} is asymptotically stable in the replicator dynamics. For (3.5) gives $\dot{x}_2 = 2(1 - 2x_2)x_3x_2$. Hence the population share x_2 converges to its Nash equilibrium value from any initial state that is neither on the boundary where $x_2 = 0$ nor at the vertex where $x_2 = 1$.

---

19. Thomas (1985a) incorrectly suggests that this set, in an equivalent game, is an ES set.

(a)

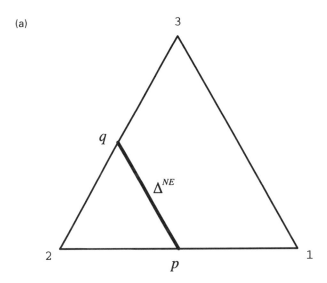

(b)

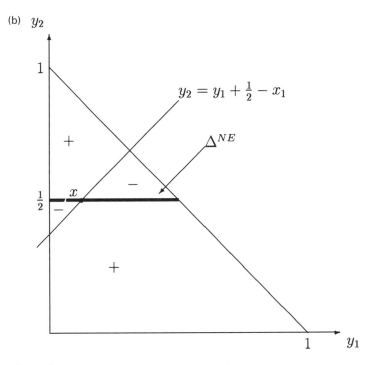

Figure 3.9
(a) The set Δ^{NE} in the game of example 3.12. (b) Projection of the same set to the (y_1, y_2)-plane.

Note also that while the asymptotically stable set $X = \Delta^{NE}$ in this example is not an ES* set, it nevertheless has the following weak evolutionary stability property: For every $y \notin X$ there is some $x \in X$ such that $u(x - y, y) > 0$.

3.6 Doubly Symmetric Games

According to a famous biological result (Fisher 1930), usually referred to as *the fundamental theorem of natural selection,* in some contexts evolutionary selection induces a monotonic increase over time in the *average* population fitness. In a sense, since more fit behaviors (strategies) are selected for, it may a priori be more surprising that this should not always be the case. In particular, the replicator dynamics increases the population shares of pure strategies with higher than average payoff and reduces the population shares of pure strategies with lower than average payoffs. Hence one might expect that average payoff $u(x, x)$ should increase as the population state $x \in \Delta$ moves according to the replicator dynamics (3.5). However, this is not generally the case. For instance, in the Prisoner's Dilemma Game (example 1.1), if initially virtually all individuals in the population play "cooperate," then average fitness is high (near 4). The population share of those who play "defect" increases monotonically over time until, in the long run, virtually all play "defect," and then average fitness is lower (near 3). Hence average fitness cannot be monotonically increasing over time. As will be seen, these efficiency considerations are not invariant under local shifts of payoff functions.

3.6.1 The Fundamental Theorem of Natural Selection

Losert and Akin (1983) show that the fundamental theorem does apply to all *doubly* symmetric games. More precisely, they show that in such a game, average payoff increases along every nonstationary solution path to the replicator dynamics. Consequently, in doubly symmetric games, evolution, as modeled in the replicator dynamics (3.5), does induce a steady increase in social efficiency over time (see section 2.5).

To state and prove this result, suppose that the game under study is doubly symmetric, and let the time derivative of average payoff (fitness) $u(x, x)$ along the solution path to the replicator dynamics (3.5) through any given state $x \in \Delta$, be written

$$\dot{u}(x, x) = \frac{d}{dt} u \left[\xi(t, x), \xi(t, x) \right]_{t=0} . \tag{3.26}$$

Using the symmetry of the payoff matrix A, we can show

$$\dot{u}(x, x) = 2 \sum_{i=1}^{k} x_i \left[u(e^i, x) - u(x, x) \right]^2 . \tag{3.27}$$

Hence $\dot{u}(x, x) \geq 0$, with equality if and only if $x \in \Delta^o$. Moreover the rate $\dot{u}(x, x)$ at which average payoff increases is twice the *variance* of the payoff distribution in the population: The more uneven this distribution is across pure strategies, the higher is the rate at which average payoff increases.

It remains to derive (3.27) from (3.26). First note that symmetry gives

$$\dot{u}(x, x) = \sum_{i,j \in K} \left[\dot{x}_i u(e^i, e^j) x_j + x_i u(e^i, e^j) \dot{x}_j \right]$$

$$= 2 \sum_{i,j \in K} \dot{x}_i u(e^i, e^j) x_j$$

$$= 2 \sum_{i \in K} \dot{x}_i u(e^i, x) . \tag{3.28}$$

Substitution of $x_i \left[u(e^i, x) - u(x, x) \right]$ for $\dot{x}_i$ gives (3.27).[20]

We have established the following version of the fundamental theorem of natural selection (Losert and Akin 1983):

Proposition 3.14   *For any doubly symmetric game, $\dot{u}(x, x) \geq 0$ with equality if and only if $x \in \Delta^o$.*

Note that although the average payoff (fitness) always increases in doubly symmetric games, this does not mean that average payoff in the long run necessarily approaches its global maximum value in the game. For instance, we saw in section 3.1 that both strict equilibria in a 2×2 Coordination Game are asymptotically stable. In particular, if the initial state is sufficiently near one of these equilibria, then the population state converges to that equilibrium, whether or not its payoff is higher or lower than that of the other strict equilibrium.

Example 3.13   Consider any 2×2 game with payoff matrix

$$A = \begin{pmatrix} a_1 & 0 \\ 0 & a_2 \end{pmatrix} .$$

---

20. To see this, expand the square in equation (3.27) and use the bilinearity of u.

For any $x \in \Delta$,

$$u(x, x) = (a_1 + a_2)\, x_1^2 - 2a_2 x_1 + a_2 \,.$$

Hence, in the case of a Coordination Game, $a_1, a_2 > 0$, and thus average payoff $u(x, x)$, viewed as a function of the population share x_1, is a parabola with *minimum* at the mixed-strategy Nash equilibrium value $x_1 = \lambda = a_2 / (a_1 + a_2)$; see figure 3.10 (a). Likewise, in the case of a Hawk-Dove Game, $a_1, a_2 < 0$, average payoff $u(x, x)$ is a parabola in x_1 with *maximum* at the mixed-strategy Nash equilibrium value $x_1 = \lambda$; see figure 3.10 (b). From our studies of the replicator dynamics, it follows that average payoff increases monotonically along every nonstationary solution trajectory in both cases.

3.6.2 Characterization of Asymptotically Stable States

A consequence of the preceding result is that in doubly symmetric games evolutionary stability is *equivalent* with asymptotic stability in the replicator dynamics (Hofbauer and Sigmund 1988). Putting this result together with the characterization of evolutionary stability in section 2.5, we obtain:

Proposition 3.15 *For any doubly symmetric game the following statements are equivalent:*

a. $x \in \Delta^{ESS}$.

b. $x \in \Delta$ *is locally strictly efficient.*

c. $x \in \Delta$ *is asymptotically stable in the replicator dynamics.*

Proof The equivalence of (a) and (b) was established in proposition 2.14. The implication (a)$\Rightarrow$(c) was established in proposition 3.10, so it is sufficient to prove the implication (c)$\Rightarrow$(b). But this follows immediately from the fundamental theorem, for if $x \in \Delta$ is asymptotically stable, it has some neighborhood U such that $\xi(t, y)_{t \to \infty} \to x$ for all initial states y in U. By proposition 3.14, we then have $u(y, y) < u(x, x)$ for all $y \neq x$ in U. ∎

Moreover, since by proposition 2.16 every locally efficient set $X \subset \Delta$ in a doubly symmetric game is an ES set, and every ES set is asymptotically stable (proposition 3.13), every locally efficient set $X \subset \Delta$ in a doubly symmetric game is asymptotically stable in the replicator dynamics.

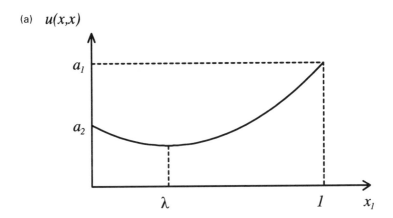

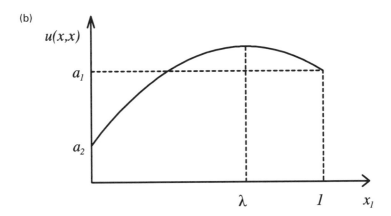

Figure 3.10
(a) Average payoff in a Coordination Game. (b) Average payoff in a Hawk-Dove Game.

3.6.3 Convergence of Solution Trajectories

The fundamental theorem implies that every nonstationary solution trajectory
to the replicator dynamics (3.5) in any doubly symmetric game converges
over time to the subset Δ^o of stationary states. Losert and Akin (1983) show
that each solution trajectory in such a game in fact converges to some *point*
in Δ^o. Combining this result with those in propositions 3.5 and 3.14, we
obtain the following efficiency *cum* equilibrium conclusion for doubly sym-

metric games: Evolutionary selection, as modeled by the replicator dynamics, induces a monotonic increase in social efficiency over time and, granted that the initial state is interior, convergence of aggregate behavior to some symmetric Nash equilibrium.

In subsection 3.1.2 we saw that the solution trajectories to the replicator dynamics are unaffected by local shifts in the payoff function, and that positive affine transformations of the payoff function do not change the induced solution orbits. Hence convergence of solution trajectories is unaffected also by such payoff transformations. Consequently Losert's and Akin's (1983) convergence result can be extended to any symmetric two-player game that can be *made* doubly symmetric by means of these two types of payoff transformation. Call the payoff matrix of such a game *symmetrizable*. Formally,

Definition 3.2 *A payoff matrix A is* symmetrizable *if A can be transformed to a symmetric matrix A' by a finite number of local shifts and affine transformations of payoffs.*

For instance, all symmetric 2×2 games are symmetrizable in this sense.

Proposition 3.16 *Every solution trajectory to the replicator dynamics (3.5) in a two-player game with symmetrizable payoff matrix converges to some point $x \in \Delta^o$.*

Note, however, that average payoff is a quadratic function and hence in general affected by affine transformations and local shifts in the payoff function. While average transformed payoff will increase monotonically over time, average payoff, as defined in the original game, need not increase monotonically. This is, for instance, the case in the Prisoner's Dilemma Game.

Example 3.14 Reconsider the Prisoner's Dilemma Game of example 1.1. Let u denote the payoff function in the original payoffs, and $\bar{u}$ those in the normalized payoffs:

$$u(x, x) = x_1(2x_1 - 1) + 3,$$

$$\bar{u}(x, x) = 2x_1(x_1 - 3) + 3.$$

Hence, as x_1 decreases monotonically in the replicator dynamics toward 0, average payoff increases monotonically in the normalized payoffs; in the original payoffs, average payoff first falls (when $x_1 > \frac{1}{4}$) and thereafter increases.

3.7 Pure-Strategy Subsets Closed under Better Replies

In some applications it is of interest to know which pure strategies survive in
the long run. We know from theorem 3.1 that if initially all pure strategies are
present, then the set of surviving pure strategies is a subset of strategies that
are not iteratively strictly dominated. However, the subset of survivors may
be smaller, depending on the initial population state. For instance, in a 2×2
Coordination Game, precisely one of the pure strategies will survive unless the
initial population state happens to coincide with the unique and dynamically
unstable interior Nash equilibrium strategy. By contrast, in the Hawk-Dove
Game, or the Rock-Scissors-Paper Game, all pure strategies survive in the
long run. Also strictly dominated pure strategies may survive if the initial
population state is not interior.

Building on the multipopulation model in Ritzberger and Weibull (1993),
to be discussed in chapter 5, we here provide a sufficient condition for a
subset $H \subset K$ of pure strategies to be a long-run survivor set in the sense
of being minimal with respect to the property that if initially virtually no
other pure strategies are present (i.e., their population shares are sufficiently
small), then all pure strategies not in H will vanish over time. The condition
in question is simple and based solely on the payoff matrix A of the game. In
particular, no computation of dynamics is necessary. Indeed, as will be shown
in subsection 4.3.3, these results easily generalize to a fairly large class of
dynamics containing the replicator dynamics (3.5) as a special case.

To make these claims precise, consider a finite and symmetric (not necessarily doubly symmetric) two-player game with pure-strategy set K, mixed-
strategy simplex Δ, and payoff matrix A. For any subset $H \subset K$ of pure
strategies, let $\Delta(H)$ denote the *face* (or subsimplex) of Δ spanned by the
pure strategies in H:

$$\Delta(H) = \{x \in \Delta : C(x) \subset H\} . \tag{3.29}$$

Such a subset $X = \Delta(H) \subset \Delta$ is a *boundary* face if H is a proper subset of
K. The extreme case is when H is a singleton and thus $\Delta(H)$ is a vertex of Δ.
(See subsection 1.1.1 for a discussion of the geometry of Δ.)

We here call a pure strategy $i \in K$ a *weakly better reply* to a mixed strategy $x \in \Delta$ if i does not give a lower payoff against x than x does itself.
Accordingly,

Definition 3.3   *A subset $H \subset K$ is* closed under weakly better replies *if*

$$[x \in \Delta(H) \text{ and } u(e^i, x) \geq u(x, x)] \Rightarrow i \in H. \tag{3.30}$$

In terms of mixed strategies, a subset H is closed under weakly better replies if and only if, for any mixed strategy x with support in H, all pure strategies outside H do worse against x than x does against itself. In terms of population states, a subset H is closed under weakly better replies if and only if, for any population state x in which all present pure strategies belong to H, all pure strategies outside H earn below the population average. The maximal subset, $H = K$, clearly meets this condition, since, by definition, there is no pure strategy outside K. Also a singleton subset $H = \{h\}$ meets this condition if and only if pure strategy h is its own unique *best* reply, that is, if and only if the strategy profile $(e^h, e^h) \in \Theta$ constitutes a strict Nash equilibrium. In this sense closure under weakly better replies is a setwise generalization of symmetric strict Nash equilibrium. Hence the following result, which generalizes the earlier noted asymptotic stability of such strategies, is not very surprising:

Proposition 3.17   *If H is closed under weakly better replies, then $\Delta(H)$ is asymptotically stable in (3.5).*

To prove this proposition, we first establish that if a subset of pure strategies is closed under weakly better replies, then it also contains the weakly better replies to all population states *near* the face it spans:

Lemma 3.2   *If $H \subset K$ is closed under weakly better replies, then $\Delta(H) \subset U$ for some open set U such that*

$$[y \in U \cap \Delta \text{ and } u(e^i, y) \geq u(y, y)] \Rightarrow i \in H. \tag{3.31}$$

Proof   Suppose that $H \subset K$ is closed under weakly better replies. Thus, if $j \notin H$, then $u(e^j, x) < u(x, x)$ for all $x \in \Delta(H)$. By continuity of u and compactness of $\Delta(H)$, there is an open set U_j containing $\Delta(H)$ such that $u(e^j, y) < u(y, y)$ for all $y \in U_j \cap \Delta$. Let $U = \cap_{j \notin H} U_j$. Since the set K of pure strategies is finite, U is the finite intersection of open sets containing $\Delta(H)$, and thus U is as claimed in the statement of the lemma. (The case $H = K$ is trivial.) ∎

Proof of Proposition 3.17   Suppose that $H \subset K$ is closed under weakly better replies, and let U be as in the lemma. There then is some $\bar{\varepsilon} > 0$ such that for any $\varepsilon \in (0, \bar{\varepsilon})$, the ε-slice

$$B(\varepsilon) = \left\{ x \in \Delta : x_j < \varepsilon \;\; \forall j \notin H \right\}$$

contains the face $\Delta(H)$, and the closure $\bar{B}(\epsilon)$ is contained in U such that for any $x \in \Delta \cap B(\varepsilon)$ and $j \notin H$, $u(e^j - x, x) < -\delta$. By continuity of u and compactness of $\bar{B}(\epsilon)$, there exists some $\delta > 0$. Hence for any such x and j, $\dot{x}_j = u(e^j - x, x)x_j < -\delta x_j$, which implies that $\xi_j(t, x^o)$ for each $j \notin H$ decreases monotonically to zero from any initial state x^o in $\Delta \cap B(\varepsilon)$. Thus $\Delta(H) \subset \Delta$ is asymptotically stable. ∎

The converse of the statement in proposition 3.17 is not valid. For instance, the following game has a pure-strategy subset that is not closed under weakly better replies, and yet it spans an asymptotically stable boundary face of the mixed-strategy simplex.

Example 3.15 Consider the doubly symmetric 3×3 game given by the payoff matrix

$$A = \begin{pmatrix} 2 & 0 & 1 \\ 0 & 2 & 1 \\ 1 & 1 & 0 \end{pmatrix}.$$

Here pure strategies 1 and 2 together constitute a coordination game, whose unique mixed-strategy Nash equilibrium gives payoff 1, exactly what pure strategy 3 earns against each of these two pure strategies. Let $H = \{1, 2\}$. Then $x = (\frac{1}{2}, \frac{1}{2}, 0) \in \Delta(H)$, and $u(x, x) = 1 = u(e^3, x)$. Consequently H is not closed under weakly better replies. However, $\Delta(H)$ is asymptotically stable in the replicator dynamics (3.5) because $\dot{x}_3 = -[x_1 + x_2 + (x_1 - x_2)^2]x_3$, and thus $\xi_3(t, x^o) \to 0$ for any $x^o \in \Delta$; see figure 3.11.

Hence, for asymptotic stability in the replicator dynamics, it is not necessary that the subset $H \subset K$ contain all weakly better replies to all mixed strategies in the face $\Delta(H)$. However, it *is* necessary that H contain the *strictly* better replies to all *vertices* in $\Delta(H)$, that is, to all pure strategies $j \in H$. Otherwise, there would be some vertex of the face $\Delta(H)$ that has an outgoing edge along which there is a local evolutionary pull away from $\Delta(H)$. Since edges are invariant under the replicator dynamics, this contradicts that $\Delta(H)$ is even Lyapunov stable.

More precisely, let

$$\alpha(H) = \{i \in K : u(e^i, x) \geq u(x, x) \text{ for some } x \in \Delta(H)\} \qquad (3.32)$$

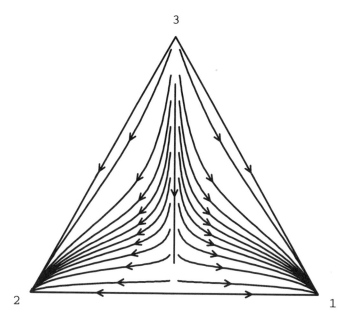

Figure 3.11
Replicator solution orbits in the game of example 3.15.

and

$$\alpha^0(H) = \{i \in K : u(e^i, e^j) > u(e^j, e^j) \text{ for some } j \in H\}. \tag{3.33}$$

Then $\alpha(H) \subset H$ if and only if H is closed under weakly better replies, and $\alpha^0(H) \subset H$ means that H contains the strictly better replies to strategies in H.

Proposition 3.18 *If $\Delta(H)$ is Lyapunov stable in (3.5), then $\alpha^0(H) \subset H$.*

Proof Suppose that $\alpha^0(H)$ is not contained in H. Then there is some $i \notin H$ and $j \in H$ such that $u(e^i, e^j) > u(e^j, e^j)$. The subset $L = \{i, j\} \subset K$ spans the face $\Delta(L)$, which is the edge of Δ connecting the vertex e^i with the vertex e^j. Each face of Δ is invariant in (3.5), so a solution trajectory starting in $\Delta(L)$ remains forever in $\Delta(L)$. Moreover, for any $x \in \Delta(L)$, $\dot{x}_i = u(e^i - x, x)x_i$, so for any $x_i > 0$ sufficiently small, $\dot{x}_i > 0$ by continuity of u. Thus $\xi_i(t, x^0) \geq x_i^0$ for any $x_i^0 > 0$ sufficiently small, and $\Delta(H)$ is not Lyapunov stable for all $t \geq 0$. ∎

The above-mentioned "long-run survivor sets" can be formally defined as follows:

Definition 3.4 $H \subset K$ is a long-run survivor set *if $\Delta(H)$ is asymptotically stable and H does not properly contain a nonempty subset L for which $\Delta(L)$ is asymptotically stable.*

Since there are finitely many pure strategies, every (finite) game possesses at least one long-run survivor set. In particular, if no nonempty proper subset of K spans an asymptotically stable boundary face of Δ, then the full set K itself is a long-run survivor set. The following sufficient condition for a set $H \subset K$ to be a long-run survivor set follows immediately from propositions 3.17 and 3.18:

Proposition 3.19 $H \subset K$ *is a long-run survivor set in the replicator dynamics (3.5) if H is closed under weakly better replies and does not properly contain any nonempty subset L for which $\alpha^0(L) \subset L$.*

Example 3.16   Expand a generalized Rock-Scissors-Paper Game, as defined in subsection 3.1.5, by addition of a fourth pure strategy that earns a low payoff against the other strategies but is in strict Nash equilibrium with itself. For example, let the payoff matrix be

$$
A = \begin{pmatrix} 1 & 2+a & 0 & b \\ 0 & 1 & 2+a & b \\ 2+a & 0 & 1 & b \\ d & d & d & c \end{pmatrix}
$$

for some $a > -1$, $b < c$, and $d < 0$. Then $H = \{1, 2, 3\}$ is closed under weakly better replies and contains no proper subset such that $\alpha^0(L) \subset L$. By proposition 3.19, H is a long-run survivor set. As was seen in subsection 3.1.5, the solution trajectories in the relative interior of this face oscillate forever if $a \in (-1, 0)$, swirling out toward its relative boundary. If initially strategy 4 is present in a sufficiently small population share, then the solution trajectory will approach the face $\Delta(H)$ and swirl around forever in this fashion. The average payoff $u(x, x)$ will then, in the long run, fluctuate between 0 and $2 + a$. The second long-run survivor set of this game is the singleton $H\prime = \{4\}$ containing the unique strict Nash equilibrium strategy of the game. If pure strategy 4 is initially present in a sufficiently large population share, then the population state will converge to the vertex e^4.

3.8 Appendix

Proposition 3.20 *The replicator dynamics (3.5) has a unique solution*
$\xi(\cdot, x^o) : R \to \Delta$ *through any initial state* $x^o \in \Delta$. *The solution mapping*
$\xi : R \times \Delta \to \Delta$ *is continuous, and it is continuously differentiable with re-*
spect to time. Each of the two subsets $bd(\Delta) \subset \Delta$ *and* $\text{int}(\Delta) \subset \Delta$ *are invari-*
ant under the solution mapping ξ.

Proof By force of propositions 6.1 and 6.2, it is sufficient to show that if
$x^o \in \Delta$, then $\xi(t, x^o) \in \Delta$ at all times $t \in R$. For this purpose, first note that
(3.5) leaves the sum of all coordinates x_i constantly equal to one:

$$\frac{d}{dt} \sum_i \xi_i(t, x^o) = \sum_i \dot{x}_i = \sum_i u(e^i - x, x)x_i = u(x - x, x) = 0 .$$

Hence the hyperplane $H = \left\{ x \in R^k : \sum_i x_i = 1 \right\}$ is invariant in this dynamics. The relevant state space $C = \Delta$ is the intersection of this hyperplane with
the closed positive orthant $P = R_+^k$ of $X = R^k$, so it remains to show that
no solution in $H \cap P$ leaves P. If, on the contrary, there is an initial state
$x^o \in \Delta = H \cap P$ and a time $t \in R$ such that $\xi(t, x^o) \notin P$, then, by continuity
of ξ, there is some strategy $i \in K$ and time $s \in R$ such that $\xi_i(s, x^o) = 0$ and
$\xi_i(t', x^o) < 0$ for some t'. But this contradicts the uniqueness of the solution of
(3.5) through the point $x^1 = \xi(s, x^o)$. Suppose that we set $x_i = \eta_i(t, x^1) = 0$
for all t and solve (3.5) for all x_j, $j \neq i$. Then we obtain another solution
$\eta(\cdot, x^1)$ through x^1, in contradiction to the Picard-Lindelöf theorem. Thus
$\xi(t, x^o) \in \Delta$ for all $t \in R$. (Incidentally the same argument can be used
to show that the interior of Δ, as well as each of its boundary faces, is
invariant.) ∎

4 Other Selection Dynamics

In the preceding chapter we found that Lyapunov stability in the single-population replicator dynamics in continuous time implies Nash equilibrium. We also found that convergence in the same dynamics implies Nash equilibrium, provided that all pure strategies of the game are present in the initial population. Finally, strictly dominated pure strategies were seen to vanish in the long run, even if the dynamic solution path does not converge, again provided that all pure strategies are initially present. The present chapter investigates the validity of these implications, from evolutionary selection to game-theoretic rationality, in alternative model environments to the standard setting studied in chapter 3.

In section 4.1 we consider biological replication in discrete time. In such models each time period usually represents a generation. Since the whole population shifts strategy simultaneously, a certain volatility or overshooting may arise in the dynamic adjustment. In fact, by way of an example, it is demonstrated that strictly dominated strategies need not get wiped out in this version of the replicator dynamics. We study the effect of time discretization within an overlapping generations (OLG) version of the usual replicator dynamics, a discrete-time model which spans the range from the mentioned extreme case when all individuals reproduce simultaneously to the limiting case of the continuous-time replicator dynamics (3.5). Incidentally this OLG dynamics is also useful for computer calculations.

In sections 4.2 through 4.4 we return to continuous-time modeling. Section 4.2 studies the replicator dynamics when applied to symmetric two-player cheap-talk games. In such a game each player sends a costless message before the base game is played. As was seen in section 2.6, this gives some scope for coordination of actions. The replicators are here the pure strategies of the cheap-talk extension of the base game. Hence we imagine that each individual is programmed to a *message* and a *decision rule*, a rule that prescribes some base-game action to be taken for each message received from one's opponent. Since the message sent by any individual is fixed in the biological interpretation of the replicator dynamics, one may alternatively think of the messages as distinct physical traits. In this interpretation individuals are allowed to be discriminating in their behavior; their actions may be conditioned on their opponent's message or physical trait. As a special case we consider the constant or undiscriminating decision rules that prescribe one and the same action for all messages or physical traits. This is precisely the standard setting studied in chapter 3. By way of an example it is shown that when evolutionary selection

operates at this level of messages and decision rules, long-run aggregate behavior need not conform with Nash equilibrium and may even involve the use
of strictly dominated strategies. However, it is also shown that if all possible
decision rules are allowed for, then the earlier implications from evolutionary
selection to game-theoretic rationality are restored, albeit in a more complex
form involving nonsymmetric Nash equilibrium play.

Sections 4.3 and 4.4 study some classes of nonbiological replication of
strategies in a large population of interacting individuals. Here payoffs need
not represent fitness. Instead, they may be decision makers' utility or profit,
just as in noncooperative game theory, and the transmission mechanism is here
based on imitation and reinforcement of successful behaviors (pure strategies
in the game in question). The two sections attack this as of today not much
studied issue from two angles. Section 4.3 examines a few broad classes of
pure-strategy selection dynamics in continuous time, all containing the replicator dynamics. Some of the replicator dynamics' positive implications for
game-theoretic rationality are established for these classes. These results require some positive connection between growth rates and payoffs to pure
strategies. Section 4.4 instead examines a few examples of imitation processes
that generate selection dynamics of the sort studied in section 4.3. Also shown
is how the replicator dynamics itself may arise in certain imitation processes.
For more results on the topics covered in this chapter, see Nachbar (1990),
Dekel and Scotchmer (1992), Robson (1990), Samuelson and Zhang (1992),
and Cabrales and Sobel (1992).

4.1   Discrete-Time Versions of the Replicator Dynamics

In some biological models evolutionary selection is modeled in discrete time
with each time period $t = 0, 1, 2, \ldots$ representing a generation. Just as in the
standard continuous-time replicator dynamics of chapter 3, suppose that payoffs represent the *fitness gain* from the interaction in question, where fitness
is simply taken to be the number of offspring. Suppose also that each offspring inherits its single parent's strategy, and let $\alpha \geq 0$ be the background
(lifetime) birthrate for an individual. If $p_i(t)$ is the number of individuals in
generation t who are programmed to pure strategy $i \in K$, then the associated
population share is $x_i(t) = p_i(t)/p(t)$, where $p(t) = \sum_i p_i(t) > 0$ is the total
population in generation t. Each individual who is programmed to pure strat-
egy i in generation t thus gets $\alpha + u\left[e^i, x(t)\right]$ offspring, where $x(t) \in \Delta$ is the

tth generation's distribution over pure strategies in the game.[1] We obtain the following population dynamics:

$$p_i(t + 1) = \left(\alpha + u\left[e^i, x(t)\right]\right) p_i(t).$$ (4.1)

Summing over all pure strategies $i \in K$, we have

$$p(t + 1) = \left(\alpha + u\left[x(t), x(t)\right]\right) p(t),$$ (4.2)

where $u[x(t), x(t)]$ is the average payoff to an individual in generation t. Dividing both sides in (4.1) by the associated total population numbers in (4.2), we obtain the discrete-time replicator dynamics

$$x_i(t + 1) = \frac{\alpha + u[e^i, x(t)]}{\alpha + u[x(t), x(t)]} x_i(t), \qquad t = 0, 1, 2, \ldots.$$ (4.3)

In chapter 3 it was shown that any Lyapunov stable population state $x \in \Delta$ in the continuous-time replicator dynamics (3.5), viewed as a strategy, is in Nash equilibrium with itself, that is, $x \in \Delta^{NE}$. Likewise any population state which is the limit of some interior solution path to the same dynamics is again a point in the set Δ^{NE}. As shown by Nachbar (1990), these two implications are valid also in the above discrete-time replicator dynamics (4.3). However, the set of dynamically stable population states, and convergent interior solution trajectories, respectively, may differ from the corresponding sets in the continuous-time replicator dynamics. In particular, due to the possibility of overshooting in the discrete-time model (4.3), these two implications for Nash equilibrium behavior may be weaker in discrete time (see below).

In the continuous-time replicator dynamics of chapter 3, all pure strategies that are iteratively strictly dominated vanish over time. Nachbar established the following weaker result for the discrete-time dynamics (4.3): If only one pure strategy remains after those pure strategies that are strictly dominated by other *pure* strategies have been iteratively eliminated, then the dynamics (4.3) converges from any interior initial population state $x(0) \in \text{int}(\Delta)$ toward the population state in which all individuals use that pure strategy. That the

---

1. In this discrete-time model we assume that $u(e^i, x) + \alpha$ is positive for each $i \in K$ and $x \in \Delta$. The random element in payoffs earned in matchings in a finite population is ignored. However, the law of large numbers applies if all subpopulations are large, in which case the present deterministic dynamics is an approximation of the expected numbers of individuals in each subpopulation, within any given finite time span.

stronger result for the continuous-time replicator dynamics, theorem 3.1, does not carry over to the discrete-time dynamics (4.3) was shown, by way of a counterexample, by Dekel and Scotchmer (1992). This example is analyzed in subsection 4.1.2 below. However, we first embed the dynamics (4.3) in a more general discrete-time framework.

4.1.1 Overlapping Generations

In the dynamics (4.3) all interactions take place within one generation at a time. It is as if all individuals in one generation are born and die simultaneously at times $t = 0, 1, 2, 3. \ldots$ Suppose instead that generations overlap in time so that births and deaths take place $r \geq 1$ times per time units, each time involving only the share $\tau = 1/r$ of the total population, where $\tau \in (0, 1]$ is the length of the time interval between two successive population changes.[2] Moreover suppose that the reproducing and dying individuals are drawn at random, with equal probability for all individuals in the population. When an individual is so drawn, she dies and is replaced by her offspring.

In this setting the life-span of an individual is a random multiple of the interval length τ. More exactly, it is a geometrically distributed random variable with mean value $\mu = 1$ and variance $\sigma^2 = (1 - \tau)/\tau = r - 1$. Note that this variance is zero when $\tau = r = 1$, corresponding to the dynamics (4.3), and is linearly increasing in r.

Suppose that each individual who is programmed to pure strategy i and reproduces at time t is replaced by $u\left(e^i, x(t)\right) + \beta \geq 0$ offspring, where $\beta \geq 0$ is the background (lifetime) birthrate.[3] This induces the following population dynamics:

$$p_i(t + \tau) = (1 - \tau)p_i(t) + \tau \left(\beta + u\left[e^i, x(t)\right]\right) p_i(t), \qquad (4.4)$$

where $p_i(t)$ is the number of individuals who at time t are programmed to strategy i, $p(t) > 0$ is the total number of individuals at that time, and $x_i(t) = p_i(t)/p(t)$. Adding all population shares and using the bilinearity of the payoff function, we obtain that the total population changes according to

---

2. It is not important that the length of these time intervals equal the size τ of the simultaneously switching population fraction; the associated solution orbits in the state space Δ are independent of the length of the time steps. We let the time step equal the size of the concerned population fraction in order to normalize the expected life-span of an individual to 1.

3. Again, the random element in payoffs earned in matchings in a finite population is ignored, and we rely on the law of large numbers.

$$p(t + \tau) = (1 - \tau)p(t) + \tau \left(\beta + u\left[x(t), x(t)\right]\right) p(t). \tag{4.5}$$

The associated replication dynamics in terms of population shares is obtained by division of each side in equation (4.4) by the corresponding side in equation (4.5):

$$x_i(t + \tau) = \frac{1 - \tau + \tau \left(\beta + u\left[e^i, x(t)\right]\right)}{1 - \tau + \tau \left(\beta + u\left[x(t), x(t)\right]\right)} x_i(t), \tag{4.6}$$

Note that the numerator can be interpreted as the expected number of copies of an individual programmed to strategy i at time t. The individual reproduces and dies with probability τ, in which case her number of copies is $\beta + u\left[e^i, x(t)\right]$, and she does not reproduce and die with probability $1 - \tau$, in which case she continues as one copy of herself. Granted the common denominator in these equations is positive, the system (4.6) of difference equations maps each state $x(t) \in \Delta$ to a new state $x(t + \tau) \in \Delta$. We will refer to (4.6) as the *overlapping-generations replicator dynamics (of order r)*.

When $r = 1$, this is just (4.3) with $\alpha = \beta$. Conversely, in the limit as $r \to \infty$, (4.6) becomes the continuous-time replicator dynamics (3.5). To see this, first rewrite (4.6) as

$$\frac{x_i(t + \tau) - x_i(t)}{\tau} = \frac{u\left[e^i - x(t), x(t)\right]}{1 - \tau + \tau \left(\beta + u\left[x(t), x(t)\right]\right)} x_i(t). \tag{4.7}$$

Letting the population fraction τ of simultaneously reproducing individuals approach zero, we obtain

$$\lim_{\tau \to 0} \frac{x_i(t + \tau) - x_i(t)}{\tau} = \dot{x}_i = u\left(e^i - x, x\right) x_i. \tag{4.8}$$

The overlapping-generations dynamics (4.6) thus spans the whole range from the generationwise discrete-time replicator dynamics (4.3), when $r = 1$, to the continuous-time replicator dynamics (3.5), when $r \to \infty$.

Note also that the solution orbits to the overlapping-generations dynamics (4.6) are identical to those of the generationwise replicator dynamics (4.3) with $\alpha = \beta + r - 1$. The only difference is that the OLG dynamics moves along each solution orbit $r \geq 1$ times per time unit, and the generationwise dynamics only once per time unit. By (4.8), the solution orbits to the generationwise dynamics (4.3) thus approach those of the continuous-time replicator dynamics as $\alpha \to \infty$ (an observation due to Hofbauer and Sigmund 1988). If the background birthrate α is high, then it is as if few individuals replicate according to the endogenous payoffs of the game while all the others replicate at the same exogenous and constant rate.

The geometry of temporal discreteness is illustrated in the following example, due to Björnerstedt et al. (1993), illustrating that convergence and stability in continuous-time dynamics does not imply convergence and stability in corresponding discrete-time dynamics.

Example 4.1 Starting from the same initial state x^o, three solution orbits for the OLG dynamics (4.6) in a generalized Rock-Scissors-Paper Game in subsection 3.1.5 are shown in figure 4.1 (the successive states $x(0)$, $x(\tau)$, $x(2\tau)$, etc., have been connected with straight-line segments). The payoff parameters value is $a = 0.35$, and the orbits correspond to OLG discretizations with $\beta = 0$ and $\tau = 0.05$, $\tau = 0.6$, and $\tau = 1$, respectively. From our study of the continuous-time replicator dynamics in subsection 3.1.5, we know that all its interior solution orbits converge to the Nash equilibrium strategy $x^* = (\frac{1}{3}, \frac{1}{3}, \frac{1}{3})$ when $a > 0$. Indeed the discrete-time orbit for $\tau = 0.05$ does converge to x^*. In contrast, the two other orbits do not. The reason is that discrete-time orbits essentially make straight-line jumps in the direction of the *tangent* of the continuous-time orbit (i.e., in the direction of its vector field). For sufficiently large τ these jumps are long enough to carry the successive states further and further away from x^*, approaching instead the boundary of the simplex.

4.1.2 The Dekel-Scotchmer Example

In this example there is a strictly dominated pure strategy which, however, is not dominated by any pure strategy. Hence no subpopulation of individuals is always doing better than those programmed to the strictly dominated strategy. In fact the latter strategy earns more than the population average in certain population states. Nevertheless, we know from proposition 3.1 that such a strategy is wiped out in the continuous-time replicator dynamics. Dekel and Scotchmer (1992) show that this is not the case in the discrete-time dynamics (4.3), unless all of the other pure strategies in the game happen to initially be present in exactly equal shares.

As pointed out by Cabrales and Sobel (1992), the reason why this counterexample works is not temporal discreteness per se, but its special form (4.3). Indeed they show that if the time discretization is made sufficiently fine, then

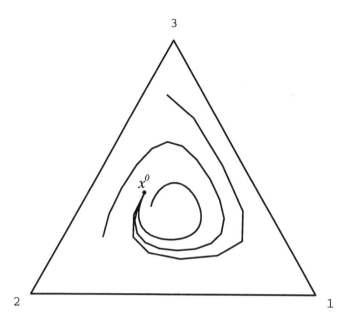

Figure 4.1
The overlapping-generations replicator dynamics in a generalized Rock-Scissors-Paper Game
with parameter $a > 0$; see example 4.1.

the third positive result is restored: All strictly dominated strategies are wiped
out along all interior solution paths.[4]

More precisely, the Dekel-Scotchmer example is the special case $a = 0.35$
and $c = 0.1$ of the following extension of the generalized Rock-Scissors-Paper
games in subsection 3.1.5:

$$A = \begin{pmatrix} 1 & 2+a & 0 & c \\ 0 & 1 & 2+a & c \\ 2+a & 0 & 1 & c \\ 1+c & 1+c & 1+c & 0 \end{pmatrix}, \tag{4.9}$$

where $0 < 3c < a$. The fourth pure strategy is strictly dominated by the unique
Nash equilibrium strategy $x^* = (\frac{1}{3}, \frac{1}{3}, \frac{1}{3}, 0) \in \Delta^{NE}$. To see this, observe that
for any strategy $y \in \Delta$ that player 2 may use, the payoff to strategy $i = 4$

---

4. Cabrales and Sobel (1992) use a different discretization than the above OLG dynamics,
however.

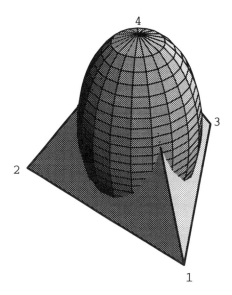

Figure 4.2
The region in the polyhedron Θ of the Dekel-Scotchmer Game where the strictly dominated strategy 4 earns below average.

is $(1 + c)(1 - y_4)$ while the payoff to x^* is $(1 + a/3)(1 - y_4) + cy_4$. Since $3c < a$, the latter payoff exceeds the former, for all $y_4 \in [0, 1]$. However, strategy 4 is not dominated by any pure strategy. Moreover, since c is positive, strategy 4 does better than the population average x when x is near any one of the vertices associated with the three first pure strategies. In fact, when $a < 4c$, as in Dekel and Scotchmer's example, the region $E = \{x \in \Delta : u(e^4, x) \le u(x, x)\}$ where strategy 4 does *not* earn more than average is an egg-shaped set containing the Nash equilibrium strategy x^*; see figure 4.2 (Björnerstedt et al. 1993).

Hence, if along a dynamic solution path the population state now and then spends sufficiently long time intervals outside this egg-shaped region, then the population share x_4 need not converge to zero. To see how this is possible, recall that on the face of the mixed-strategy simplex Δ where x_4 is zero, the OLG-dynamics spirals outward, toward the relative boundary of this face (or subsimplex) when the share τ of simultaneously reproducing individuals is large (e.g., $\tau = r = 1$); see figure 4.1. If τ is large, then the dynamics leads the population state out of the egg-shaped region in figure 4.2. This makes strategy 4's gain above average, and x_4 does *not* converge to zero. In fact, this popula-

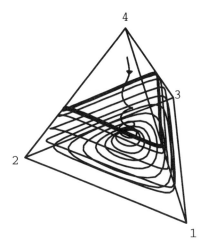

Figure 4.3
A nonconvergent solution orbit to the overlapping-generations replicator dynamics in the Dekel-Scotchmer Game (τ large).

tion share recurrently approaches the value $\frac{1}{2}$; see figure 4.3. In contrast, all interior solution trajectories sooner or later enter the egg-shaped region and converge to the Nash equilibrium strategy x^* when τ is small, just as in the continuous-time replicator dynamics (3.5). (For details, see Björnerstedt et al. 1993.)

4.2   The Replicator Dynamics in Cheap-Talk Games

Robson (1990), Dekel and Scotchmer (1992), Banerjee and Weibull (1992, 1995), and Stahl (1993) have pointed out that the evolutionary support for aggregate Nash equilibrium behavior, and even for the elimination of strictly dominated strategies, may be in trouble if the population of interacting individuals is heterogeneous with respect to sophistication.[5]

4.2.1   Cheap Talk in the Biologist's Lab

To illustrate this point, consider the following thought experiment (Banerjee and Weibull 1992, 1995). A biologist studies evolutionary selection in a

---

5. This section follows to a large extent Banerjee and Weibull (1993).

large population of programmed individuals who are randomly matched to play some finite and symmetric two-player game. However, without the biologist's knowledge, an economist comes by and injects a few individuals of the species *homo oeconomicus* in the sample population. These new agents are endowed with the capacity to recognize the type of agent they meet. In particular, they correctly predict at each encounter the strategy to be used by each of their biologically programmed opponents. They also recognize each other, and then play the unique pure strategy that is not iteratively strictly dominated. In contrast, the original, biologically programmed agents go on using their inherited pure strategies as before. What will happen?

Suppose that the payoff matrix of the game is as in example 1.4:

$$A = \begin{pmatrix} 3 & 1 & 6 \\ 0 & 0 & 4 \\ 1 & 2 & 5 \end{pmatrix}. \tag{4.10}$$

This game is strictly dominance solvable: Strategy 2 is strictly dominated, both by strategy 1 and 3, and once strategy 2 has been eliminated, strategy 3 is strictly dominated by strategy 1. Hence, by theorem 3.1, the biologist expects the population to converge from any interior initial population state to the monomorphic population state in which *all* agents use strategy 1 in every encounter.

What if the initial population is mixed and, for instance, contains many biological agents programmed to the strictly dominated strategy 2, few biological agents programmed to strategies 1 and 3, and some *homo oeconomicus*? The latter would earn payoff 3 when meeting each other and payoff 2 when meeting biological agents of *type* 2, namely programmed to strategy 2. In contrast, type 2 agents would earn zero when meeting each other but payoff 4 when meeting *homo oeconomicus*. Thus, in the presence of *homo oeconomicus*, type 2 agents benefit from their commitment to the strictly dominated but aggressive strategy 2. For a sufficiently large population share of *homo oeconomicus*, and low shares of biological agents programmed to strategies 1 and 3, biological agents programmed to strategy 2 may earn even *more* than *homo oeconomicus*.

In fact, one can show that starting from any initial population mixture containing positive shares of all three types of biological agents and of *homo oeconomicus*, the population share of biological agents of type 3 vanishes asymptotically in the continuous-time replicator dynamics as applied to this setting (see below). Once this population share is small, two things can happen, depending on the initial population state. Either the population state moves toward a continuum of states in which *all* agents use strategy 1, as predicted by evolutionary and noncooperative game theory alike. In this case the survivors are some *homo oeconomicus* mixed with some biological agents who happen to be programmed to strategy 1. As put by Stahl (1993): "being right is just as good as being smart." Alternatively, the population state moves toward the state at which $\frac{2}{3}$ of the population belong to *homo oeconomicus* and $\frac{1}{3}$ are programmed to the strictly dominated strategy 2. In the latter case the three pure strategies of the game are used in proportions $\frac{4}{9}$, $\frac{1}{3}$, and $\frac{2}{9}$, respectively; definitely at variance with the biologist's expectation! Moreover, even if the distressed biologist perturbs this population state by injecting, say, a few "good" biological agents (i.e., programmed to strategy 1), the replicator dynamics leads the population back toward its "bad" habit of, in aggregate, playing the strictly dominated mixed strategy $x = (\frac{4}{9}, \frac{1}{3}, \frac{2}{9})$.

To see how this can be established, note that the situation in the biologist's laboratory is equivalent to letting a population of *programmed* agents play the following 4×4 game:

$$A^* = \begin{pmatrix} 3 & 1 & 6 & 3 \\ 0 & 0 & 4 & 4 \\ 1 & 2 & 5 & 1 \\ 3 & 2 & 6 & 3 \end{pmatrix}. \tag{4.11}$$

To be a *homo oeconomicus* in the original base game is equivalent to being programmed to strategy 4 in this meta game; this strategy earns the best-reply payoff against all strategies, and all other strategies earn that payoff against strategy 4 which they get when meeting their best replies. The replicator dynamics (3.5) can be applied to the meta game, and the claimed results follow by standard arguments, as developed in chapter 3. In particular, the population share $\xi_3(t, x^o)$ decreases to zero along any interior solution path in the mixed-strategy simplex of the meta game, and the replicator dynamics on the boundary face where strategy 3 is extinct looks as in figure 4.4.

4.2.2   Cheap-Talk Strategies as Replicators

The preceding example can be embedded in a richer model framework. Then the positive implications of evolutionary dynamic selection for "game-theoretic rationality," established in chapter 3, can be restored, albeit in a somewhat weaker and more complex form. In particular, the dynamic stability, shown in figure 4.4, of the strictly dominated mixed base-game strategy will be destroyed.

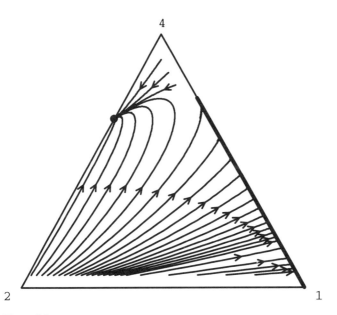

Figure 4.4
Replicator solution orbits when a few *homo oeconomicus* are injected into the biologist's sample population, and pure strategy 3 becomes extinct.

First, suppose that we have, as usual, a population of individuals who are randomly matched to play a symmetric two-player game. However, now each individual has one of finitely many observable and distinct physical *traits* or, equivalently, at each matching is programmed to send one and the same of finitely many, distinct signals or *messages* before play of the game. Suppose that these individuals are genetically or otherwise programmed to *decision rules* prescribing which strategy in the game to play depending on the message received before play of the game. Formally, the situation is identical with that of a cheap-talk game, so all of that machinery applies directly to the present setting.

In the notation of subsection 2.6.1, let G be the base game with pure strategy set $K = \{1, \ldots, k\}$ and pure-strategy payoff function π, and let M be the finite set of *messages* (or physical traits). A *decision rule* is a function $f : M \to K$ which says that if the opponent's message is $\mu \in M$, then use pure strategy $i = f(\mu)$, and so on. Let F be the set of all such functions. A *pure strategy* in the associated *cheap-talk game* G_M is a pair $(\mu, f) \in M \times F$, and the payoff to a pure-strategy profile $((\mu, f), (\nu, g))$ is $\pi\left[f(\nu), g(\mu)\right].$[6] To avoid confusion between strategies in the base game G and in the cheap-talk game G_M, we will call the base-game strategies *actions*.

Example 4.2   Applied to the thought experiment in subsection 4.2.1, the set M could consist of four messages, one for each type of biologically programmed agent and one for *homo oeconomicus*, $M = \{1, 2, 3, 4\}$. Moreover each agent of type $\mu = i \leq 3$ is programmed to the *constant* (or nondiscriminating) decision rule that prescribes action i for all encounters, and each agent of type $\mu = 4$ (*homo oeconomicus*) is programmed to the best-reply rule f defined by $f(2) = 3$, and otherwise $f(\mu) = 1$.

The results derived for the replicator dynamics all apply to the cheap-talk game so defined. Evolutionary selection thus has the usual implications concerning dominated and Nash equilibrium strategies in the cheap-talk game G_M. The implications for the resulting decisions or base-game *actions* are not immediately transparent, however.

To investigate these implications, some more notation is needed. For each pure strategy $h = (\mu, f)$ in the cheap-talk game, let p_h be the population share of individuals programmed to play h. The vector $p = (p_h)$ is then the population *state*, a point on the unit simplex Δ_M of mixed strategies in the cheap-talk game, and one may study the workings of the replicator dynamics on this simplex, just as in chapter 3. When the population state is $p \in \Delta_M$, the payoff of any pure strategy $h = (\mu, f)$ in the cheap-talk game is $u_M(e^h, p)$, and the average payoff in the population is $u_M(p, p)$. The replicator dynamics (3.5), as applied to the space Δ_M of mixed strategies in the cheap-talk game, thus is

$$\dot{p}_h = u_M(e^h - p, p)p_h. \tag{4.12}$$

For any message $\mu \in M$, we will say that an individual who sends this message is of *sender-type* μ, and the associated subpopulation will be called *subpopulation* μ. Individuals in the same subpopulation $\mu \in M$ differ only with respect to their decision rule $f \in F$, and when matched with any particular individual from the population, they all face the *same* action (base-game strategy): if the opponent's decision rule is $g \in F$, then any individual from

---

6. Without loss of generality one may assume that players condition their base-game strategy choice only on their opponent's message; see subsection 2.6.1.

subpopulation μ faces action $j = g(\mu)$. Let p^μ denote the *population share* of individuals of sender type μ (i.e., p^μ is the sum of all p_h such that $h = (\mu, f)$ for some $f \in F$).

It turns out to be analytically convenient to decompose the matchings between individuals in the population into batches, one batch for each message-pair. For each action $i \in K$, message-pair $(\mu, \nu) \in M^2$ and population state $p \in \Delta_M$ with $p^\mu > 0$, let $p_i^{\mu\nu} \in [0, 1]$ be the share of individuals in subpopulation μ who take action i when meeting an individual of type ν. Clearly the associated vector $p^{\mu\nu} = (p_i^{\mu\nu})_{i \in K}$ is a point on the unit simplex Δ of the base game G, so $p^{\mu\nu}$ may be viewed as the randomized action (mixed base-game strategy) facing any individual of type ν when matched with an individual of type μ. Put differently, $p^{\mu\nu} \in \Delta$ is the equivalent randomized action used by subpopulation $\mu \in M$ against subpopulation $\nu \in M$.

4.2.3   Strictly Dominated Base-Game Strategies

We know from proposition 3.1 that all strictly dominated cheap-talk strategies vanish in the long run, along any interior solution path to the replicator dynamics as applied to Δ_M. However, as was shown in example 3.4, the same is not true for weakly dominated strategies. This observation is relevant to the present setting, since, if the set M contains at least two messages, then any action $i \in K$ that is strictly dominated in G is part of cheap-talk strategies $h = (\mu, f) \in K_M$ which are only weakly dominated in G_M. For such a cheap-talk strategy h may prescribe the strictly dominated action i only against some opponent messages $\nu \in M$. Therefore one cannot invoke proposition 3.1 to establish that pure base-game strategies i that are strictly dominated in G will be wiped out in the cheap-talk replicator dynamics (4.12). However, in force of proposition 3.2, one may show that in the long run strictly dominated base-game actions are virtually never used in the matchings (Banerjee and Weibull 1993). The following result is the first step toward this claim:

Proposition 4.1 *Suppose that a base-game strategy $i \in K$ is strictly dominated in G, and let $\mu, \nu \in M$. Then the product $p_i^{\mu\nu} p^\nu$ converges to zero along some interior solution path to the replicator dynamics (4.12) in Δ_M.*

Proof Suppose, first, that action $i \in K$ is strictly dominated by $y \in \Delta$. For any messages $\mu, \nu \in M$, let $H_i^{\mu\nu} = \{(\mu, f) \in K_M : f \in F \text{ and } f(\nu) = i\}$ and $H^\nu = \{(\nu, g) \in K_M : g \in F\}$. Then $p_i^{\mu\nu}$ is the sum of all p_h with $h \in H_i^{\mu\nu}$

and p^v is the sum of all p_k with $k \in H^v$. From now on, fix any pure cheap-talk strategy $h = (\mu, f) \in H_i^{\mu v}$, and let $q \in \Delta_M$ be such that, for each action $j \in C(y)$, the sum of the cheap-talk probabilities $q_{\mu,g}$, over all $g \in F$ such that $g(v) = j$ and $g(\omega) = f(\omega)$ for all $\omega \neq v$, is y_j. In other words, the mixed cheap-talk strategy $q \in \Delta_M$ assigns zero probability to all pure cheap-talk strategies $k = (\omega, g) \in K_M$ that have messages $\omega \neq \mu$ and/or decision rules g that differ from f when facing other messages than v and/or have decision rules g that use actions $j \in K$ outside the support of $y \in \Delta$. Moreover q randomizes the action against message v in such a way that the induced distribution over the set K coincides with that of $y \in \Delta$. It follows that the cheap-talk pure strategy $h \in (\mu, f) \in K_M$ is weakly dominated by the cheap-talk mixed strategy $q \in \Delta_M$, since h does worse than q against pure cheap-talk strategies $k \in H^v$ and equally well against all other pure cheap-talk strategies k. Formally, $u_M(q - e^h, e^k) > 0$ for all $k \in H^v$ and $u_M(q - e^h, e^k) = 0$ for all $k \notin H^v$. By proposition 3.2, $p_h(t, p^o)p_k(t, p^o)_{t \to \infty} \to 0$ for any $k \in H^v$ and initial state $p^o \in \text{int}(\Delta_M)$. Summing over all $k \in H^v$, we get $p_h(t, p^o)p^v(t, p^o) \to 0$. This is true for any $h \in H_i^{\mu v}$, so we may sum over all these, yielding $p_i^{\mu v}(t, p^o)\bar{p}^v(t, p^o)_{t \to \infty} \to 0$. ∎

From a descriptive viewpoint the population shares of individuals programmed to different cheap-talk strategies may be less interesting than the frequency by which different base-game strategies are actually used in the interactions. Formally, let $z_i(p)$ be the share of *matchings* at which action $i \in K$ is used in an interior population state $p \in \Delta_M$:

$$z_i(p) = \sum_{\mu \in M} p^\mu \left[\sum_{v \in M} p_i^{\mu v} p^v \right]. \tag{4.13}$$

Then $z(p) \in \Delta$ represents the induced aggregate base-game behavior, and the following result is an immediate implication of proposition 4.1:

Corollary 4.1.1 *If a pure base-game strategy $i \in K$ is strictly dominated, then its relative frequency $z_i(p)$ goes to zero along any interior solution path to (4.12).*

In other words, even if some surviving decision rule involves some strictly dominated base-game action, such actions will virtually never be used in the long run. In particular, in the laboratory experiment in subsection 4.2.1, the strictly dominated action 2 vanishes along all interior solution paths in the associated cheap-talk game G_M defined in example 4.2. How can this be reconciled with the vector field shown in figure 4.4? The answer is that the associated solution trajectories are not interior to the full cheap-talk simplex Δ. For there are four messages in G_M. With three base-game actions this results in $3^4 = 81$ decision rules $f : M \to K$, out of which only three are represented in the face of Δ_M shown in figure 4.4. If instead all 81 decision rules had been initially present (in combination with each of the four messages), then the frequency $z_2(p)$ of base-game action 2 would tend to zero, by corollary 4.1.1. For instance, the cheap-talk strategy to send message 2—just to look like a biological agent who is programmed to the strictly dominated but aggressive strategy 2—and to use instead the best-reply decision rule would outrival the biological agents of type 2 and thereby reduce the usage of the strictly dominated strategy 2.

4.2.4 Base-Game Nash Equilibrium

By proposition 3.4, any population state $p \in \Delta_M$ that is Lyapunov stable in the replicator dynamics (3.5) on the cheap-talk strategy space Δ_M is a best reply to itself, that is, $p \in \Delta_M^{NE}$. Moreover, as shown in Banerjee and Weibull (1993), if subpopulations μ and ν, where possibly $\mu = \nu$, are nonextinct in such a Lyapunov stable population state p, then these subpopulations necessarily play some, possibly nonsymmetric, Nash equilibrium of the base game against each other:

Proposition 4.2 *Suppose that $p \in \Delta_M$ is Lyapunov stable in (4.12). If $p^\mu, p^\nu > 0$, then $(p^{\mu\nu}, p^{\nu\mu}) \in \Theta^{NE}$.*

Proof Suppose that $p \in \Delta_M$ is stationary in (4.12), $p^\mu, p^\nu > 0$, and that $p^{\mu\nu} \in \Delta$ is *not* a best reply in G to $p^{\nu\mu} \in \Delta$. Then some action $i \in C(p^{\mu\nu})$ earns a suboptimal payoff against $p^{\nu\mu}$. Let $h = (\mu, f) \in K_M$ satisfy $f(\nu) = i$ and $p_h > 0$; such a cheap-talk strategy h exists since $p^\mu > 0$ and $p_i^{\mu\nu} > 0$. Let $k = (\mu, g) \in K_M$ be another cheap-talk pure strategy such that $g(\nu) \in K$ is a best reply against $p^{\nu\mu} \in \Delta$ and $g(\omega) = f(\omega)$ for all other messages $\omega \neq \nu$. In other words, the cheap-talk pure strategy $k = (\mu, g)$ plays a best reply against the population mixture in the subpopulation of sender-type ν, hence earning a higher payoff than the cheap-talk pure strategy $h = (\mu, f)$ in such encounters, and otherwise k plays exactly like h. Since $p^\nu > 0$, we have $u_M(e^k, p) > u_M(e^h, p)$. By stationarity of $p_h > 0$, $u_M(e^h - p, p) = 0$, so $u_M(e^k - p, p) >$

0, implying that $p_k = 0$ by stationarity. However, by continuity of u_M, $\dot{q}_k = u_M(e^k - q, q)q_k > 0$ for all population states $q \in \text{int}(\Delta_M)$ near p. Hence p is not Lyapunov stable. ∎

In other words, when allowing for all possible decision rules, and not just constant (nondiscriminatory) decision rules as in the standard setup of evolutionary game theory, evolution selects, insofar as Lyapunov stability in the replicator dynamics is concerned, symmetric base-game Nash equilibrium play within each subpopulation and symmetric or nonsymmetric base-game Nash equilibrium play between any two subpopulations.[7] Consequently the total population's aggregate base-game play is some *convex combination* of symmetric and/or asymmetric Nash equilibria. Formally, let $\Theta_1^{NE} \subset \Delta$ be the subset of mixed strategies $x \in \Delta$ such that $(x, y) \in \Theta^{NE}$ for some mixed strategy $y \in \Delta$, and let $\text{co}(\Theta_1^{NE}) \subset \Delta$ be the convex hull of this set.[8] In this notation, proposition 4.2 implies that

Corollary 4.2.1 *For $p \in \Delta_M$ Lyapunov stable in (4.12): $z(p) \in \text{co}(\Theta_1^{NE})$.*

That the converse of this result is not generally true—that certain convex combinations of base-game Nash equilibria may constitute a dynamically unstable cheap-talk population state—is seen in the Coordination Game of example 1.10. We saw in subsection 3.1.4 that no interior mixed strategy, $x \in \text{int}(\Delta)$, viewed as a population state in the replicator dynamics (3.5), is Lyapunov stable. However, here *any* mixed strategy is a convex combination of (the two strict) Nash equilibria: $\Theta_1^{NE} = \Delta$. Moreover, since the cheap-talk replicator dynamics (4.12) coincides with the base-game replicator dynamics (3.5) in the special case when there is only one message (M a singleton), we do have a whole continuum of base-game strategies in $\text{co}(\Theta_1^{NE})$ each of which correspond to a dynamically unstable cheap-talk population state.

As shown in chapter 3, a sufficient condition for Lyapunov stability is neutral stability, so any neutrally stable cheap-talk game strategy $p \in \Delta_M$ corresponds to some convex combination of base-game Nash equilibria. The following example shows how such a neutrally stable cheap-talk strategy may

---

7. In particular, it follows from proposition 4.2 that the non-Nash equilibrium outcome in the laboratory experiment in subsection 4.2.1 is not Lyapunov stable in the full cheap-talk game as defined in example 4.2. The stability observed in this laboratory experiment is due to the above-mentioned fact that only a few of all possible decision rules were present.

8. Formally, the set Θ_i^{NE} is the *projection* of the set Θ^{NE} to the mixed-strategy space of player position i. In a symmetric two-player game, $\Theta_1^{NE} = \Theta_2^{NE}$. The *convex hull* of a set X is the set of all convex combinations from X or, equivalently, the smallest convex set containing X.

involve the play of *asymmetric* base-game Nash equilibria and, in this example, may result in a higher payoff than without communication.

Example 4.3 Reconsider the Hawk-Dove Game of example 2.3. This game has three Nash equilibria, one symmetric and interior, and two asymmetric and strict. The symmetric Nash equilibrium results in payoff $\frac{2}{3}$ to each player, and each of the asymmetric equilibria results in payoff 2 to one player and payoff 0 to the other. As shown in subsection 3.1.4, the symmetric Nash equilibrium strategy $x = \left(\frac{2}{3}, \frac{1}{3}\right)$ is asymptotically, and hence also Lyapunov, stable in the replicator dynamics (3.5). Now suppose that costless messages can be sent before the game is played, and suppose that the number of messages is odd, say, $M = \{\mu, \nu, \omega\}$. One may construct a neutrally stable cheap-talk strategy, and hence a dynamically stable population state, resulting in payoff $8/9 > 2/3$ to all individuals in the population, as follows. The idea is to let each sender type play the above randomized action x with itself and play the two asymmetric Nash equilibria with the two other sender types.

To make this precise, one may use two decision rules for each sender type, resulting in a symmetric constellation of actions as indicated in figure 4.5, where H signifies base-game action 1, hawk, and D signifies base-game action 2, dove. Formally, let subpopulation μ use the decision rules f and g in subpopulation shares $\frac{2}{3}$ and $\frac{1}{3}$, respectively, where $f(\mu) = f(\nu) = H$ and $f(\omega) = D$, and $g(\mu) = g(\omega) = D$ and $g(\nu) = H$. Then subpopulation μ plays the symmetric Nash equilibrium with itself, and letting the two other subpopulations behave likewise (see figure 4.5), distinct subpopulations play the two asymmetric Nash equilibria with each other. If moreover all subpopulations are equally large, $p^\mu = p^\nu = p^\omega = \frac{1}{3}$, then all pure cheap-talk strategies used in p earn the same payoff, and so $p \in \Delta_M$ is stationary in (4.12). In fact $p \in \Delta_M^{NSS}$, since p is a best reply to itself. Any alternative best reply $q \in \Delta_M$ has to use the same decision rules as p between distinct sender types and can make no postentry payoff gain by using other decision rules within sender types. Since all sender types are equally common and behave symmetrically in p, no change in message frequencies can increase the postentry payoff to q above that of p. Since p thus is neutrally stable in G_M, it is Lyapunov stable in the replicator dynamics on Δ_M, by proposition 3.12.

4.2.5 Social Efficiency in Doubly Symmetric Games

In doubly symmetric games, every locally efficient set is an ES set (proposition 2.16), and hence it is asymptotically stable in the replicator dynamics

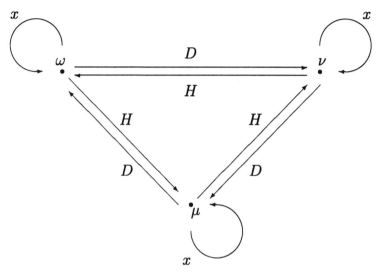

Figure 4.5
The construction of a Lyapunov stable population state in the cheap-talk game of example 4.3.

(by proposition 3.13). If the base game G is doubly symmetric, so is any cheap-talk game G_M based on it, and hence these implications apply also to cheap-talk games based on doubly symmetric games. Moreover, by proposition 2.17, a cheap-talk population state $p \in \Delta_M$ that does not use all messages belongs to an ES set if and only if it is globally efficient. Hence, under the proviso of not using all messages, there is a close connection between global social efficiency and (setwise) asymptotic stability in cheap-talk extensions of doubly symmetric games (see Schlag 1993a for more results).

4.3 General Selection Dynamics

For many applications replication by way of biological reproduction is not a compelling parable for how behaviors spread in a population. In the social sciences in general and economics in particular, replication by way of imitation and enforcement of successful behaviors seems more appropriate. Before studying, in the next section, some explicit models of such mechanisms of social evolution, we will consider a few classes of continuous-time selection dynamics that include the replicator dynamics (3.5) as a special case. In these dynamics the replicators are the pure strategies of a symmetric two-player game with mixed-strategy simplex Δ and payoff function u. Examples are collected in section 4.4.

More specifically, we focus on dynamics defined on the mixed-strategy simplex Δ in terms of *growth-rates* for the population shares associated with each pure strategy $i \in K$ of the game, as follows:

$$\dot{x}_i = g_i(x)x_i \,, \tag{4.14}$$

where g is a function with open domain X containing Δ. The function g specifies every population share's growth rate per time unit, $\dot{x}_i/x_i = \lim_{\Delta t \to 0} (\Delta x_i/x_i \cdot 1/\Delta t) = g_i(x)$. Thus $g_i(x) \in R$ is the rate at which pure strategy i replicates when the population is in state x. In the special case of the replicator dynamics (3.5), $g_i(x) = u(e_i - x, x)$.

Dynamics of the form (4.14) represent selection, as opposed to mutation, in the sense that (4.14) favors some *present* behaviors (pure strategies) over other *present* behaviors, while absent behaviors remain absent. As mentioned in the context of the replicator dynamics (subsection 3.3.2), mutations can indirectly be taken care of by the way of dynamic stability considerations.

Note that the growth rates $g_i(x)$ in (4.14) are functions of the *current* population state. In particular, we do not here allow growth rates to depend on past population states and thereby on pure strategies' past performances.[9] Before considering the connection between payoffs and growth rates, we need to ensure that the considered growth rate function g is well-behaved in terms of dynamic implications.

4.3.1   Regularity

More precisely, being well-behaved here means to induce a unique solution to the associated system of differential equations (4.14) through any initial population state in Δ, a solution which remains in the simplex at all times. By force of the Picard-Lindelöf theorem (theorem 6.1), existence and uniqueness of a solution is guaranteed if the vector field in (4.14) is Lipschitz continuous, a sufficient condition for which is that g be Lipschitz continuous. It is easily verified that the population state remains in the simplex at all times if the weighted sum of growth rates $\sum_i g_i(x)x_i$ is constantly equal to zero. This

---

9. Part of the present analysis can be extended to selection dynamics with memory by expanding the state space; see Swinkels (1993) for suggestions in this direction.

keeps the sum of population shares constant (equal to one):

$$\frac{d}{dt}\left[\sum_{i \in K} x_i\right] = \sum_{i \in K} \dot{x}_i = \sum_{i \in K} g_i(x)x_i = g(x) \cdot x . \tag{4.15}$$

Geometrically the condition $g(x) \cdot x = 0$ means that the growth-rate vector $g(x) \in R^k$ always has to be orthogonal to the associated population vector $x \in \Delta$.

Definition 4.1 *A regular growth-rate function is a Lipschitz continuous function $g : X \to R^k$ with open domain X containing Δ, such that $g(x) \cdot x = 0$ for all $x \in \Delta$.*

The growth-rate function in the replicator dynamics (3.5) is clearly regular in this sense. The equation $g_i(x) = u(e^i - x, x)$ defines a Lipschitz continuous function g on $X = R^k$, and for any $x \in \Delta$:

$$g(x) \cdot x = \sum_i \left[u(e^i, x) - u(x, x)\right]x_i = u(x, x) - u(x, x) = 0 . \tag{4.16}$$

When we showed in subsection 3.1.3 (and the appendix at the end of chapter 3) that the replicator dynamics induces a continuous solution mapping $\xi : R \times \Delta \to \Delta$ that leaves the simplex Δ, as well as its interior and boundary, invariant, we actually only used the regularity of the associated growth-rate function g. Hence, as an immediate corollary to proposition 3.20, we have that if g is regular, then (4.14) has a unique solution $\xi(\cdot, x^o) : R \to \Delta$ through any initial state $x^o \in \Delta$, the solution mapping $\xi : R \times \Delta \to \Delta$ being continuous, and each of the subsets $\text{bd}(\Delta) \subset \Delta$ and $\text{int}(\Delta) \subset \Delta$ being invariant under this mapping ξ. We will refer to a system of differential equations (4.14) as a *regular selection dynamics* if the associated growth-rate function g is regular.

It is easily verified that in any regular selection dynamics (4.14), the growth rate of the *ratio* between any two population shares $x_i > 0$ and $x_j > 0$ equals the difference between the two growth rates:[10]

$$\frac{d}{dt}\left[\frac{\xi_i(t, x)}{\xi_j(t, x)}\right]_{t=0} = \frac{\dot{x}_i}{x_j} - \frac{x_i \dot{x}_j}{x_j x_j} = [g_i(x) - g_j(x)]\frac{x_i}{x_j} . \tag{4.17}$$

Moreover it is evident from equation (4.14) that a population state $x \in \Delta$ is stationary if and only if all pure strategies that are in use in x have zero growth

---

10. See equation (3.6) in subsection 3.1.1 for the standard replicator dynamics.

rate, that is, if and only if $g_i(x) = 0$ for all $i \in C(x)$. What about stability? The following result provides a sufficient condition for asymptotic stability, and instability, respectively.[11]

Proposition 4.3 *Suppose that g is a regular growth-rate function. If x has some neighborhood U such that $g(y) \cdot x > 0$ for all population states $y \neq x$ in U, then x is asymptotically stable in (4.14). If x has some neighborhood U such that $g(y) \cdot x < 0$ for all $y \neq x$ in U, then x is unstable in (4.14).*

Proof Suppose, first, that $U \subset \Delta$ is a neighborhood of x such that $g(y) \cdot x > 0 \ \forall y \neq x, \ y \in U \cap \Delta$. It is sufficient to show that the relative-entropy function H_x in subsection 3.5.1 is decreasing along every solution path to (4.14) in $V = U \cap Q_x$, where $Q_x \subset \Delta$ is the domain of H_x. The same technique as in the proof of lemma 3.1 yields

$$\dot{H}_x(y) = \sum_i \frac{\partial H_x(y)}{\partial y_i} \dot{y}_i = -\sum_i \frac{x_i}{y_i} g_i(y) y_i = -g(y) \cdot x < 0 \,.$$

If instead U is a neighborhood of x such that $g(y) \cdot x < 0$ for all $y \neq x$, $y \in U \cap \Delta$, then $\dot{H}_x(y) > 0$ for all $y \in V = U \cap Q_x$. ∎

By the so-called cosine law for the inner product, the condition in this result is geometric in nature, requiring for asymptotic stability that the growth-rate vector $g(y)$, at any state $y \neq x$ near x, should make an acute angle with the population-state vector x (while $g(x)$ always is orthogonal to x, by regularity).[12] This guarantees a local drift toward x. See figure 4.6 for illustrations of stability (a) and instability (b) in the case $k = 2$.

In the special case of the replicator dynamics (3.5), the condition that $g(y) \cdot x > 0$ for all nearby states $y \neq x$ is equivalent with evolutionary stability of x. By proposition 2.6, $x \in \Delta^{ESS}$ if and only if $u(x, y) > u(y, y)$ for all nearby states $y \neq x$, and in the replicator dynamics

$$g(y) \cdot x = \sum_i u(e^i - y, y) x_i = u(x, y) - u(y, y) \,. \tag{4.18}$$

Hence the above proposition is a generalization of proposition 3.10 to any regular selection dynamics. Moreover, just as proposition 3.10 could be gener-

---

11. A state x is *unstable* if it is not Lyapunov stable.

12. The *cosine law* states that if ω is the angle between two vectors x and y in some euclidean space, then $x \cdot y = \|x\| \|y\| \cos(\omega)$.

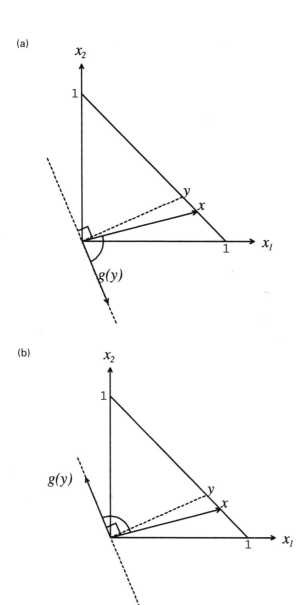

Figure 4.6
The geometry of the stability conditions in proposition 4.3: (a) Asymptotic stability at x, (b) instability at x.

alized from evolutionarily stable states to evolutionarily stable* sets in proposition 3.13, proposition 4.3 can be turned setwise as follows:

Proposition 4.4 *Suppose that g is a regular growth-rate function. If $X \subset \Delta$ is a closed set and every $x \in X$ has some neighborhood U such that $g(y) \cdot x > 0$ for all $y \in U \cap \sim X$, then X is asymptotically stable in (4.14).*

The proof is parallel to that of proposition 3.13, and in the special case of the replicator dynamics, the stability condition in the above proposition is equivalent to the requirement that $X \subset \Delta$ be an ES* set.

4.3.2 Payoff Monotonicity

So far no relation between growth rates and payoffs has been imposed, and therefore no connection between dynamic properties and criteria in noncooperative game theory can be expected. If, however, high growth rates are associated with high payoffs, then such connections can be established. The intuition is simply that if more successful pure strategies replicate at a higher rate than less successful, then poorly performing strategies are weeded out, and in the long run only best replies are present (i.e., the population state is in Nash equilibrium with itself). It turns out, however, that the weeding out of strictly dominated strategies along nonconvergent solution paths may be weaker than in the replicator dynamics.

The formal requirement is here that a pure strategy with a higher payoff grows at a higher rate. Formally:

Definition 4.2 *A regular growth-rate function g is* payoff monotonic *if, for all $x \in \Delta$,*

$$u(e^i, x) > u(e^j, x) \Leftrightarrow g_i(x) > g_j(x) . \tag{4.19}$$

The associated population dynamics (4.14) will be called *payoff monotonic*.[13] Clearly the replicator dynamics is payoff monotonic. The relation $u(e^i, x) > u(e^j, x)$ is equivalent with $u(e^i - x, x) > u(e^j - x, x)$ which, in (3.5), is precisely $g_i(x) > g_j(x)$.

Geometrically payoff monotonicity requires the vector field of (4.14) to point into a certain *cone*, determined by pure-strategy payoffs, in the simplex

---

13. This property is called *relative monotonicity* in Nachbar (1990), *order compatibility of predynamics* in Friedman (1991), and simply *monotonicity* in Samuelson and Zhang (1992).

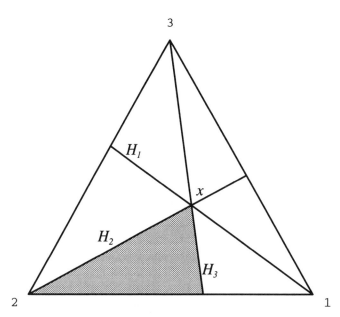

Figure 4.7
The geometry of payoff monotonicity in the case of three pure strategies. For each pure strategy i, H_i is the straight line where the ratio between the other two pure-strategy shares is constant.

Δ of mixed strategies. This is illustrated for the case $k = 3$ in figure 4.7. If the payoffs to strategies 1, 2, and 3 in a state $x \in \Delta$ are ordered $u(e^2, x) > u(e^1, x) > u(e^3, x)$, then it follows from (4.17) and (4.19) that the vector field of any payoff-monotonic population dynamics at x points into the (relative) interior of the shaded sector.

2×2 **Games** In symmetric two-player games where each player position has only two pure strategies, *all* results for the replicator dynamics (3.5) carry over to any payoff monotonic population dynamics (4.14). The reason is that then being better than average, and hence having a positive growth rate in the replicator dynamics, is the same as being better than the other strategy, and hence having a positive growth rate in any payoff-monotonic selection dynamics. Formally,

$$u(x, x) = x_1 u(e^1, x) + (1 - x_1) u(e^2, x), \qquad (4.20)$$

so the replicator dynamics (3.5) can be written

$$\dot{x}_1 = \left[u(e^1, x) - u(e^2, x)\right](1 - x_1)x_1 \quad \text{and} \quad \dot{x}_2 = -\dot{x}_1. \tag{4.21}$$

Hence the replicator growth-rate of the subpopulation playing strategy 1 is positive (negative) if and only if its payoff exceeds that of strategy 2. But this is exactly the condition for any payoff monotonic dynamics to induce a positive (negative) growth-rate for the same subpopulation. Hence the qualitative results in subsection 3.1.4 for the replicator dynamics apply to any payoff-monotonic selection dynamics.

$k \times k$ **Games**   It turns out that some fundamental results for the replicator dynamics are valid for all payoff-monotonic selection dynamics also in games with an arbitrary (finite) number of pure strategies. In section 3.2 it was shown that the replicator dynamics wipes out all strictly dominated strategies along all interior solution paths, convergent and divergent. It turns out that this result is *not* valid for all payoff-monotonic selection dynamics. More precisely, for payoff-monotonic selection dynamics we only have the result that pure strategies that are strictly dominated by other *pure* strategies vanish in the long run. The validity of this weaker claim is intuitively fairly obvious. If a subpopulation uses a pure strategy that is strictly dominated by another pure strategy, then there exists another subpopulation (in interior population states) that always does strictly better. Since the latter subpopulation share is bounded from above by one, the former population share has to decrease toward zero over time (Nachbar 1990):

Proposition 4.5   *If strategy $i \in K$ is strictly dominated by a pure strategy, then the population share $\xi_i(t, x^o)$ converges to zero in any payoff-monotonic dynamics (4.14), from any interior initial state $x^o \in \text{int}(\Delta)$.*

Proof   Suppose that $u(e^i, x) < u(e^j, x) \ \forall x \in \Delta$. Then $g_i(x) - g_j(x) < 0$ $\forall x \in \Delta$, by (4.19). By continuity of g and compactness of Δ, there exists some $\epsilon > 0$ such that $g_i(x) - g_j(x) < -\epsilon \ \forall x \in \Delta$. Suppose that $x^o \in \text{int}(\Delta)$. By (4.17),

$$\frac{d}{dt}\left[\frac{\xi_i(t, x^o)}{\xi_j(t, x^o)}\right] < -\epsilon \cdot \frac{\xi_i(t, x^o)}{\xi_j(t, x^o)} \qquad \forall t \geq 0,$$

and hence

$$\frac{\xi_i(t, x^o)}{\xi_j(t, x^o)} < \frac{x_i^o}{x_j^o}\exp(-\epsilon t) \qquad \forall t \geq 0.$$

Since $\xi_j(t, x^o) < 1 \ \forall t, \xi_i(t, x^o) \to 0$. ∎

Björnerstedt (1993) provides an example of a payoff-monotonic selection dynamics in which a strictly dominated pure strategy (not dominated by any pure strategy) survives along interior solution paths. These solution paths oscillate forever, and every now and then the strictly dominated pure strategy appears in a significant population share (see example 4.4 below).

In analogy with theorem 3.1, the above proposition can be strengthened to yield the conclusion that if a pure strategy does not survive the *iterated* elimination of strategies that are strictly dominated by another pure strategy, then the strategy does not survive under a payoff-monotonic selection dynamics. This follows from a result due to Samuelson and Zhang (1992):[14]

Proposition 4.6 *If a pure strategy i does not survive the iterated elimination of pure strategies dominated by pure strategies, then its population share $\xi_i(t, x^o)$ converges to zero in any payoff-monotonic dynamics (4.14), from any initial state $x^o \in \text{int}(\Delta)$.*

Turning to connections with aggregate Nash equilibrium behavior, first note that all payoff-monotonic selection dynamics have the same set of stationary states. The replicator dynamics being one such dynamics, this common set is

$$\Delta^o = \left\{ x \in \Delta : u(e^i - x, x) = 0 \ \ \forall i \in C(x) \right\} . \tag{4.22}$$

Proposition 4.7 *Δ^o is the set of stationary states under any payoff-monotonic selection dynamics (4.14).*

Proof   First, suppose that $x \in \Delta^o$. Then $u(e^i, x) = u(x, x)$ for all $i \in C(x)$. By monotonicity (4.19) there exists some $\mu \in R$ such that $g_i(x) = \mu$ for all $i \in C(x)$. But then $g(x) \cdot x = \mu$, and so $\mu = 0$ by orthogonality. Hence $x \in \Delta$ is stationary in (4.14). Second, suppose that $y \in \Delta$ is stationary in some payoff-monotonic dynamics (4.14). Then $g_i(y) = 0$ for all $i \in C(y)$. By (4.19), this implies that there exists some $\lambda \in R$ such that $u(e^i, y) = \lambda$ for all $i \in C(y)$. But then $u(y, y) = \sum_i y_i u(e^i, y) = \lambda$, and thus $y \in \Delta^o$. ∎

Consequently, by proposition 3.3, all population states in the subset Δ^{NE} are stationary in any payoff-monotonic selection dynamics, and the set of interior stationary states coincides with the set $\Delta^{NE} \cap \text{int}(\Delta)$, and so on. In section 3.3 it was shown that dynamic stability in the replicator dynamics, as well as interior convergence, implies Nash equilibrium behavior. Generalizations

---

14. A related (weaker) result is given in Nachbar (1990).

of these results to payoff-monotonic selection dynamics are straightforward (Nachbar 1990):[15]

Proposition 4.8 *If $x \in \Delta$ is Lyapunov stable in some payoff-monotonic selection dynamics (4.14), then $x \in \Delta^{NE}$.*

Proof Following the proof of proposition 3.4, suppose that $x \in \Delta^o$ and that $x \notin \Delta^{NE}$. Then all pure strategies in the support $C(x)$ earn the same suboptimal payoff against x. Hence there exists some $i \notin C(x)$ such that $u(e^i, x) > u(e^j, x)$ for all $j \in C(x)$. By stationarity and payoff monotonicity, $g_i(x) > g_j(x) = 0$ for all $j \in C(x)$. Hence by continuity of g there is a $\delta > 0$ and a neighborhood U of x such that $g_i(y) \geq \delta$ for all $y \in U \cap \Delta$. But then $\xi_i(t, x^o) \geq x_i^o \exp(\delta t)$ for any $x^o \in U \cap \Delta$ and all times $t > 0$ such that $\xi(t, x^o) \in U \cap \Delta$. Thus $\xi_i(t, x^o)$ initially increases exponentially from any $x^o \in U \cap \text{int}(\Delta)$, and yet $x_i = 0$, so x is not Lyapunov stable. ■

Proposition 4.9 *If there is some $x^o \in \text{int}(\Delta)$ and payoff-monotonic selection dynamics (4.14) such that $\xi(t, x^o)_{t \to \infty} \to x$, then $x \in \Delta^{NE}$.*

Proof Following the proof of proposition 3.5, assume that $x^o \in \text{int}(\Delta)$ and $\xi(t, x^o) \to x$, in some payoff-monotonic selection dynamics (4.14). Then x is stationary in that dynamics, by proposition 6.3. Hence $g_j(x) = 0$ for all $j \in C(x)$, and by proposition 4.7, $u(e^j, x) = u(x)$ for all $j \in C(x)$. If $x \notin \Delta^{NE}$, then there exists some strategy $i \notin C(x)$ such that $u(e^i, x) > u(x, x)$, and thus $g_i(x) > g_j(x) = 0$ for all $j \in C(x)$. By continuity of g there exists some neighborhood U of x such that $g_i(y) > 0$ for all population states y in $U \cap \Delta$. However, this contradicts the hypothesis that $\xi(t, x^o)$ converges to x. The latter implies that there exists a time $T > 0$ such that $\xi(t, x^o) \in U \cap \text{int}(\Delta)$ for all $t \geq T$. Since $x_i = 0$, there must be some $t \geq T$ such that $d\xi_i(t, x^o)/dt < 0$, a contradiction to g_i being positive on $U \cap \Delta$. Hence $x \in \Delta^{NE}$. ■

In other words, if a population state $x \in \Delta$ is the limit state to any interior solution trajectory, under any payoff-monotonic selection dynamics, then this is sufficient to guarantee that x is in Nash equilibrium with itself. (Note that any interior stationary state is trivially reachable in this sense.)

---

15. Friedman (1991) establishes proposition 4.8 in a more general setting under the slightly stronger hypothesis that x is *asymptotically* stable.

4.3.3 Payoff Positivity

Instead of payoff monotonicity, which requires that the growth rates $g_1(x)$, $\ldots, g_k(x) \in R$ always have the same internal ordering (in the usual ordering of R) as the payoffs $u(e^1, x), \ldots, u(e^k, x) \in R$, some applications call for other connections between growth rates and payoffs. One alternative broad class of growth rate functions are those that respect the signs of the excess payoffs $u(e^i - x, x) \in R$. The requirement here is that pure strategies that earn above (below) average have positive (negative) growth rates:[16]

Definition 4.3 *A regular growth-rate function g is* payoff positive *if, for all $x \in \Delta$ and $i \in K$,*

$$\text{sgn}\left[g_i(x)\right] = \text{sgn}\left[u(e^i - x, x)\right]. \tag{4.23}$$

Besides payoff monotonicity, payoff positivity is another property of the replicator growth-rate function: In (3.5) we have $g_i(x) = u(e^i, x) - u(x, x)$ for all $i \in K$. Moreover in 2×2 games the classes of payoff-monotonic and payoff-positive growth-rate functions coincide, since being better than average is the same as being better than the other pure strategy. In particular, the qualitative observations in subsection 4.3.2 about such games carry over to payoff-positive selection dynamics. However, for other games these two classes may be distinct: Pure strategies that are better than average but not optimal may have negative growth rates under payoff monotonicity, and so forth.

In section 3.7 we established a sufficient condition for a subset $H \subset K$ of pure strategies to be a long-run survivor set under the replicator dynamics (3.5). It is not difficult to show that this condition is in fact valid for any payoff-positive selection dynamics (4.14). To see this, recall that a subset $H \subset K$ was defined to be closed under weakly better replies if all pure strategies that are weakly better replies to any state x in the face $\Delta(H) \subset \Delta$ belong to H. Recall also the definition of $\alpha^0(H)$. As a generalization of the definition given in section 3.7, we call a set $H \subset K$ a *long-run survivor set* in a regular selection dynamics (4.14) if $\Delta(H)$ is asymptotically stable in this dynamics and H does not properly contain a nonempty subset L with this property.

Proposition 4.10 *Consider a payoff-positive growth-rate function g and the associated selection dynamics (4.14):*

---

16. Nachbar (1990) calls the associated dynamics (4.14) *sign-preserving*.

a. If $\Delta(H)$ is Lyapunov stable, then $\alpha^0(H) \subset H$.

b. If H is closed under weakly better replies, then $\Delta(H)$ is asymptotically stable.

c. If $H \subset K$ is closed under weakly better replies and does not properly contain any nonempty subset L for which $\alpha^0(H) \subset L$, then H is a long-run survivor set.

Proof These claims can be proved along the same lines as in the special case of the replicator dynamics (3.5). (a) If $\alpha^0(H)$ is not contained in H, there is some $x = e^i \in \Delta(H)$ and $j \notin H$ such that $u(e^j - x, x) > 0$. By payoff positivity, $g_j(x) > 0$, and by continuity of g_j, there is a $\delta > 0$ and neighborhood U of x such that $g_j(y) > \delta$ for all $y \in U \cap \Delta$. Since the edge $\Delta(\{i, j\})$ is invariant, (4.14) has solution trajectories in $U \cap \Delta$ that start arbitrarily near x and forever move away from $\Delta(H)$, and $\Delta(H) \subset \Delta$ is not Lyapunov stable. (b) Suppose that $H \subset K$ is closed under weakly better replies, and let U be as in lemma 3.2. There then is some $\bar{\varepsilon} > 0$ such that for any $\varepsilon \in (0, \bar{\varepsilon})$, the ε-slice $B(\varepsilon) = \{x \in \Delta : x_j < \varepsilon \; \forall j \notin H\}$ contains the face $\Delta(H)$ and the closure $\bar{B}(\epsilon)$ is contained in U. On $\bar{B}(\varepsilon)$, a compact set $u(e^j - x, x)$ is negative and hence, by payoff positivity, so is the continuous function g_j. By Weierstrass's maximum theorem, the maximum of g_j over this set is negative. Hence there is some $\delta > 0$ such that, for any such x and j, $\dot{x}_j = g_j(x)x_j < -\delta x_j$, which implies that $\xi_j(t, x^o)$ for each $j \notin H$ decreases monotonically to zero from any initial state x^o in $\Delta \cap B(\varepsilon)$. Thus $\Delta(H) \subset \Delta$ is asymptotically stable. (c) follows directly from (a) and (b). ∎

4.3.4 Weak Payoff Positivity

It turns out that the implications from payoff-monotonic selection dynamics to aggregate Nash equilibrium behavior, established in subsection 4.3.2, are in fact valid for a wider class of selection dynamics that also includes all payoff-positive selection dynamics. As can be seen in the proofs of these results, it is sufficient that whenever there exists a pure strategy $i \in K$ that gives a payoff above average, some such pure strategy has a positive growth rate. This is the case, for instance, if all pure strategies that earn above average have positive growth rates or if some pure *best* reply has a positive growth rate whenever such a strategy gives an above-average payoff.

More exactly, suppose that g is a regular growth-rate function. The required connection between growth rates and payoffs is that if not all pure strategies in the game earn the same payoff, then at least one of the pure strategies that earns above average has a positive growth rate. Formally, for any state $x \in \Delta$, let $B(x)$ denote the (possibly empty) subset of pure strategies that earn above average,

$$B(x) = \left\{ i \in K : u(e^i, x) > u(x, x) \right\}. \tag{4.24}$$

Definition 4.4 *A regular growth-rate function g is* weakly payoff positive *if, for all $x \in \Delta$: $B(x) \neq \emptyset \Rightarrow g_i(x) > 0$ for some $i \in B(x)$.*

Clearly payoff positivity implies weak payoff positivity: *Every* pure strategy $i \in B(x)$ has a positive growth rate under payoff positivity. To see that this also is a weakening of payoff monotonicity, let g be a payoff-monotonic growth-rate function, and assume that $B(x) \neq \emptyset$. If all pure strategies in the support of x earn the same payoff, then all their growth rates must be the same, by monotonicity, and this common growth rate must be zero, by orthogonality, $g(x) \cdot x = 0$. Hence in this case every pure strategy in $B(x)$ has a positive growth rate, by monotonicity. Suppose, instead, that not all pure strategies in the support of x earn the same payoff. By monotonicity the best earning among these have a higher growth rate than the least earning, and again by orthogonality, the best earning must have a positive growth rate. These clearly earn above average and hence belong to $B(x)$. Thus all payoff-monotonic growth-rate functions are weakly payoff positive.

We are now in a position to establish the claimed generalized implications for Nash equilibrium behavior:

Proposition 4.11 *Suppose that g is weakly payoff positive:*

a. *If $x \in \mathrm{int}(\Delta)$ is stationary in (4.14), then $x \in \Delta^{NE}$.*

b. *If $x \in \Delta$ is Lyapunov stable in (4.14), then $x \in \Delta^{NE}$.*

c. *If $x \in \Delta$ is the limit to some interior solution to (4.14), then $x \in \Delta^{NE}$.*

Proof   (a) Suppose that $x \in \mathrm{int}(\Delta)$ is stationary in (4.14). Then $B(x) = \emptyset$ by weak payoff positivity, and $x \in \Delta^{NE}$. (b) Suppose that $x \in \Delta$ is stationary in (4.14). Then $g_i(x) = 0$ for all $i \in C(x)$. If $x \notin \Delta^{NE}$, then $B(x) \neq \emptyset$, and by weak payoff positivity, there is some $j \in B(x)$ such that $g_j(x) > 0$. Consequently $j \notin C(x)$, that is, $x_j = 0$. By continuity of g_j there is a $\delta > 0$ and a neighborhood U of x such that $g_j(y) > \delta$ for all $y \in U \cap \Delta$, and by the argument given in the proof of proposition 4.8, x is not Lyapunov stable. (c) Suppose that $x^o \in \text{int}(\Delta)$ and $\xi(t, x^o)_{t \to \infty} \to x$ in some weakly payoff-positive dynamics (4.14). Then x is stationary, by proposition 6.3, and $g_j(x) = 0$ for all $j \in C(x)$. If $x \notin \Delta^{NE}$, then $B(x) \neq \emptyset$, and there is some $j \in B(x)$ such that $g_j(x) > 0$ and $x_j = 0$. By the same argument as in the proof of proposition 4.9, this leads to a contradiction, so $x \in \Delta^{NE}$. ∎

4.4   Replication by Imitation

We now enter yet another not much researched arena, formal modeling of social evolution of behaviors in a population of strategically interacting agents. These may be individuals, firms, or other social or economic units. We will here sketch a few continuous-time pure-strategy selection dynamics arising from adaptation by myopic imitation. In these models we imagine that all agents in the population are infinitely lived and interact forever. Each agent sticks to some pure strategy for some time interval, and now and then reviews her strategy, sometimes resulting in a change of strategy.[17]

There are two basic elements common to these models. The first is a specification of the *time rate* at which agents in the population review their strategy choice. This rate may depend on the current performance of the agent's pure strategy and of other aspects of the current population state. We will write $r_i(x)$ for the average review rate of an agent who uses pure strategy $i \in K$—an i-strategist. The second element is a specification of the *choice probabilities* of a reviewing agent. The probability that a reviewing i-strategist will switch to some pure strategy j may here depend on the current performance of these strategies and other aspects of the current population state. This probability is written $p_i^j(x)$, where $p_i(x) = (p_i^1(x), \ldots, p_i^k(x))$ is the resulting probability distribution over the set K of pure strategies, $p_i(x) \in \Delta$.[18] In particular, $p_i^i(x)$ is the probability that a reviewing i-strategist does not change strategy.

In a finite population one may imagine that the review times of an agent are the arrival times of a Poisson process with arrival rate $r_i(x)$ and that, at each such time, the agent selects a pure strategy according to the probability

---

17. The discussion in this section follows Björnerstedt and Weibull (1993).

18. Alternatively, what is here called reviewing could be reinterpreted as the exit of one agent who is instantly replaced by a new agent.

distribution $p_i(x)$ over the set K. Assuming that all agents' Poisson processes are statistically independent, the aggregate of reviewing times in the subpopulation of i-strategists is itself a Poisson process with (population size normalized) arrival rate $x_i r_i(x)$. If strategy switches are statistically independent random variables across agents, then the arrival rate of the aggregate Poisson process of switches from strategy i to strategy j in the whole population is $x_i r_i(x) p_i^j(x)$.[19]

We now imagine a continuum of agents and, by the law of large numbers, model these aggregate stochastic processes as deterministic flows. The outflow from subpopulation i thus is $\sum_{j \neq i} x_i r_i(x) p_i^j(x)$, and the inflow is $\sum_{j \neq i} x_j r_j(x) p_j^i(x)$. Rearranging terms, we obtain

$$\dot{x}_i = \sum_{j \in K} x_j r_j(x) p_j^i(x) - r_i(x) x_i . \tag{4.25}$$

To guarantee that this system of differential equations induces a well-defined dynamics on the state space Δ, we henceforth assume that $r_i : X \to R_+$ and $p_i : X \to \Delta$ are Lipschitz continuous functions with open domain X containing Δ. By the Picard-Lindelöf theorem, (4.25) then has a unique solution through any initial state $x^o \in \Delta$, and such a solution trajectory is continuous and never leaves Δ.[20]

4.4.1 Pure Imitation Driven by Dissatisfaction

For a model of pure imitation, assume that all reviewing agents adopt the strategy of "the first man they meet in the street." Independently of which strategy the reviewing agent has used so far, she draws an agent at random from the population, according to a uniform probability distribution across agents and adopts the pure strategy of the so sampled agent. Formally, for all population states $x \in \Delta$ and pure strategies $i, j \in K$:

$$p_i^j(x) = x_j . \tag{4.26}$$

---

19. A *Poisson process* is a stochastic point process in continuous time, the points usually being called *arrival times*. The probability distribution of these is given by a function $\lambda : R \to R$, the *arrival rate* (or *intensity*) of the process such that $\lambda(t)dt$ is the probability for an arrival in the infinitesimal time interval $(t, t + dt)$. Superposition of statistically independent Poisson processes is again a Poisson process, and its arrival rate is the sum of the constituent arrival rates. Likewise statistically independent decomposition of a Poisson process, such as at the above strategy switchings, again results in a Poisson process.

20. The state space Δ is *forward* invariant in this dynamics; see section 6.3.

If the review rates were independent of the current strategy i, then such an imitation process would lead to no change at all in the population state; all population states $x \in \Delta$ are then stationary in (4.25). However, if agents with less successful strategies on average review their strategy at a higher rate than agents with more successful strategies, then a payoff-monotonic selection dynamics arises. More precisely, suppose that

$$r_i(x) = \rho \left[u(e^i, x), x \right] \tag{4.27}$$

for some (Lipschitz continuous) function ρ that is strictly decreasing in its first (payoff) argument. Note that this monotonicity assumption does not presume that an agent necessarily *knows* the expected payoff to her current pure strategy and the population state. It is sufficient that some or all agents in the population have some noisy empirical data on their current (expected) payoff.

Under assumptions (4.26) and (4.27), the population dynamics (4.25) becomes

$$\dot{x}_i = \left(\sum_{h \in K} x_h \rho \left[u(e^h, x), x \right] - \rho \left[u(e^i, x), x \right] \right) x_i . \tag{4.28}$$

Here the growth rate of the population share of i-strategists, by monotonicity of ρ, is higher than that of the population share of j-strategists if and only if the current payoff to the former, $u(e^i, x)$, exceeds that of the second, $u(e^j, x)$. Hence (4.28) constitutes a payoff-monotonic selection dynamics (4.14), and all results in subsection 4.3.2 apply to this form of social evolution by way of imitation.

As a special case, let the review rate of an agent be *linearly* decreasing in her current payoff. Then the average review rate is linearly decreasing in the average payoff:

$$\rho \left[u(e^i, x), x \right] = \alpha - \beta u(e^i, x) \tag{4.29}$$

for some $\alpha, \beta \in R$ such that $\beta > 0$ and $\alpha/\beta \geq u(e^i, x)$ for all x and i. Under these assumptions all review rates are nonnegative and (4.28) boils down to

$$\dot{x}_i = \beta \left[u(e^i, x) - u(x, x) \right] x_i , \tag{4.30}$$

a mere (constant) rescaling of time in the replicator dynamics (3.3)![21] Hence

---

21. This observation is due to Björnerstedt (1993).

all results for the replicator dynamics are valid for this special case of replication by way of pure imitation.

The following example (Björnerstedt 1993) suggests that if instead review rates are highly nonlinear in payoffs, then a strictly dominated pure strategy (which is not strictly dominated by any pure strategy) may survive in the long run.

Example 4.4 Suppose that virtually only those agents who use the *worst* performing pure strategies review their strategy and that all imitation is pure, (4.26). (Alternatively, imagine a bank that now and then weeds out the worst performing firms in a market, subject to a small observational error as to performance, and imagine that now and then naive entrant firms appear who mimic the existing firms' behaviors.) Formally, suppose that $\rho\left[u(e^i, x), x\right] = \psi\left[u(e^i, x) - w(x)\right]$, where $w(x) = \min_j u(e^j, x)$, and ψ is (Lipschitz continuous and) positive and strictly decreasing with $\psi(0) = 1$. Under pure imitation (4.26) this results in the payoff-monotonic selection dynamics

$$\dot{x}_i = \left(\sum_{j \in K} x_j \psi\left[u(e^j, x) - w(x)\right] - \psi\left[u(e^i, x) - w(x)\right]\right) x_i .$$

In the Dekel-Scotchmer example (subsection 4.1.2), the fourth pure strategy is strictly dominated by the mixed Nash equilibrium strategy but by no pure strategy. However, the fourth pure strategy is the worst performing only when the other three strategies are mixed approximately as in the Nash equilibrium; see the cylinder-shaped region in figure 4.8 (a). Moreover, on the boundary face where the fourth pure strategy is extinct, all solution trajectories to the above dynamics, except the one starting at the Nash equilibrium point, lead out toward the (relative) boundary of this face. This is illustrated in figure 4.8 (b), which has been drawn for the limiting case when ψ is the (not Lipschitz continuous) unit step function that takes the value $\psi(z) = 0$ for all $z > 0$ (corresponding to no observational error).

4.4.2   Imitation of Successful Agents: Model 1

To model a process of directed imitation in a finite but large population, we could proceed as follows: Suppose that each reviewing agent samples another agent at random from the population, with equal probability for all agents, and observes with some noise the average payoff to her own and to the sampled agent's strategy, respectively. If an i-strategist samples a j-strategist,

(a)

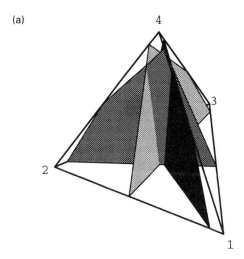

(b)

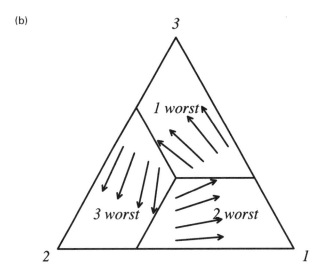

Figure 4.8
(a) The region in the polyhedron Θ, in the Dekel-Scotchmer Game, where the strictly dominated strategy 4 earns the lowest payoff among pure strategies. (b) The limiting vector field (in the absence of observational errors) of the selection dynamics in example 4.4, on the boundary face of the simplex where strategy 4 is extinct.

then she observes payoff $u(e^i, x) + \varepsilon$ to strategy i and payoff $u(e^j, x) + \varepsilon'$ to strategy j, where ε and ε' are random variables such that their difference, the random variable $\varepsilon - \varepsilon'$, has a continuously differentiable (and hence Lipschitz continuous) probability distribution function $\phi : R \to [0, 1]$.[22] Having made such a pairwise payoff comparison, the reviewing agent switches to the sampled agent's strategy if and only if the observed payoff difference is positive, $u(e^j, x) + \varepsilon' > u(e^i, x) + \varepsilon$. The conditional probability that the agent will switch to strategy j, given that she sampled strategy j, is thus $\phi[u(e^j, x) - u(e^i, x)]$. Since the probability that the agent will sample strategy j is x_j, the resulting conditional choice probability distribution, $p_i(x) \in \Delta$, is given by

$$p_i^j(x) = \begin{cases} x_j \phi[u(e^j - e^i, x)] & \text{if } j \neq i, \\ 1 - \sum_{j \neq i} x_j \phi[u(e^j - e^i, x)] & \text{otherwise.} \end{cases} \tag{4.31}$$

The random variables ε and ε' may alternatively be interpreted as idiosyncratic preference differences between agents in the population: Then $u(e^i, x) + \varepsilon$ and $u(e^j, x) + \varepsilon'$ are the true average payoffs to pure strategies i and j, respectively, according to the preferences of a randomly drawn agent from the population. In this interpretation the choice probabilities (4.31) result from individual differences in preferences across agents and not from observation errors made by agents with identical preferences.

To isolate the effect of choice probabilities as in (4.31), assume that all review rates are constantly equal to one:

$$r_i(x) \equiv 1. \tag{4.32}$$

Inserted into (4.25), this results in the following selection dynamics:

$$\dot{x}_i = \left[\sum_{j \in K} x_j \left(\phi[u(e^i - e^j, x)] - \phi[u(e^j - e^i, x)] \right) \right] x_i. \tag{4.33}$$

If ϕ is strictly increasing over the (bounded) range of possible payoff differences in the game, then (4.33) is payoff monotonic, and all results for that class of replication dynamics apply (see subsection 4.3.2).

---

22. Note that this probability distribution is assumed to be functionally independent of i, j, and x; in fact it is a heroic simplification from the viewpoint of statistical sampling.

Consider population states x near some interior state x^* that is stationary in (4.33). Since this dynamics is payoff monotonic, $x^* \in \Delta^{NE}$ (proposition 4.7). In particular, all pure strategies earn the same payoff against x^*. Consequently at states x near x^* all pure-strategy payoff differences in (4.33) are small. Linearization in (4.33) of the (continuously differentiable) probability distribution function ϕ, at states x near x^*, results in

$$\dot{x}_i \approx \sum_{j \in K} x_j \phi'(0) \left[u(e^i - e^j, x) - u(e^j - e^i, x) \right] x_i$$

$$= 2\phi'(0) u(e^i - x, x) x_i \, .$$

(4.34)

Hence, in a neighborhood of an interior stationary state, the vector field of the imitation dynamics (4.33) is approximately just a positive constant times that of the replicator dynamics (3.5)!

As a special case of (4.33), suppose that all error terms (or idiosyncratic preference differences) are *uniformly* distributed with a support containing the range of all possible payoff differences in the game. Then ϕ is an affine function over the relevant interval, namely $\phi(z) = \alpha + \beta z$ for some $\alpha, \beta \in R$ where $\beta > 0$, and (4.33) becomes a mere scaling of time in the replicator dynamics:

$$\dot{x}_i = 2\beta [u(e^i, x) - u(x, x)] x_i \, .$$

(4.35)

4.4.3 Imitation of Successful Agents: Model 2

As a generalization of pure imitation we might assume that the choice probabilities $p_i^j(x)$ are proportional to j's popularity x_j, where the proportionality factor (or weight) may be positively related to the current payoff to strategy j. It is thus as if a reviewing agent would imitate another agent from the population, drawn at random but possibly with a higher probability for relatively more successful agents (perhaps due to their conspicuous consumption or visible well-being). Let the weight factor that a reviewing i-strategist attaches to pure strategy j be $\omega_i \left[u(e^j, x), x \right] > 0$, where ω_i is a (Lipschitz continuous) function which is nondecreasing in its first (payoff) argument. Then

$$p_i^j(x) = \frac{\omega_i \left[u(e^j, x), x \right] x_j}{\sum_{h \in K} \omega_i \left[u(e^h, x), x \right] x_h} \, .$$

(4.36)

As in the earlier case of differentiated review rates (subsection 4.4.1), the informational assumption behind choice probabilities such as these is not that a reviewing agent necessarily knows the current average payoffs to all pure strategies in the game, nor does she have to know the current population state. It is sufficient that some agents have some, perhaps noisy, empirical information about payoffs to some pure strategies in current use, and, on average, are more likely to imitate an agent with higher current average payoff than one with lower average payoff.

As a special case of (4.36) we have pure imitation: If the weight function ω_i is completely payoff insensitive, then $p_i^j(x) = x_j$ for all pure strategies j and population states x. Conversely, by making the weight functions in (4.36) sufficiently payoff sensitive, we may have virtually all reviewing agents adopt one of the best pure strategies currently in use.

Combining choice probabilities of the form (4.36) with the assumption (4.32) of unit review rates results in the following selection dynamics (see (4.25)):

$$\dot{x}_i = \left(\sum_{j \in K} \frac{\omega_j \left[u(e^i, x), x \right] x_j}{\sum_{h \in K} \omega_j \left[u(e^h, x), x \right] x_h} - 1 \right) x_i . \tag{4.37}$$

If the weight functions are strictly increasing in payoffs, pure strategies i with higher payoffs $u(e^i, x)$ have higher growth rates in (4.37) than pure strategies with lower payoffs, so this imitation dynamics is again payoff monotonic.

As a special case suppose that the weight factors are *linear* in the target payoff, namely $\omega_i(z, x) = \lambda + \mu z$ for some $\lambda, \mu \in R$ such that $\mu > 0$ and $\lambda + \mu u(e^i, x) > 0$ for all population states x and pure strategies i. Then (4.37) becomes

$$\dot{x}_i = \frac{\mu}{\lambda + \mu u(x, x)} \left[u(e^i, x) - u(x, x) \right] x_i , \tag{4.38}$$

a (payoff-dependent) rescaling of time in the replicator dynamics (3.5)! Hence the solution orbits to (4.38) coincide with those of (3.5), and except for results on time averages (subsection 3.3.4), all results in chapter 3 apply to this model of replication by payoff-weighted imitation. In the special case where the weights are *proportional* to payoffs ($\lambda = 0$), we obtain growth rates $g_i(x) = \left[u(e^i, x) - u(x, x) \right] / u(x, x)$ in (4.38) (here assume that all payoffs are positive). In this special case it is as if reviewing individuals draw a payoff unit, from the current stream of payoffs, at random; the probability

(a)

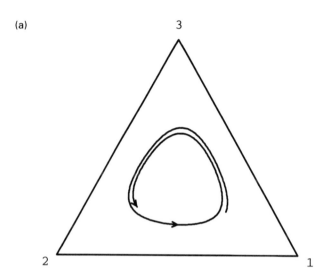

(b)

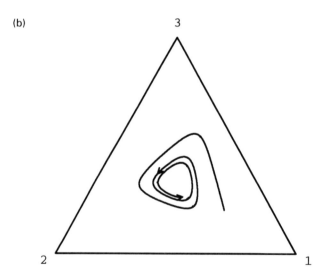

Figure 4.9
Solution orbits to the imitation dynamics in example 4.6, applied to a generalized Rock-Scissors-Paper Game with payoff parameter $a = 1$: (a) For sensitivity parameter $\sigma = 1$, (b) for sensitivity parameter $\sigma = 10$.

that the so drawn payoff unit has been earned by pure strategy i is precisely $x_i u(e^i, x)/u(x, x)$.

Example 4.5 Consider choice probabilities (4.36) with weight factors $\omega_i(z, x) = \exp(\sigma z)$ for some $\sigma > 0$. With unit reviewing rates (4.32) the induced payoff-monotonic selection dynamics (4.37) becomes

$$\dot{x}_i = \left(\frac{\exp\left[\sigma u(e^i, x)\right]}{\sum_h x_h \exp\left[\sigma u(e^h, x)\right]} - 1 \right) x_i \,.$$

The boundary case $\sigma = 0$ corresponds to pure imitation, and the limit case $\sigma \to \infty$ corresponds to pure best-reply adaptation at all interior population states x in the sense that all reviewing agents then switch to currently best replies. Figures 4.9 (a) and (b) show computer simulations for the generalized Rock-Scissors-Paper Game in subsection 3.1.5 with payoff parameter $a = 1$ and payoff sensitivity $\sigma = 1$ and $\sigma = 10$, respectively.

5 Multipopulation Models

So far the studied interactions have all been modeled as symmetric and pair-wise random matchings between individuals in a single population. However, many relevant strategic interactions—in biology, economics, and other social sciences—are not symmetric; they may take place between two or more individuals from distinct populations. For instance, individuals from different biological species may interact, or buyers and sellers may interact in markets. Moreover, even if the game representing the interaction is itself symmetric, the players of the game may nevertheless be drawn from distinct populations. We are led to studies of evolutionary selection in multiple populations who interact in an arbitrary n-player game—the topic of the present chapter.

In the same spirit as in the single-population setting, we can imagine large (technically infinite) populations of individuals, one such population for each player position of the game. Over and over again, individuals are randomly drawn from these populations to play the game—one individual from each player population. The game can be symmetric or asymmetric; the only restriction imposed is that it be a finite game in normal form.

For the purpose of extending the static single-population criterion of evolutionary stability (chapter 2) to such a multipopulation setting, we imagine that all individuals in a player population are initially programmed to the same pure or mixed strategy available to that player position in the game. We then imagine that some mutant strategy arises in a small population share in some or all of these player populations. However, unlike in the single-population setting, here a mutant strategy never meets itself, for the simple reason that each individual in any of the n player populations is always matched with individuals from the *other* $n - 1$ player populations. Consequently a nonstrict Nash equilibrium is vulnerable to "invasions" by alternative best replies. Indeed, it turns out that suggested criteria for multipopulation evolutionary stability are met *only* by strict Nash equilibria (see also section 2.7). Multipopulation criteria for evolutionary stability, along with robustness against equilibrium entrants and equilibrium evolutionary stability of sets of strategy profiles, are analyzed in section 5.1.

The rest of the chapter is devoted to explicitly dynamic models of evolutionary selection. In the spirit of chapters 3 and 4 it is here imagined that each individual is, at each instant, programmed to one of the *pure* strategies available to the player position of her population. Hence each player population can, at every moment in time, be divided into as many subpopulations as there are pure strategies for the player position in question. The evolutionary selection dynamics to be studied are concerned with the growth rates of these subpopulation shares. Formally, a player-population state is identical with a (pure or mixed) strategy for the player position. Taken together, these player-population states constitute a (pure or mixed) strategy profile of the game. However, in this dynamic setting there arise some new issues not present in the single-population setting.

To begin with, there are *two* multipopulation extensions of the continuous-time replicator dynamics studied in chapter 3. These two versions are studied in section 5.2. The emphasis is on examples and on comparisons in symmetric two-player games with the single-population dynamics. Section 5.3 derives a variety of evolutionary selection dynamics, including the two replicator dynamics, from simple models of individual adaptation by way of imitation. In section 5.4 the perspective is shifted from the interacting individuals to the replicators, the pure strategies of the game in question. In a simple statistical-mechanical model of competition among such replicators for hosts, within each player population a class of evolutionary selection dynamics is derived.

Section 5.5 defines a few broad classes of evolutionary selection dynamics. Each contains both versions of the multipopulation replicator dynamics along with many of the other selection dynamics derived in sections 5.3 and 5.4. Implications from selection dynamics in these classes for noncooperative solution criteria are examined in section 5.6. It turns out that the results from the single-population setting in chapters 3 and 4 carry over. In particular, the results concerning survival of dominated strategies are straight-forward extensions of those for single-population selection dynamics, and dynamic stability and interior convergence again imply aggregate Nash equilibrium behavior.

It may thus seem that models of evolutionary dynamic selection lend strong support to the Nash equilibrium paradigm. However, to obtain robust dynamic predictions, stronger dynamic stability is needed. More precisely, in view of the possibility of unmodeled evolutionary drift caused by occasional mutations or mistakes in individual behavior or by small-scale experimentation with alternative behaviors, it is desirable that dynamic stability properties are not destroyed by small perturbations of (the vector field that defines) the dynamics in question. One such classical structurally robust dynamic stability property is asymptotic stability.[1] Unfortunately, few Nash equilibria are asymptotically stable in multipopulation dynamics. In particular, in one of the two multi-

---

1. In contrast, mere Lyapunov stability can be destroyed by arbitrarily small perturbations of the population state.

population versions of the replicator dynamics, *only* strict Nash equilibria are asymptotically stable. Hence in this benchmark dynamics we are essentially back to square one, just as in the above-mentioned multipopulation extension of the evolutionary stability criterion. Moreover all Nash equilibria are stationary in the studied selection dynamics (with the exception of some weakly positive selection dynamics), so no Nash equilibrium that belongs to a non-singleton component of the set of Nash equilibria is asymptotically stable. And nonsingleton components of Nash equilibria are endemic in normal form games derived from extensive forms. These issues are discussed in the first part of section 5.7.

Since the existence problem for asymptotic stability concerns individual strategy profiles, it is natural to turn to *sets* of strategy profiles instead. Section 5.7 provides a characterization of asymptotic stability for a certain class of sets, the *faces* of the polyhedron of strategy profiles. A wide class of evolutionary selection dynamics agree concerning asymptotic stability of such sets. Asymptotic stability of such sets can be used for robust dynamic predictions in terms of subsets of pure strategies, one subset for each player position in the game. The necessary and sufficient condition in question is operational, and its cutting power is illustrated in a few examples.

Readers interested in more results on multipopulation models may consult Hofbauer and Sigmund (1988), Cressman (1992a), Samuelson and Zhang (1992), and Swinkels (1992a, 1993).

5.1 Evolutionary Stability Criteria

Using the notation of chapter 1 for n-player games, let $I = \{1, \ldots, n\}$ be the set of players, S_i the pure-strategy set of player $i \in I$, Δ_i her mixed-strategy set, Θ the polyhedron of mixed-strategy profiles, and $u_i(x)$ the payoff to player i when $x \in \Theta$ is played.

5.1.1 Evolutionarily Stable Strategy Profiles

There appears to be no consensus as to how the criterion of evolutionary stability should be extended to multipopulation interactions. Suppose that each player role in an n-player game is represented by a large population of individuals and that each interaction takes place among a randomly drawn n-tuple of individuals, one from each player population. Suppose moreover that every individual in each population $i \in I$ is programmed to one and the same (pure or mixed) strategy x_i. It appears that a minimal requirement for a strategy profile $x \in \Theta$ to be evolutionarily stable is that each strategy x_i be a best reply to x, since otherwise some player population i would be vulnerable to invasions by some mutant strategy y_i that would earn a higher payoff than x_i in these same matchings. By definition, no alternative best reply exists for any player population if the profile x in question happens to be a strict Nash equilibrium, so such profiles should qualify. The question then arises whether there are nonstrict Nash equilibria that should be considered evolutionarily stable. Suppose, for instance, that $x \in \Theta$ is a Nash equilibrium and that y_i is an alternative best reply for player position i to x. What protects the strategy x_i against invasion of a few mutants playing y_i? Irrespective of their share ϵ_i of the ith player population, these mutants earn precisely the same payoff as the incumbents, who play x_i. For this reason even weak evolutionary stability criteria in multipopulation settings tend to reject all nonstrict Nash equilibria.

The following relatively weak criterion for evolutionary stability is equivalent to a definition in Cressman (1992a; see also Swinkels 1992a):

Definition 5.1 $x \in \Theta$ is evolutionarily stable *if for every strategy profile* $y \neq x$ *there exists some* $\bar{\epsilon}_y \in (0, 1)$ *such that for all* $\epsilon \in (0, \bar{\epsilon}_y)$, *and with* $w = \epsilon y + (1 - \epsilon)x$,

$$u_i\left(x_i, w_{-i}\right) > u_i\left(y_i, w_{-i}\right) \qquad \text{for some } i \in I \tag{5.1}$$

In other words, a strategy profile x is evolutionarily stable if there for every mutant profile $y \neq x$ exists an invasion barrier $\bar{\epsilon}_y$ such that if y comes in a smaller dose (population share), then at least one of the incumbent strategies x_i does better in the postentry population mix than its mutant strategy y_i. Alternatively, one might want to require this "immunity" from *all* constituent strategies x_i rather than from some. An intermediate criterion, between "all" and "some," was suggested in Taylor (1979), where the incumbent strategies x_i are required to do better than their respective mutant strategies, y_i, *in the aggregate* (see also Schuster et al. 1981b). Taylor's definition is obtained if one replaces condition (5.1) by

$$\sum_{i \in I} u_i\left(x_i, w_{-i}\right) > \sum_{i \in I} u_i\left(y_i, w_{-i}\right). \tag{5.2}$$

Clearly (5.2) implies (5.1).

However, as suggested earlier, even weak criteria of evolutionary stability in multipopulation settings reject all but strict Nash equilibria. Formally (see Selten 1980; van Damme 1987; Swinkels 1992a):

Proposition 5.1 $x \in \Theta$ *is evolutionarily stable if and only if x is a strict Nash equilibrium.*

Proof[2] First, assume that $x \in \Theta$ is evolutionarily stable, and fix any player position $i \in I$. Let $y_i \in \tilde{\beta}_i(x)$, and for all $j \neq i$, $y_j = x_j$. Let $w = \epsilon y + (1 - \epsilon)x$, where $\epsilon \in \left(0, \bar{\epsilon}_y\right)$. Then $u_i\left(x_i, w_{-i}\right) = u_i\left(y_i, w_{-i}\right)$ and $u_j\left(x_j, w_{-j}\right) = u_j\left(y_j, w_{-j}\right)$ for all $j \neq i$, so $y = x$ by evolutionary stability. Thus $\tilde{\beta}_i(x) = \{x_i\}$, and since $i \in I$ was arbitrary, $\tilde{\beta}(x) = \{x\}$. Second, assume that $x \in \Theta$ is a strict Nash equilibrium, and let $y \neq x$. Then $y_i \neq x_i$ for some player position $i \in I$, and $u_i\left(x_i, x_{-i}\right) = u_i(x) > u_i\left(y_i, x_{-i}\right)$. By continuity of u_i there exists some $\bar{\epsilon}_y \in (0, 1)$ such that for all $\epsilon \in \left(0, \bar{\epsilon}_y\right)$, and with $w = \epsilon y + (1 - \epsilon)x$, $u_i\left(x_i, w_{-i}\right) > u_i\left(y_i, w_{-i}\right)$, showing that x is evolutionarily stable. ■

Since any strict Nash equilibrium meets Taylor's stability criterion, it is immaterial if one defines evolutionary stability as above or as suggested in Taylor (1979): Both are equivalent with strict Nash equilibrium. However, many games of interest lack strict Nash equilibria, in which case the above evolutionary stability criteria are of no help.

In section 2.7 a definition was given of evolutionary stability of role-conditioned behaviors in two-player games where individuals can identify their player position. A behavior strategy in that setting was seen to be formally identical with a strategy profile in the underlying game. According to a result due to Selten (proposition 2.18 above), such a behavior strategy is evolutionarily stable if and only if the associated (base game) strategy profile is a strict Nash equilibrium. In two-player games the present two-population definition of evolutionary stability thus coincides, in terms of strategy profiles in the game, with the role-conditioned single-population definition in section 2.7. Let $\Theta^{ESS} \subset \Theta$ denote the (possibly empty) set of evolutionarily stable strategy profiles (or, equivalently, the set of strict Nash equilibria).

5.1.2 Strategy Profiles That Are Robust against Equilibrium Entrants

Evolutionary stability places no restrictions on the mutant strategy profiles. In particular, these may themselves be unstable or for other reasons implausible in the given context. In some applications to economics, for instance, Swinkels (1992a) argues that it may be reasonable to require stability only against mutant strategies which are optimal in the postentry population. Such a

2. This proof follows Swinkels (1992a).

weaker stability criterion for the single-population symmetric two-player setting was studied in subsections 2.3.2 (pointwise) and 2.4.2 (setwise). These criteria readily extend to the present n-population setting for arbitrary (finite) n-player games (see the mentioned sections for interpretations).

If the incumbent strategy profile is $x \in \Theta$, the mutant profile $y \in \Theta$, and the population share of mutants is ϵ, then the postentry strategy profile is $w = \epsilon y + (1 - \epsilon)x \in \Theta$, and y is called an *equilibrium entrant profile* if it is a best reply to w (Swinkels 1992a).

Definition 5.2 $x \in \Theta$ *is* robust against equilibrium entrants (REE) *if there exists some $\bar{\epsilon} \in (0, 1)$ such that condition (5.3) below holds for all profiles $y \neq x$ and $\epsilon \in (0, \bar{\epsilon})$:*

$$y \notin \tilde{\beta}\left[\epsilon y + (1 - \epsilon)x\right] . \tag{5.3}$$

It follows that every ESS profile is robust against equilibrium entrants in this sense and it can be shown that every REE profile, by continuity of the payoff function, is a Nash equilibrium. Writing Θ^{REE} for the (possibly empty) set of REE profiles: $\Theta^{ESS} \subset \Theta^{REE} \subset \Theta^{NE}$ (see proposition 2.8).

5.1.3 Equilibrium Evolutionarily Stable Sets of Strategy Profiles

Turning the REE criterion setwise (Swinkels 1992a):

Definition 5.3 *A set $X \subset \Theta$ is* equilibrium evolutionarily stable (EES) *if it is minimal with respect to the following property: X is a nonempty and closed subset of Θ^{NE} for which there is some $\bar{\epsilon} \in (0, 1)$ such that if $x \in X$, $y \in \Theta$, $\epsilon \in (0, \bar{\epsilon})$, and $y \in \tilde{\beta}\left((1 - \epsilon)x + \epsilon y\right)$, then $(1 - \epsilon)x + \epsilon y \in X$.*

In other words, an EES set X is a minimal closed set of Nash equilibria such that no small-scale invasion of equilibrium entrants can lead the population out of X. In the special case of a singleton set $X = \{x\}$, X is an EES set if and only if x is an REE profile.

We noted in chapter 1 that the set $\Theta^{NE} \subset \Theta$ of Nash equilibria of a (finite n-player) game is the finite union of disjoint, connected, and closed sets, the *components* of Θ^{NE}. Swinkels (1992a) shows that these components are the only candidates for EES sets:

Proposition 5.2 *Every EES set $X \subset \Theta^{NE}$ is a component of Θ^{NE}.*

(This proposition can be proved along the same lines as proposition 2.12.)

Since payoffs are constant on each Nash equilibrium component in generic extensive form games (see subsection 1.3.2), all strategy profiles in an EES set generically result in the same payoff outcome. In this respect not much precision is lost when going from predictions in terms of individual strategy profiles to predictions in terms of such sets of strategy profiles.

The following result, due to Swinkels (1992a), establishes a link from evolutionary stability with respect to "rational" mutants, as formalized in REE profiles and EES sets, to the noncooperative solution concept of proper equilibrium—the refinement that requires robustness against "rational" trembles (see subsection 1.4.2):

Proposition 5.3 *Suppose that $X \subset \Theta$ is an EES set. If X is a singleton, or $G = (I, \Theta, u)$ is the normal form of a generic two-player extensive-form game, then X contains a proper Nash equilibrium.*

The next example (Swinkels 1992a) shows how the EES criterion selects the "intuitive" Nash equilibrium component in a classical testing game for noncooperative refinements, the so-called Beer-Quiche Game due to David Kreps (Kohlberg and Mertens 1986; Cho and Kreps 1987; see also van Damme 1987). Although developed for economic analysis, the game has a certain biological flavor.

Example 5.1 The Beer-Quiche Game builds on a game related to the Entry Deterrence Game of example 1.6. Here player 1 (the monopolist or owner) observes a random move by nature assigning one of two types to her; either S (strong), with probability 0.9, or W (weak), with probability 0.1. Having learned her own type, player 1 sends one of two signals to player 2: either s ("I am strong") or w ("I am weak"). A true signal is costless, whereas a false signal costs 10 payoff units. Upon receiving this signal, player 2 (the entrant, or intruder) decides whether to "fight" or "retreat." If he fights, he will win or lose 10 payoff units depending on whether player 1 is weak or strong. Player 1, on the other hand, loses 20 payoff units whenever there is a fight (irrespective of her type).

Each player position thus has four pure strategies. For player 1: "always s," "s when S, w when W," "s when W, w when S," and "always w." For player 2: "retreat when s, fight when w," "always retreat," "always fight," and "fight when s, retreat when w." The payoff matrices are

$$
A = \begin{pmatrix} -1 & -1 & -21 & -21 \\ -2 & 0 & -20 & -18 \\ -28 & -10 & -30 & -12 \\ -29 & -9 & -29 & -9 \end{pmatrix} \quad \text{and} \quad B = \begin{pmatrix} 0 & 0 & -8 & -8 \\ 1 & 0 & -8 & -9 \\ -9 & 0 & -8 & 1 \\ -8 & 0 & -8 & 0 \end{pmatrix}.
$$

The set Θ^{NE} of Nash equilibria consists of two components. In the first, player 1 always says she is strong, and player 2 retreats when hearing this; otherwise, he fights with a probability of at least $\frac{1}{2}$. Denoting mixed strategies for player position 1, $x \in \Delta_1$, and those for player position 2, $y \in \Delta_2$, this component is

$$
C = \left\{ (x, y) \in \Theta : x_1 = 1, \ y_1 + y_2 = 1, \ y_1 \geq \frac{1}{2} \right\}.
$$

In the second component, player 1 always says she is weak, and player 2 retreats when hearing this; otherwise, he fights with a probability of at least $\frac{1}{2}$. Formally, this component is

$$
C' = \left\{ (x, y) \in \Theta : x_4 = 1, \ y_2 + y_4 = 1, \ y_4 \geq \frac{1}{2} \right\}.
$$

The equilibria in this component do not appear sensible in that player 2's prior probability that player 1 is strong is 0.9, while his posterior probability that she is strong falls below 0.5 if player 1 deviates and says that she is strong.[3] Nevertheless, *all* Nash equilibria in the game are perfect, even proper.

According to proposition 5.3 above, C and C' are the only candidates for being an EES set. However, the second component C' fails for the reason that the strong signal is not sent in equilibrium, and hence any response to that signal is optimal. The second player's strategy y can thus "costlessly drift" toward his second pure strategy "always retreat." But once $y_2 > \frac{1}{2}$, it is optimal for player 1 to deviate toward her less costly truth-telling strategy 2. This can be shown to invalidate C' as an EES set. In contrast, the Nash equilibrium component C does constitute an EES set. Here the weak signal is not sent in equilibrium, so any response to that signal is optimal. However, if costless drift occurs toward the second player's second pure strategy, and finally $y_2 > \frac{1}{2}$, then player 1 should deviate to her second pure strategy and player 2 should move back to his equilibrium strategy. For this reason no equilibrium entrant can take the population state out of the Nash equilibrium component C.

---

3. This issue is actually quite subtle; see Cho and Kreps (1987) or van Damme (1987) for a discussion.

For an interesting application of the EES criterion to symmetric and asymmetric two-player communication games in which one or both players can send a preplay message before playing the underlying game, see Blume, Kim, and Sobel (1993). Sending a message is there either costless (cheap talk) or costs little. They find that many such communication games lack EES sets and therefore suggest that the criterion of equilibrium evolutionary stability be weakened by way of dropping the condition that the set be a subset of Θ^{NE}. With this condition removed, existence is guaranteed for all games (by Zorn's lemma). Swinkels (1992b) discusses a modified EES criterion for a wide class of sets (including all convex subsets $X \subset \Theta$), which implies that the set contains a subset of Nash equilibria that is strategically stable in the sense of Kohlberg and Mertens (1986).

5.2 The Standard and Adjusted n-Population Replicator Dynamics

5.2.1 Definitions and Preliminaries

Just as in the single-population replicator dynamics, in its multipopulation counterpart we imagine that individuals during their lifetimes always use some fixed pure strategy. Hence the population of individuals in each player role i can at each instant be subdivided into m_i subpopulations, one for each pure strategy $h \in S_i$ available to player position i. A *population state* now is a point $x = (x_1, \ldots, x_n)$ in the polyhedron Θ of mixed-strategy profiles, where each component x_i is a point in the corresponding mixed-strategy simplex Δ_i, representing the distribution of individuals in player population i across the pure strategies available to that player position. The vector x_i may thus be thought of as the state of player population $i \in I$ at time t, where $x_{ih} \in [0, 1]$ is the proportion of individuals in population i who are currently programmed to pure strategy $h \in S_i$.

Each player population is imagined to be infinite, and individuals are randomly matched to play the game. However, unlike in the single-population setting, one individual is drawn from each player population. At every matching exactly n individuals play the game, each individual being assigned the player position of her population.

Unlike in the single-population setting, there are two versions of the continuous-time replicator dynamics. Its most commonly used form was suggested by one of the pioneers for the single-population replicator dynamics

(3.5), Peter Taylor (see Taylor 1979), and it is of the same form as (3.5):

$$\dot{x}_{ih} = \left[u_i(e_i^h, x_{-i}) - u_i(x) \right] x_{ih} . \tag{5.4}$$

In other words, for each population state $x \in \Theta$, player position $i \in I$ and pure strategy $h \in S_i$ available to that player position, the growth rate $\dot{x}_{ih}/x_{ih}$ of the associated population share equals its excess payoff, $u_i(e_i^h, x_{-i}) - u_i(x)$, over the average payoff in its player population.

The vector field on the right-hand side in (5.4) is in general quadratic.[4] Hence the vector field in (5.4) is a Lipschitz continuous function on the whole euclidean space R^m containing the state space Θ. By the Picard-Lindelöf theorem, the associated system of differential equations (5.4) has a unique solution $\xi(\cdot, x^o) : R \rightarrow \Theta$ through every initial state $x^o \in \Theta$. It is easily verified that the polyhedron Θ, as well as its interior and boundary, are invariant in this dynamics. The dynamics defined by (5.4) will henceforth be called the *standard n-population replicator dynamics*.

In some studies the right-hand side in (5.4) is divided by $u_i(x)$, the player-population's average payoff. This version of the multipopulation replicator dynamics was introduced by Maynard Smith 1982 (see also Hofbauer and Sigmund 1988):

$$\dot{x}_{ih} = \frac{1}{u_i(x)} \left[u_i(e_i^h, x_{-i}) - u_i(x) \right] x_{ih} . \tag{5.5}$$

In other words, for each population state $x \in \Theta$, player position $i \in I$ and pure strategy $h \in S_i$, the growth rate $\dot{x}_{ih}/x_{ih}$ of the associated population share equals its relative excess payoff, $u_i(e_i^h, x_{-i})/u_i(x) - 1$, over the average payoff in its player population. In this dynamics a given absolute payoff difference has a stronger dynamic effect if average payoff is low than if it is high.

Unlike in (5.4), it is here presumed that all payoffs are positive, $u_i(x) > 0$ for all $i \in I$ and $x \in \Theta$. Under this assumption, and for essentially the same reasons as for (5.4), (5.5) uniquely defines a well-behaved dynamics on Θ, to be called the *(payoff-)adjusted n-population replicator dynamics*.

Which of these two versions of the replicator dynamics, if any, is appropriate to a given modeling task? Does the choice really matter for the con-

---

4. More exactly, there is a term $-u_i(e_i^h, x_{-i})x_{ih}^2$, unless $u_i(e_i^h, x_{-i}) = 0$. In contrast, the single-population replicator dynamics is generally cubic because there individuals programmed to a certain pure strategy also interact with each other.

clusions? Indeed, in the biology literature "there is . . . room for doubt as to which form is more appropriate . . . " (Maynard Smith 1982, p. 201).[5] Rather than advocating one or the other, we will in this chapter explore general properties of fairly wide classes of selection dynamics that contain both the standard and the adjusted replicator dynamics. Moreover, in the context of a few simple models of social evolution by way of imitation, each of the two dynamics (5.4) and (5.5) will be derived as a special case. However, we first examine some similarities and differences between the two versions.

It follows immediately from equations (5.4) and (5.5) that if all players have the same payoff function, if $u_i(x) = u_j(x)$ for all $i, j \in I$ and $x \in \Theta$, then these two dynamics induce the same solution orbits in Θ, and hence the same stability properties. In such special games the only difference between the two dynamics is the velocity at which the population state moves along these same orbits.

For other games, however, the standard and adjusted replicator dynamics induce distinct solution orbits in Θ, so given states and sets of states may have different stability properties in the two dynamics. Nevertheless, the set of stationary states is the same in both dynamics. A population state $x \in \Theta$ is stationary in any one of these dynamics if and only if, for each player-population i, every pure strategy $h \in S_i$ *in use* earns the same payoff. Hence the common set of stationary states is

$$\Theta^o = \left\{ x \in \Theta : u_i(e_i^h, x_{-i}) = u_i(x) \ \ \forall i \in I, \ h \in C(x_i) \right\} . \tag{5.6}$$

Consequently all interior stationary states are Nash equilibria, and all Nash equilibria are stationary in both dynamics:

$$\Theta^o \cap \text{int}(\Theta) \subset \Theta^{NE} \subset \Theta^o . \tag{5.7}$$

---

5. Starting from alternative discrete-time models, such as multipopulation versions of those in section 4.1, each of the two continuous-time dynamics can be obtained in the limit. However, unlike in the single-population setting, there is an issue here of the *relative sizes* of the player populations, causing differences in individual matching rates and hence payoff streams, between the different player populations. Consider, for instance, a two-player game played by one large but finite population in player position 1 and another finite population in player position 2, where the latter population is half the size of the former. If individuals are randomly paired at any given time, then the time rate at which any given individual in the second population is drawn to play the game is twice the rate at which any individual in the first population is drawn to play the game. Hence individuals in player population 1 earn their payoffs from the game at only half the rate by which individuals in player population 2 earn theirs.

Unlike in the single-population setting, these multipopulation replicator dynamics are not invariant under arbitrary positive affine transformation of payoffs. If a constant α_i is added to all payoffs to some player position i, then the standard replicator dynamics (5.4) is unaffected, while the solution orbits to the adjusted replicator dynamics (5.5) in general change under such a payoff transformation. If, instead, all payoffs to some player position i are multiplied by a positive constant β_i, then the adjusted dynamics (5.5) is unaffected while the solution orbits to the standard version (5.4) change. However, if in the latter dynamics, the payoffs to *all* player positions are multiplied by one and the same positive constant, then the effect is equivalent to a change of time scale by the same factor β for all players i and pure strategies h. Hence all orbits to the standard replicator dynamics remain unchanged.

Just as in its single-population counterpart (3.5), local shifts of payoff functions, as defined in subsection 1.3.3, have no effect at all on the standard n-player replicator dynamics (5.5). In contrast, such shifts do in general affect the solutions to the adjusted n-player replicator dynamics (5.5). While the numerator in the expression on the right-hand side in (5.5) is unchanged, the denominator—the average payoff—does change by such a payoff transformation (see subsection 1.3.3).

5.2.2 Two-Player Games

In the notation of subsection 1.1.2, let A be the payoff matrix of player 1 and B that of player 2. Thus $a_{hk} \in R$ is the payoff to player 1 and $b_{hk} \in R$ the payoff to player 2 when player 1 uses pure strategy $h \in S_1$ and player 2 uses pure strategy $k \in S_2$. Here $u_1(x, y) = x \cdot Ay$, and $u_2(x, y) = y \cdot B^T x$ signify the expected payoffs to the two players when player 1 uses mixed strategy $x = (x_h)_{h \in S_1} \in \Delta_1$ and 2 mixed strategy $y = (y_k)_{k \in S_2} \in \Delta_2$.

In this notation the standard two-population replicator equations (5.4) can be written

$$\dot{x}_h = \left[e^h \cdot Ay - x \cdot Ay \right] x_h = \left[\sum_{k \in S_2} a_{hk} y_k - \sum_{j \in S_1} \sum_{k \in S_2} x_j a_{jk} y_k \right] x_h , \qquad (5.8)$$

$$\dot{y}_k = \left[e^k \cdot B^T x - y \cdot B^T x \right] y_k = \left[\sum_{h \in S_1} b_{hk} x_h - \sum_{j \in S_2} \sum_{h \in S_1} y_j b_{hj} x_h \right] y_k. \qquad (5.9)$$

Since this version of the replicator dynamics is invariant under local shifts in payoff functions, we may, without loss of generality, suppose that both matrices have zeros off their diagonals in the special case when each player position has only two pure strategies:[6]

$$A = \begin{pmatrix} a_1 & 0 \\ 0 & a_2 \end{pmatrix}, \quad B = \begin{pmatrix} b_1 & 0 \\ 0 & b_2 \end{pmatrix}. \tag{5.10}$$

In this special case the standard replicator equations (5.8) and (5.9) boil down to

$$\dot{x}_1 = (a_1 y_1 - a_2 y_2) x_1 x_2, \tag{5.11}$$

$$\dot{y}_1 = (b_1 x_1 - b_2 x_2) y_1 y_2, \tag{5.12}$$

where $x_2 = 1 - x_1$ and $y_2 = 1 - y_1$.

We proceed to show that in this special case no interior population state $(x, y) \in \Theta = \Delta_1 \times \Delta_2$ is asymptotically stable in (5.4), irrespective of the payoffs in the game. We do this by means of a general and powerful technique that will later be used on arbitrary (finite) n-player games. The technique, developed by Amann and Hofbauer (1985) and Hofbauer and Sigmund (1988), is based on Liouville's formula (see section 6.6).

Since division of a vector field by a positive function (the same for all components of the vector field) does not alter the solution orbits, only the velocity along these, we may divide the right-hand sides in (5.11) and (5.12) by the product $x_1 x_2 y_1 y_2$ without affecting the solution orbits in the *interior* of Θ. The resulting system of differential equations,

$$\dot{x}_1 = \frac{a_1 y_1 - a_2 y_2}{y_1 y_2} \quad \text{and} \quad \dot{x}_2 = -\dot{x}_1, \tag{5.13}$$

$$\dot{y}_1 = \frac{b_1 x_1 - b_2 x_2}{x_2 x_2} \quad \text{and} \quad \dot{y}_2 = -\dot{y}_1, \tag{5.14}$$

clearly has a continuously differentiable vector field at all $(x, y) \in \text{int}(\Theta)$, and hence Liouville's formula applies to the interior of the state space Θ. Since the right-hand side of each of the four variables' differential equation does not contain the variable itself, the vector field in (5.13)–(5.14) is divergence free.[7]

---

6. Here $a_1 = a_{11} - a_{21}, a_2 = a_{22} - a_{12}, b_1 = b_{11} - b_{12}$, and $b_2 = b_{22} - b_{21}$; see subsection 1.5.3.

7. The *divergence* of a vector field is the trace of its Jacobian; see section 6.6.

Hence the system (5.13)–(5.14) represents a volume-preserving flow, implying that no interior population state (x, y) is asymptotically stable. Formally, this follows from proposition 6.6. Since the solution orbits are the same as in the standard replicator dynamics, we have established the claim that no interior population state is asymptotically stable in that dynamics. The following example illustrates the possibility that an interior stationary population state—hence a Nash equilibrium—may nevertheless be Lyapunov stable in the standard replicator dynamics.

Example 5.2   A prototype asymmetric 2×2 game is the Matching Pennies Game of example 1.5. The game was seen to have a unique Nash equilibrium, and in this equilibrium both players use each of their two strategies with probability $\frac{1}{2}$. Rewriting the standard replicator equations (5.11)–(5.12) in terms of x_1 and y_1 only, we get

$$\dot{x}_1 = 2(2y_1 - 1)(1 - x_1)x_1 \,,$$
$$\dot{y}_1 = 2(1 - 2x_1)(1 - y_1)y_1 \,.$$

The state space of this reduced dynamics is the unit square $[0, 1]^2$, and the latter can be usefully subdivided into four equally large subsquares. Figure 5.1 shows some typical solution orbits. As suggested by this diagram, all solution orbits to the standard replicator dynamics are closed curves, and the game's unique Nash equilibrium, represented by the midpoint in the unit square, is Lyapunov, but not asymptotically, stable.

The next example compares the solution orbits in the preceding example to those of the adjusted replicator dynamics (5.5). However, not all payoffs in the game studied there—the Matching Pennies Game—are positive, and so (5.5) is not well defined. Adding a positive constant to each payoff in the game has no effect on the solution orbits to the standard replicator dynamics and, if the constant exceeds 1, renders the adjusted replicator dynamics well defined.

Example 5.3   Addition of $1 + c$ to each payoff in the Matching Pennies Game of example 1.5 results in payoff matrices

$$A = \begin{pmatrix} 2 + c & c \\ c & 2 + c \end{pmatrix}, \quad B = \begin{pmatrix} c & 2 + c \\ 2 + c & c \end{pmatrix}.$$

For any $c > 0$ all payoffs are positive, and so the (payoff-)adjusted replicator dynamics (5.5) is well defined. The solution orbits to the standard replicator dynamics are precisely the same as in example 5.1, and division of the

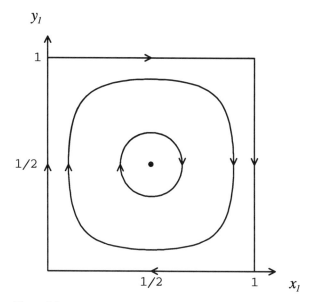

Figure 5.1
Solution orbits to the standard two-population replicator dynamics in the Matching Pennies Game
of examples 1.5 and 5.2.

right-hand sides in equations (5.11)–(5.12) by the corresponding average payoff, $x \cdot Ay$ and $yB^T x$, respectively, result in the following payoff-adjusted
replicator equations:

$$\dot{x}_1 = \frac{2(2y_1 - 1)(1 - x_1)}{c + 2\left[x_1 y_1 + (1 - x_1)(1 - y_1)\right]} x_1 ,$$

$$\dot{y}_1 = \frac{2(1 - 2x_1)(1 - y_1)}{c + 2\left[x_1(1 - y_1) + (1 - x_1)y_1\right]} y_1 .$$

The effect of this payoff adjustment of the standard replicator vector field is
to bend the vector field somewhat inward, toward the Nash equilibrium point
$(x_1, y_1) = (\frac{1}{2}, \frac{1}{2})$, *less* so the larger $c > 0$ is. Hence all interior solution curves
now swirl inward, and the Nash equilibrium is asymptotically stable. As c
increases, the pull toward this equilibrium point is weakened. (In the limit
as $c \to \infty$, the solution orbits coincide with those of the standard replicator
dynamics.) Figure 5.2 shows some solution orbits for $c = 0.1$ and $c = 3$, respectively.

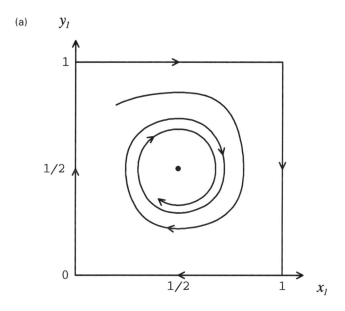

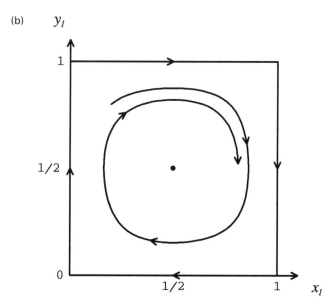

Figure 5.2
Solution orbits to the (payoff) adjusted two-population replicator dynamics in the re-scaled
Matching Pennies Game of example 5.3: (a) For payoff parameter $c = 0.1$, (b) for payoff pa-
rameter $c = 3$.

The next example is again an asymmetric 2×2 game. This game has two Nash equilibrium components. One is a continuum, and the other a singleton, both situated on the boundary of the mixed-strategy space Θ. In the standard replicator dynamics (5.4), all but one point in the continuum component is Lyapunov stable, and yet that component is not a Lyapunov stable set. Moreover some interior solution trajectories converge to the Lyapunov stable points in this component, while others converge to the singleton component, which consists of a strict Nash equilibrium.

Example 5.4   Reconsider the Entry Deterrence Game of example 1.6. The set Θ^{NE} of Nash equilibria was seen to consist of two components; one (subgame perfect) singleton, in which the entrant (intruder) enters and the monopolist (owner) yields, and a continuum of (subgame imperfect) Nash equilibria in which the first stays out and the second threatens to fight entry. Applying the standard replicator dynamics (5.11)–(5.12) to this game, we implicitly imagine a large population of potential entrants (intruders) and a distinct, large population of monopolists (owners). Pairs of individuals, one from each population, are randomly matched to play this game. No rationality is presumed on behalf of the individuals. Instead, these are all programmed to one of the two pure strategies available to their player position. The payoff of the game represents the expected number of offspring, and the standard replicator dynamics describes how the population shares of each of the four pure strategies evolve over time. With x_1 denoting the population share (in chapter 1 denoted x_{11}) of potential entrants who are programmed to strategy E (enter), and y_1 the population share (earlier denoted x_{21}) of potential monopolists who are programmed to strategy Y (yield), the standard replicator dynamics (5.4) becomes

$$\dot{x}_1 = (2y_1 - 1)(1 - x_1)x_1$$

$$\dot{y}_1 = 2x_1(1 - y_1)y_1$$

It is immediate from these equations that y_1 increases monotonically along any interior solution orbit and that x_1 decreases (increases) when y_1 is below (above) $\frac{1}{2}$. In particular, it follows that the unique subgame perfect strategy pair $(x_1, y_1) = (1, 1)$, a *strict* Nash equilibrium, is asymptotically stable; see figure 5.3. Note also that the vector field points outward along the Nash equilibrium component on the edge where $x_1 = 0$: There $\dot{y}_1/\dot{x}_1 = (2y_1 - 1)/[(1 - y_1)2y_1] < 0$. Hence interior solution trajectories starting near this component

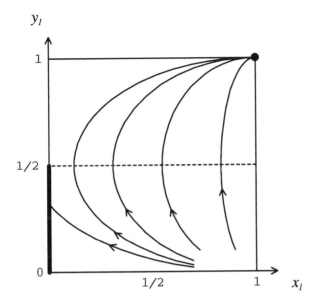

Figure 5.3
Solution orbits to the standard two-population replicator dynamics in the Entry Deterrence Game
of examples 1.6 and 5.4.

and/or near the edge where $y_1 = 0$, converge to Nash equilibria in that component; see figure 5.3. The evolutionary selection pressure against the weakly dominated pure strategy (fight) is thus weak for such initial states.

To enable a direct comparison with the single-population replicator dynamics, we now focus on the special case of the two-population standard replicator dynamics (5.8)–(5.9) when applied to *symmetric* games. In the notation of chapter 3, let the common pure-strategy set be $K = \{1, 2, \ldots, k\}$ and the associated mixed-strategy simplex be Δ. Hence the polyhedron of mixed-strategy profiles (x, y) here is $\Theta = \Delta^2$. By symmetry of payoff functions $(u_2(x, y) = u_1(y, x)$ for all $x \in \Delta$ and $y \in \Delta)$, it suffices to use the payoff function u_1, denoted u in chapter 3.

In the present two-population setting, a population *state* is a point $(x, y) \in \Theta$, where $x \in \Delta$ is the pure-strategy distribution in player population 1 and $y \in \Delta$ the pure-strategy distribution in player population 2. The associated average payoff in population 1 is $u(x, y)$ and that of population 2 $u(y, x)$. The standard replicator dynamics (5.4) can therefore be written

$$\dot{x}_h = u(e^h - x, y)x_h ,\qquad(5.15)$$

$$\dot{y}_h = u(e^h - y, x)y_h .\qquad(5.16)$$

For any initial state $(x^o, y^o) \in \Theta$, let the solution to these differential equations be denoted ξ for population 1 and η for population 2; namely $\xi(t, x^o, y^o) \in \Delta$ is the state of population 1 at any time $t \in R$ and likewise for $\eta(t, x^o, y^o) \in \Delta$. Note, in particular, that if the two population distributions initially are the same, then, by symmetry, they remain identical forever:

$$x^o = y^o \Rightarrow \xi(t, x^o, y^o) = \eta(t, x^o, y^o) \qquad \forall t \in R.$$

To see this formally, just note that $x = y$ in (5.15)–(5.16) implies that $\dot{x}_h = \dot{y}_h = u(e^h - x, x)x_h$. In other words, the diagonal $D = \{(x, y) \in \Theta : x = y\}$ of the state space Θ is invariant in the standard replicator dynamics. Moreover on D the standard replicator dynamics (5.4) is identical with the single-population dynamics studied in chapter 3. It follows immediately that the same is true for the orbits to the adjusted replicator dynamics (5.5), which in a symmetric two-player game can be written[8]

$$\dot{x}_h = \frac{u(e^h - x, y)x_h}{u(x, y)} ,\qquad(5.17)$$

$$\dot{y}_h = \frac{u(e^h - y, x)y_h}{u(y, x)} .\qquad(5.18)$$

In sum:

Proposition 5.4 *For any symmetric two-player game, $D \subset \Theta$ is invariant both in the standard and adjusted replicator dynamics. Moreover the solution orbits in D to these two dynamics are identical with those of the single-population replicator dynamics (3.5).*

Consequently, if, for some symmetric two-player game, a mixed strategy $x \in \Delta$, viewed as a population state in the single-population replicator dynamics, has been found to be unstable, then the associated symmetric two-population state (x, x) is necessarily unstable in the two-population standard

---

8. Here, as elsewhere, we presume positive payoffs when speaking about the (payoff-)adjusted replicator dynamics (5.5).

and adjusted replicator dynamics alike. By contrast, (Lyapunov or asymptotic) stability in the single-population replicator dynamics does not imply the corresponding property in the two-population standard or modified replicator dynamics. For instance, a mixed strategy $x \in \Delta$ may be asymptotically stable in the single-population replicator dynamics, while the corresponding strategy profile $(x, x) \in \Theta$ is a saddle point in the standard or adjusted replicator dynamics. Hence stability of symmetric Nash equilibria may be lost, but not gained, when moving from the single-population setting to the two-population setting. On the other hand, as was seen in example 5.4, asymmetric Nash equilibria, namely population states $(x, y) \notin D$, appear as new candidates for stable states when one moves from the single-population setting to the two-population setting. This will also be seen below.

Let us consider the classification of symmetric 2×2 games in subsection 1.5.3, and make a comparison between the single-population and two-population standard replicator dynamics (3.5) and (5.4), respectively. The single-populations version was analyzed in subsection 3.1.4, where payoffs were normalized so that the off-diagonal elements were zero. Since also the standard two-population replicator dynamics is invariant under local payoff shifts, we may without loss of generality also here take the payoff matrix of player 1 to be of the form

$$A = \begin{pmatrix} a_1 & 0 \\ 0 & a_2 \end{pmatrix}.$$

Equations (5.15) and (5.16) then become

$$\dot{x}_1 = (a_1 y_1 - a_2 y_2) x_1 x_2, \tag{5.19}$$

$$\dot{y}_1 = (a_1 x_1 - a_2 x_2) y_1 y_2. \tag{5.20}$$

Recall that $\dot{x}_2 = -\dot{x}_1$ and $\dot{y}_2 = -\dot{y}_1$; see equations (5.11) and (5.12).

Categories I and IV (Prisoner's Dilemma Games) If $a_1 a_2 < 0$, then the growth rates do not change sign in the interior of the state space. Hence both populations converge from any interior initial position to the dominant strategy (strategy 2 in category I and strategy 1 in category IV). In these two game categories there is no qualitative difference between the single-population and two-population dynamics. See figure 5.4 (a) for an illustration of the vector field as applied to the Prisoner's Dilemma Game of example 3.1 (the two-population differential equations are given in example 6.12). Granted all payoffs in the original payoff matrix A are positive, the same qualitative conclusions are valid also for the modified replicator dynamics (5.5) when applied directly to those payoffs.

Category II (Coordination Games)   If a_1 and a_2 are both positive, then the game has two strict Nash equilibria, both symmetric, and one symmetric mixed Nash equilibrium. In the single-population replicator dynamics, the latter is unstable; in fact it is the separation point between the two basins (intervals) of attraction of the two strict equilibria. The situation in the present dynamics is qualitatively the same. To see this, let $\lambda = a_2/(a_1 + a_2)$. For states (x, y) with $y_1 < \lambda$, x_1 decreases, while for $y_1 > \lambda$, x_1 increases, and vice versa for the movement in y_1. The mixed-strategy Nash equilibrium is a saddle point, and with the exception of a single curve through this point, all solution trajectories converge to one of the strict equilibria; see figure 5.4 (b) for an illustration of the two-population standard replicator dynamics in the Coordination Game of example 1.10. Granted all payoffs in the original payoff matrix A are positive, the orientation of the vector field in each of the four quarters of the unit square is unaffected by division of the average payoff for each population. Hence the same qualitative conclusions are valid also for the modified replicator dynamics (5.5), as applied directly to those payoffs.

Category III (Hawk-Dove Games)   If a_1 and a_2 are both negative, then the game has two strict Nash equilibria, both asymmetric, and one symmetric mixed Nash equilibrium. In this game category a qualitative difference with the earlier studied single-population replicator dynamics arises. While the mixed Nash equilibrium strategy then was seen to constitute an asymptotically stable population state, even attracting the whole (relative) interior of that state space (which here corresponds to the diagonal D), the associated mixed-strategy Nash equilibrium constitutes an *unstable* population state in the two-population standard replicator dynamics, as well as in the modified replicator dynamics. The reason for this stark qualitative contrast between the single- and two-population settings is that when the interaction takes place between two distinct populations, there arises a possibility of *polarization* in behaviors. Here the slightest deviation from identical population distributions may lead the player populations toward specialization in *different* pure strategies. In the Hawk-Dove Game of example 2.3, for instance, this means that one population will become more and more aggressive (playing the "hawk" strategy) over time, while the other population will become more and more

(a) y_1

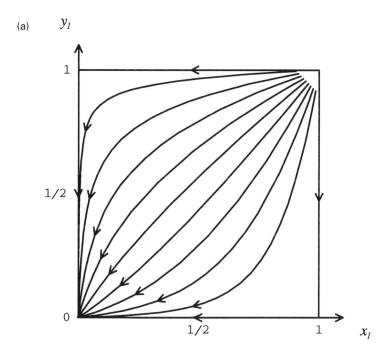

(b) y_1

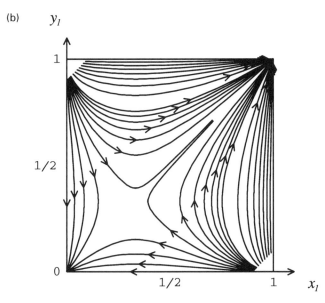

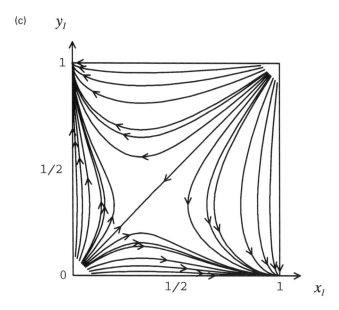

Figure 5.4
Solution orbits to the standard two-population replicator dynamics in generic symmetric 2×2 games: (a) In category I, (b) in category II, (c) in category III.

yielding (play the "dove" strategy). Which of the two possible long-run states will emerge depends on the initial population state; see figure 5.4 (c) for typical solution orbits in that example.

More formally, the symmetric mixed-strategy Nash equilibrium (x^*, x^*) again splits the state space $\Theta = [0, 1]^2$ into four quarters. Here $x_1^* = \lambda = a_2/(a_1 + a_2) \in (0, 1)$. It is easily verified that any initial state in any one of the two quarters on the diagonal D, except at this symmetric Nash equilibrium point, leaves its quarter in finite time. In contrast, again excluding the symmetric mixed Nash equilibrium point, each quarter off the diagonal is positively invariant, and all solution orbits therein converge to the corresponding corner, as seen in the computer simulations in figure 5.4 (c). Granted all payoffs in the original payoff matrix A are positive, the orientation of the vector field in each of the four quarters of the unit square is also here unaffected by division by population averages, and so the same qualitative conclusions are valid also for the modified replicator dynamics (5.5).

Certain general features are seen in these diagrams. First, in accordance with our earlier general observation, every Nash equilibrium indeed constitutes a *stationary* population state in both versions of the two-population replicator dynamics, and every *interior* stationary state in these dynamics constitutes a Nash equilibrium. Moreover in these diagrams every dynamically *stable* state is a Nash equilibrium, and so is the *limit* state to any convergent interior solution path. We will later show that these observations concerning implications of evolutionary dynamics for aggregate Nash equilibrium play are valid in all (finite) games and for a wide range of selection dynamics.

As a new feature, when moving from single- to multipopulation dynamics, we may note that mixed Nash equilibria did not fare well. Despite the fact that these equilibria are perfect Nash equilibria—indeed strictly perfect and hence strategically stable—viewed as singletons, they were seen to be unstable in the standard and modified replicator dynamics. This stark difference between the rationalistic and evolutionary paradigms concerning mixed Nash equilibria turns out to be valid for all games in the standard n-population replicator dynamics but not in the modified n-population replicator dynamics (recall examples 5.2 and 5.3).

5.3   Replication by Imitation

In this section we extend the imitation models in section 4.4 from a single population playing a symmetric two-player game to n populations playing a (symmetric or asymmetric) n-player game.[9] Just as in the setting for the standard and adjusted n-population replicator dynamics, discussed in section 5.2, a population state is here formally identical with a mixed-strategy profile $x \in \Theta$, and each component $x_i \in \Delta_i$ represents the distribution of pure strategies in player population i; namely x_{ih} is the probability that a randomly drawn agent (individual, firm, organization) in population i will use pure strategy $h \in S_i$. Moreover the replicators are also here the pure strategies available to each player position. However, instead of replication by way of biological reproduction, we now follow the approach of section 4.4 and imagine player populations of constant size in which each agent lives forever but now and then *reviews* her pure strategy. The following elaborations are straightforward

---

9. The discussion in this section follows closely Björnerstedt and Weibull (1993).

extensions of the imitation models sketched in section 4.4 (a quick look back may be helpful).

5.3.1 The Transmission Process

Let $r_{ih}(x)$ denote the average *time rate* at which an h-strategist in player population $i \in I$ reviews her strategy choice, when the population is in state $x \in \Theta$. Let $p_{ih}^k(x)$ denote the probability that such a reviewing agent will select pure strategy $k \in S_i$, and write $p_{ih}(x) = \left(p_{ih}^1(x), \ldots, p_{ih}^{m_i}(x) \right) \in \Delta_i$ for the induced probability *distribution* over the set S_i.

Imagine that in a finite population setting the review times of an h-strategist in player population i constitute the arrival times of a Poisson process with arrival rate $r_{ih}(x)$ and that, at each such arrival time, the agent selects a pure strategy according to the probability distribution $p_{ih}(x)$. If all agents' Poisson processes are statistically independent, the aggregate reviewing times among h-strategists in player population i is a Poisson process with arrival rate $x_{ih}r_{ih}(x)$ when the population is in state x.[10] If strategy choices are statistically independent random variables, the aggregate arrival rate of the Poisson process of agents switching from pure strategy $h \in S_i$ to pure strategy $k \in S_i$ is $x_{ih}r_{ih}(x)p_{ih}^k(x)$.

By the law of large numbers these aggregate stochastic processes may be approximated as deterministic flows, each such flow being equal to the arrival rate of the corresponding Poisson process.[11] This deterministic approximation results in the following system of ordinary differential equations (cf. equation (4.25) in section 4.4):

$$\dot{x}_{ih} = \sum_{l \in S_i} r_{il}(x) p_{il}^h(x) x_{il} - r_{ih}(x) x_{ih} . \tag{5.21}$$

To guarantee the existence and uniqueness of a solution through every initial population state x^o in Θ, we henceforth assume that the review functions $r_{ih} : X \to R_+$ and choice-probability functions $p_{ih} : X \to \Delta_i$ are Lipschitz continuous on an open domain $X \subset R^m$ containing Θ. By the Picard-Lindelöf

---

10. For notational simplicity it is here assumed that all player populations are equally large, and all aggregate arrival rates are computed on a per capita basis.

11. See Boylan (1992) for a critical analysis of flow approximations in random matching models.

theorem there then exists a unique and continuous solution through every initial population state $x^o \in \Theta$, a solution that never leaves the state space Θ (i.e., Θ is positively invariant; see chapter 6).

5.3.2 Pure Imitation Driven by Dissatisfaction

As a model of pure imitation, assume that all reviewing agents adopt the strategy of "the first man they meet in the street" in their own player population. Formally for all population states $x \in \Theta$, player positions $i \in I$ and pure strategies $h, k \in S_i$:

$$p_{ih}^k(x) = x_{ik}.$$

(5.22)

Suppose that agents with less successful strategies on average review their strategy at a higher rate than agents with more successful strategies. More precisely, let

$$r_{ih}(x) = \rho_i \left[u_i(e_i^h, x_{-i}), x \right]$$

(5.23)

for some (Lipschitz continuous) function ρ_i which is strictly decreasing in its first (payoff) argument. As in the single-population case this monotonicity assumption does not presume that agents necessarily know the expected payoff to their current pure strategy nor that they know the current population state x. In the present multipopulation setting it should also be noted that agents in one player population need not know anything about the payoffs to other player positions.

Under assumptions (5.22) and (5.23) the population dynamics (5.21) becomes

$$\dot{x}_{ih} = \left(\sum_{l \in S_i} x_{il} \rho_i \left[u_i(e_i^l, x_{-i}), x \right] - \rho_i \left[u_i(e_i^h, x_{-i}), x \right] \right) x_{ih}.$$

(5.24)

The growth rate $\dot{x}_{ih}/x_{ih}$ of the subpopulation of h-strategists is thus composed of two terms, one sum representing the average review rate in the player population—hence the same for all pure strategies h available to the player position—and one negative term, representing the review rate of h-strategists. By monotonicity of ρ the growth-rate of a pure strategy h in player population i is higher than that of pure strategy k if and only if strategy h earns a higher payoff than strategy k.

As a special case of (5.24), let the review rates be *linearly* decreasing in payoffs. Taking averages, we have

$$\rho_i \left[u_i(e_i^h, x_{-i}), x \right] = \alpha_i(x) - \beta_i(x) u_i(e_i^h, x_{-i}) \tag{5.25}$$

for some (Lipschitz continuous) functions α_i, β_i such that $\beta_i(x) > 0$ and $\alpha_i(x)/\beta_i(x) \geq u_i(e_i^h, x_{-i})$ for all states $x \in \Theta$ and pure strategies $h \in S_i$. Then all review rates are nonnegative, and (5.24) boils down to

$$\dot{x}_{ih} = \beta_i(x) \left[u(e_i^h, x_{-i}) - u_i(x) \right] x_{ih} . \tag{5.26}$$

In particular, if all functions β_i are constant and equal, $\beta_i(x) \equiv b > 0$, then (5.26) is a mere (constant) rescaling of time in the *standard* n-population replicator dynamics (5.4). Alternatively, presuming that all payoffs are positive and letting $\beta_i(x) \equiv c/u_i(x)$ for some $c > 0$, we obtain the *adjusted* n-population replicator dynamics (5.5). In the first special case review rates are linearly decreasing in *absolute* payoffs, $u(e_i^h, x_{-i})$, while in the second they are linearly decreasing in *relative* payoffs, $u(e_i^h, x_{-i})/u_i(x)$.

5.3.3   Imitation of Successful Agents: Model 1

Suppose that each reviewing agent samples another agent at random from her player population, with equal probability for all agents in that population, and that she observes with some noise the average payoff difference between her own and the sampled agent's strategies. More exactly, if, in player population i, an h-strategist samples a k-strategist, then she observes payoff $u_i(e_i^h, x_{-i}) + \varepsilon$ to her own strategy h and payoff $u_i(e_i^k, x_{-i}) + \varepsilon'$ to the other agent's strategy k, where ε and ε' are random variables such that their difference, the random variable $\varepsilon - \varepsilon'$, has a continuously differentiable probability distribution function $\phi_i : R \rightarrow [0, 1]$.[12] Having made such a pairwise payoff comparison, the reviewing agent switches to the sampled agent's strategy if and only if the observed payoff difference is positive, $u_i(e_i^k, x_{-i}) + \varepsilon' > u_i(e_i^h, x_{-i}) + \varepsilon$. The conditional probability that the agent will switch to strategy k, given that she sampled strategy k, is thus $\phi_i \left[u_i(e_i^k, x_{-i}) - u_i(e_i^h, x_{-i}) \right]$. Since the probability that the agent will sample strategy k is x_{ik}, the resulting conditional choice probability distribution $p_{ih}(x) \in \Delta$ is given by

---

12. See footnote 22 in chapter 4.

$$
p_{ih}^k(x) = \begin{cases} x_{ik}\phi_i\left[u_i(e_i^k - e_i^h, x_{-i})\right] & \text{if } k \neq h\,, \\ 1 - \sum_{l \neq h} x_{il}\phi_i\left[u(e_i^l - e_i^h, x_{-i})\right] & \text{otherwise}\,. \end{cases} \tag{5.27}
$$

Just as in the single-population setting the random variables ε and ε' may alternatively be interpreted as idiosyncratic preference differences between agents in the population: Then $u_i(e_i^h, x_{-i}) + \varepsilon$ and $u_i(e_i^k, x_{-i}) + \varepsilon'$ are the true average payoffs to pure strategies h and k, respectively, according to the preferences of a randomly drawn agent from player population i.

If all review rates are constantly equal to one,

$$
r_{ih}(x) \equiv 1\,, \tag{5.28}
$$

this results in the following dynamics:

$$
\dot{x}_{ih} = \left[\sum_{l \in S_i} x_{il}\left(\phi_i\left[u_i(e_i^h - e_i^l, x_{-i})\right] - \phi_i\left[u_i(e_i^l - e_i^h, x_{-i})\right]\right)\right] x_{ih}\,. \tag{5.29}
$$

If the distribution function ϕ_i is strictly increasing, then the growth rate $\dot{x}_{ih}/x_{ih}$ of the subpopulation of pure strategy h is higher than that of another pure strategy k, available to the same player position, if and only if strategy h earns a higher payoff than strategy k. As in the single-population case (section 4.4), Taylor expansion at an interior stationary state results in a time rescaling, which here may be player specific, of the standard replicator dynamics.

As a special case of (5.29), suppose that all error terms (or idiosyncratic preference differences) are uniformly distributed with a support containing the range of all possible payoff differences in the game. Then ϕ_i is an affine function over the relevant interval, namely $\phi_i(z) = \alpha_i + \beta_i z$ for some $\alpha_i, \beta_i \in R$ where $\beta_i > 0$, and (5.29) becomes

$$
\dot{x}_{ih} = 2\beta_i\left[u_i(e_i^h, x_{-i}) - u_i(x)\right]x_{ih}\,. \tag{5.30}
$$

In particular, if all player populations have the same error distribution, $\beta_i = \beta_j$ for all $i, j \in I$, then (5.30) is the standard n-population replicator dynamics (5.4), modulo a constant change of time scale.

5.3.4 Imitation of Successful Agents: Model 2

As an alternative to pure imitation we might assume that the choice probabilities $p_{ih}^k(x)$ are proportional to strategy k's popularity in the player population,

x_{ik}, where the proportionality factor is larger the higher is the current payoff to strategy k. Let the weight factor that a reviewing h-strategist in player population i attaches to pure strategy k be $\omega_{ih}\left[u_i(e_i^k, x_{-i}), x\right] > 0$, where ω_{ih} is a (Lipschitz continuous) function that is strictly increasing in its first (payoff) argument. Then

$$p_{ih}^k(x) = \frac{\omega_{ih}\left[u_i(e_i^k, x_{-i}), x\right] x_{ik}}{\sum_{l \in S_i} \omega_{ih}\left[u_i(e_i^l, x_{-i}), x\right] x_{il}}. \tag{5.31}$$

As in the single-population case the informational assumption behind such choice probabilities is not that a reviewing agent necessarily knows the current expected payoffs to all pure strategies available to the player position, nor does she have to know the current population state. Moreover, in the present multipopulation setting, no knowledge of the payoffs to other player positions is presumed.

Combining choice probabilities (5.31) with unit review rates, one obtains the following dynamics:

$$\dot{x}_{ih} = \left(\sum_{k \in S_i} \frac{\omega_{ik}\left[u_i(e_i^h, x_{-i}), x\right] x_{ik}}{\sum_{l \in S_i} \omega_{ik}\left[u_i(e_i^l, x_{-i}), x\right] x_{il}} - 1 \right) x_{ih}. \tag{5.32}$$

Again growth rates are ordered according to payoffs: One pure strategy has a higher growth rate than another (in the same player position) if the first earns a higher payoff than the second.

In the special case of affine weight functions whereby $\omega_{ih}(z, x) = \lambda_i + \mu_i z$ for some $\lambda_i, \mu_i \in R$ such that $\mu_i > 0$ and $\lambda_i + \mu_i u_i(e_i^h, x_{-i}) > 0$ for all population states x, player positions i, and pure strategies h,

$$\dot{x}_{ih} = \frac{\mu_i}{\lambda_i + \mu_i u_i(x)}\left[u_i(e_i^h, x_{-i}) - u_i(x)\right] x_{ih}. \tag{5.33}$$

In particular, if all payoffs are positive, then the *adjusted n-population replicator dynamics* (5.5) arises when weights are proportional to payoffs ($\lambda_i = 0$), that is, when reviewing agents switch strategies according to the pure strategies' shares of the total payoff "pie."

5.4   Replication by Contamination

Instead of adopting the perspective of the individuals or agents in the population, let us briefly adopt a viewpoint that brings the replicators to the foreground. Here the individuals or agents in the player population in question are merely the "hosts" for which the replicators compete.[13] Suppose that individuals in the same player population now and then randomly bounce into each other, according to, say, a Poisson process with arrival rate $b_i(x)$. All bounces being equally likely, the rate at which h- and k-strategists bounce into each other is $b_i(x)x_{ih}x_{ik}$, for any $h, k \in S_i$. Strategies are contagious, so there is a probability $q_{ih}^k(x)$ that the h-strategist will become a k-strategist, and vice versa for the k-strategist. Assuming statistical independence, we observe that when a pair (h, k) bounces together, they will part as an (h, h) pair with probability $\left(1 - q_{ih}^k(x)\right) q_{ik}^h(x)$, as a (k, k) pair with probability $q_{ih}^k(x)\left(1 - q_{ik}^h(x)\right)$, and otherwise as an (h, k) or (k, h) pair. In the first case the number of h-strategists increases by one and the number of k-strategists decreases by one, and conversely in the second case. In the last two cases no change in population shares takes place.

In terms of expected numbers, this bouncing and strategy switching results in the following dynamics in player population i:

$$\dot{x}_{ih} = b_i(x) \sum_{k \in S_i} x_{ik} \left[\left(1 - q_{ih}^k(x)\right) q_{ik}^h(x) - \left(1 - q_{ik}^h(x)\right) q_{ih}^k(x)\right] x_{ih}$$

$$= b_i(x) \left(\sum_{k \in S_i} x_{ik} \left[q_{ik}^h(x) - q_{ih}^k(x)\right]\right) x_{ih}. \tag{5.34}$$

Assuming, as usual, that the involved functions are Lipschitz continuous, this system of differential equations has a unique solution through every initial population state in Θ. Moreover Θ, its interior and boundary, are all invariant sets.

If payoffs represent the reproductive strength of a pure strategy, viewed as a contagious replicator in this epidemiological (or statistical mechanical) model, then one might assume that each contamination probability $q_{ih}^k(x)$ is increasing in the average payoff $u_i(e_i^k, x_{-i})$ to the "attacking" (foreign) strategy k and decreasing in the average payoff $u_i(e_i^h, x_{-i})$ to the "defending" (incumbent) strategy.[14] Let

13. The same perspective can of course be adopted also in the single-population setting. The related idea of "memes" competing for human hosts, as a paradigm for social evolution, is due to Dawkins (1976).

14. Such an approach neglects stochastic elements, which may nevertheless be important.

$$q_{ih}^k(x) = \theta_i \left[u_i(e_i^k, x_{-i}), u_i(e_i^h, x_{-i}) \right] \tag{5.35}$$

for some (Lipschitz continuous) function θ_i which is increasing in its first argument and decreasing in its second. Then (5.34) can be written

$$\dot{x}_{ih} = b_i(x) \left[\sum_{l \in S_i} x_{il} \left(\theta_i \left[u_i(e_i^h, x_{-i}), u_i(e_i^l, x_{-i}) \right] \right. \right.$$
$$\left. \left. - \theta_i \left[u_i(e_i^l, x_{-i}), u_i(e_i^h, x_{-i}) \right] \right) \right] x_{ih}. \tag{5.36}$$

Like many of the imitation dynamics, this epidemiological dynamics ranks growth rates of pure strategies according to their payoffs. Moreover there is a formal similarity with the earlier studied imitation dynamics (5.29). Indeed that dynamics is the special case of (5.36) which arises when the bouncing rate is constantly equal to one and contamination probabilities are functions of payoff *differences*.[15]

5.5   Classes of Selection Dynamics

We here consider certain classes of n-population selection dynamics for n-player games, each such class containing both the standard (5.4) and adjusted (5.5) replicator dynamics. Once these classes have been defined, in the present section, results for dynamics in these classes, concerning connections with solution concepts in noncooperative game theory, are established in the next section. The classification to be given is a straight-forward extension from the single-population classification given in section 4.3.

The widest class to be considered are the *regular* selection dynamics. Within this general class four subclasses will be studied. One is the class of *payoff-monotonic* selection dynamics, in which a pure strategy with a higher payoff always has a higher growth-rate than a pure strategy with a lower payoff. As was seen in the preceding sections, many models of replication by imitation (section 5.3) and contamination (section 5.4) fall in this category. Another subclass of regular selection dynamics are those that are *payoff positive*. Here the requirement is that a pure strategy has a positive growth rate if

---

15. Set $b_i(x) = 1$ and $\theta_i \left[u_i(e_i^k, x_{-i}), u_i(e_i^h, x_{-i}) \right] = \phi_i \left[u_i(e_i^k, x_{-i}) - u_i(e_i^h, x_{-i}) \right]$.

and only if its payoff is above average in its player population. Each of these two classes of regular population dynamics contains the *payoff linear* selection dynamics, to which both the standard (5.4) and adjusted (5.5) replicator dynamics belong. The largest subclass of regular selection dynamics are those that are *weakly payoff positive*. Here the only requirement is that if some pure strategy earns above average in its player population, then some such strategy has a positive growth rate. This class contains all the other classes of regular selection dynamics mentioned above.

5.5.1 Regularity

The notion of multipopulation regularity is a straightforward generalization of the corresponding single-population notion. Recall that the ith player mixed-strategy simplex Δ_i is a compact subset of R^{m_i} and that the polyhedron $\Theta = \times \Delta_i$ of mixed-strategy profiles accordingly is a compact subset of R^m, where $m = m_1 + \ldots + m_n$. Just as in the single-population setting, we specify the system of differential equations for the population state in terms of growth rates. Also here this turns out to be a convenient way to describe how selection among present behaviors (pure strategies) operates. Like in the single-population models studied in chapters 3 and 4, mutations are treated indirectly by way of dynamic stability considerations.

   In the present setting a growth-rate function g assigns to each population state x, player population i, and pure strategy h available to player i the growth rate $g_{ih}(x)$ of the associated population share x_{ih}. Write $g(x) = (g_1(x), \ldots, g_k(x))$, each component $g_i(x)$ being a vector-valued growth-rate function for player population i, and

$$\dot{x}_{ih} = g_{ih}(x)x_{ih} \qquad \forall i \in I, h \in S_i, x \in \Theta. \tag{5.37}$$

Definition 5.4 *A regular growth-rate function is a Lipschitz continuous function* $g : X \to R^m$ *with open domain* $X \subset R^m$ *containing* Θ, *such that* $g_i(x) \cdot x_i = 0$ *for all population states* $x \in \Theta$ *and player populations* $i \in I$.

   Geometrically the condition $g_i(x) \cdot x_i = 0$ requires the growth-rate vector $g_i(x)$, for player population i, always to be orthogonal to the associated player population vector x_i. This guarantees that for each player population i, the sum of its population shares x_{ih} remains constantly equal to 1, as is apparent if the condition is written coordinatewise:

$$\sum_{h \in S_i} \dot{x}_{ih} = \sum_{h \in S_i} g_{ih}(x)x_{ih} = 0 \qquad \forall i \in I, x \in \Theta. \tag{5.38}$$

The standard n-population replicator dynamics (5.4) is the special case $g_{ih}(x) = u_i(e_i^h, x_{-i}) - u_i(x)$, and when all payoffs are positive, the adjusted n-population replicator dynamics (5.5) is the special case $g_{ih}(x) = u_i(e_i^h, x_{-i})/u_i(x) - 1$. In both cases the orthogonality condition is clearly met.

Let G denote the set of regular growth-rate functions. The dynamics induced by a regular growth-rate function via the associated system (5.37) of differential equations will be called a *regular selection dynamics* on Θ.[16] All imitation dynamics studied in the preceding section are regular in this sense.

Just as in the single-population setting (subsection 4.3.1), any regular n-population growth-rate function induces a well-defined dynamics on the relevant state-space, which in the present setting is the polyhedron Θ of mixed-strategy profiles. More precisely, if $g \in G$, then (1) the system (5.37) has a unique solution $\xi(\cdot, x^o) : R \to \Theta$ through any initial state $x^o \in \Theta$, (2) each of the sets Θ, $\text{int}(\Theta)$ and $\text{bd}(\Theta)$ are invariant, and (3) the induced solution mapping $\xi : R \times \Theta \to \Theta$ is continuous.

Not so surprisingly, the chain rule of differentiation implies that the growth rate of the ratio between two (positive) population shares, in any player population, equals the difference between the two growth rates. Formally, for any player position $i \in I$, pure strategies $h, k \in S_i$, and population state $x \in \text{int}(\Theta)$,

$$\frac{d}{dt} \left[\frac{\xi_{ih}(t, x)}{\xi_{ik}(t, x)} \right]_{t=0} = \left[g_{ih}(x) - g_{ik}(x) \right] \frac{x_{ih}}{x_{ik}}. \tag{5.39}$$

For robust long-run predictions the criterion of asymptotic stability plays a key role. If a population initially is near an asymptotically stable state, then it will converge to it over time. Even if the population state in the meantime is exposed to occasional small shocks, such as mutations in small population doses, the population will remain near to this asymptotically stable state. The following result extends the general sufficient condition for asymptotic stability in regular single-population selection dynamics (proposition 4.3):

Proposition 5.5 *Suppose that $g \in G$. A profile $x \in \Theta$ is asymptotically stable in the associated dynamics (5.37) if (5.40) below holds for all profiles $y \neq x$ in some neighborhood of x:*

---

16. This definition is equivalent with the definition in Samuelson and Zhang (1992).

$$\sum_{i \in I} x_i \cdot g_i(y) > 0. \tag{5.40}$$

Proof Suppose that $x \in \Theta$. For each player $i \in I$, let the subset $Q_{x_i} \subset \Delta_i$ and associated relative-entropy function $H_{x_i} : \Delta_i \to R$ be defined as in subsection 3.5.1. Let

$$Q_x = \times_{i \in I} Q_{x_i} = \{y \in \Theta : C(x) \subset C(y)\},$$

and define the function $K_x : Q_x \to R$ as the sum of the associated relative-entropy functions

$$K_x(y) = \sum_{i \in I} H_{x_i}(y_i).$$

By lemma 3.1, $K_x(y) \geq 0$, with equality if and only if $y = x$. Moreover the argument in the second half of the proof of that lemma, as applied to any regular selection dynamics (5.37), gives

$$\dot{K}_x(y) = -\sum_{i \in I} x_i \cdot g_i(y) \qquad \forall y \in Q_x.$$

Thus K_x is a strict local Lyapunov function if (5.40) holds, implying that x is asymptotically stable, by theorem 6.4. ∎

In view of orthogonality (5.38), (5.40) is equivalent to the more geometric condition $\sum_i (x_i - y_i) \cdot g_i(y) > 0$; namely at any nearby population state y, each growth-rate vector $g_i(y)$ should, on average across populations, make an acute angle with the straight line from y_i to x_i (see the discussion in subsection 4.3.1).

5.5.2 Payoff Monotonicity

In analogy with the single-population case (subsection 4.3.3), any growth-rate function g that always ranks each player position's pure strategies in order of payoffs will be called *payoff monotonic*.[17]

Definition 5.5 $g \in G$ is payoff monotonic *if, for all population states $x \in \Theta$, player positions $i \in I$, and pure strategies $h, k \in S_i$:*

---

17. This property is called *relative monotonicity* in Nachbar (1990), *order compatibility* (of what he calls *pre-dynamics*) in Friedman (1991), and simply *monotonicity* in Samuelson and Zhang (1992).

$$u_i(e_i^h, x_{-i}) > u_i(e_i^k, x_{-i}) \Leftrightarrow g_{ih}(x) > g_{ik}(x). \tag{5.41}$$

In other words, if a pure strategy $h \in S_i$ is a better (equal, worse) reply to the current population state $x \in \Theta$ than another pure strategy $k \in S_i$, then the first population share, x_{ih}, should have a higher (equal, lower) growth rate than the second population share, x_{ik}.

We will denote the class of payoff-monotonic growth-rate functions $G^m \subset G$. The dynamics induced via (5.37) by such growth-rate functions will be called *payoff monotonic*. The imitation dynamics (5.24), (5.29), and (5.32) are examples of payoff-monotonic selection dynamics as is the contamination dynamics (5.36).

5.5.3   Payoff Positivity

An alternative compatibility property of population dynamics with respect to the payoff of the game in question is that strategies that earn above (below) average in their player population grow (decline). Letting sgn(z) denote the sign of $z \in R$:

Definition 5.6 $g \in G$ is payoff positive *if, for all population states $x \in \Theta$, player positions $i \in I$, and pure strategies $h \in S_i$:*

$$\text{sgn}\left[g_{ih}(x)\right] = \text{sgn}\left[u_i(e_i^h, x_{-i}) - u_i(x)\right]. \tag{5.42}$$

The subclass of payoff-positive growth-rate functions will be denoted $G^p \subset G$, and also the dynamics induced by such a growth-rate function g will be *payoff positive.*[18] Both the standard (5.4) and adjusted (5.5) replicator dynamics are clearly payoff positive in this sense.

Note that payoff positivity admits that one pure strategy yields a higher payoff than another and yet has a lower growth rate, provided that both strategies earn either above or below average. Hence the two classes G^p and G^m are generally distinct. Exceptions are games in which each player position has only two pure strategies. Then a pure strategy earns above (below) average in its player population if and only if it earns more (less) than the other pure strategy available to that player position. Hence $G^p = G^m$ in any such game.

---

18. Nachbar (1990) calls this class *sign-preserving.*

5.5.4 Payoff Linearity

A class of selection dynamics that has both the payoff monotonic and payoff positive properties is that in which growth rates are *linearly* related to the associated payoffs. More exactly:

Definition 5.7 $g \in G$ is payoff linear *if for each player position $i \in I$ there exist Lipschitz continuous functions $a_i : X \to R_{++}$ and $c_i : X \to R$ such that, for all population states $x \in \Theta$ and pure strategies $h \in S_i$,*

$$g_{ih}(x) = a_i(x)u_i(e_i^h, x_{-i}) + c_i(x). \tag{5.43}$$

By orthogonality, each growth rate $g_{ih}(x)$ is requested to be *proportional* to the associated excess payoff: $c_i(x) = -a_i(x)u_i(x)$, and so $g_{ih}(x) = a_i(x)$ $(u_i(e_i^h, x_i) - u_i(x))$. The positivity of the proportionality factor $a_i(x)$ implies that both monotonicity (5.41) and positivity (5.42) are met. Hence the class of payoff linear growth-rate functions, to be denoted $G^l \subset G$, is indeed a subclass of each of the two other classes:[19]

$$G^l \subset G^m \cap G^p. \tag{5.44}$$

The standard replicator dynamics (5.4) is here the special case when all proportionality factors $a_i(x)$ are constantly equal to 1. Generally, if the proportionality functions are identical across player populations but not necessarily constantly equal to one, that is, if $a_i = a_j$ for all $i, j \in I$, then the induced solution *orbits* in Θ are still identical to those of the standard replicator dynamics (5.4). The only difference is that the population state moves along these solution orbits at a different velocity (all time derivatives are multiplied by the same positive number). If different player populations have *different* proportionality functions a_i, then the induced solution orbits need not at all coincide with those of the standard replicator dynamics (5.4). Indeed such a player-specific rescaling of time arises in the *adjusted* replicator dynamics (5.5); then $a_i(x) \equiv 1/u_i(x)$, provided that all payoffs are positive. The imitation dynamics (5.26), (5.30), and (5.33) are examples of payoff-linear selection dynamics.

Example 5.5 Consider again the Matching Pennies Game of examples 5.2 and 5.3. In the notation of those examples, any payoff-linear dynamics can be

---

19. A closely related monotonicity property, called *aggregate monotonicity*, was introduced by Samuelson and Zhang (1992); see subsection 5.8.1.

written

$$\dot{x}_1 = a(x, y)(2y_1 - 1)(1 - x_1)x_1 \, ,$$

$$\dot{y}_1 = b(x, y)(1 - 2x_1)(1 - y_1)y_1 \, ,$$

where a and b are positive functions on an open domain containing the unit square. In the standard replicator dynamics, $a(x, y) \equiv b(x, y) \equiv 1$, while in the adjusted replicator dynamics, $a(x, y) \equiv \left[u_1(x, y) + c\right]^{-1}$ and $b(x, y) \equiv \left[u_2(x, y) + c\right]^{-1}$, where c is the payoff parameter given in example 5.3.

Consider, for any payoff-linear dynamics, any state (x, y) in the interior of the northwest subsquare of the unit square. The tangent of the replicator orbit through the point is the direction of the standard replicator vector field. By varying the values $a(x, y) > 0$ and $b(x, y) > 0$ of the multiplier functions a and b at the point, we obtain a vector field with any direction pointing northeast; see the indicated $90°$ cone in figure 5.5 (a). Hence a payoff-linear dynamics may bend the replicator orbits inward ($a(x, y) > b(x, y)$) or outward ($a(x, y) < b(x, y)$). The same operation can be performed in the interior of each of the four subsquares, and hence it is intuitively clear that the unique Nash equilibrium of this game (the midpoint of the square) is asymptotically stable in some payoff-linear dynamics and unstable in others; see figure 5.5 (b) and (c) for illustrations. Payoff linearity thus allows for directional deviations from the replicator vector field within a $90°$ cone, at all points (x, y) in the interior of any of the four subsquares. At a boundary point between two such subsquares, however, the replicator vector field is either horizontal or vertical, and hence all payoff-linear vector fields point in the same direction as the replicator vector field. The replicator vector field vanishes at the Nash equilibrium point, and so do all payoff-linear vector fields. Along the boundaries of the full square, all payoff-linear vector fields point in the same direction as the replicator field.

5.5.5   Weak Payoff Positivity

All the preceding classes of regular growth-rate functions are subclasses of the class of weakly payoff-positive growth-rate functions, defined, by way of a straightforward extension, as in the single-population case (subsection 4.3.4). The defining criterion is that whenever there exists a pure strategy that gives a payoff above average in its player population, then such a pure strategy should have a positive growth rate. This is the case, for instance, if all pure strategies

(a)

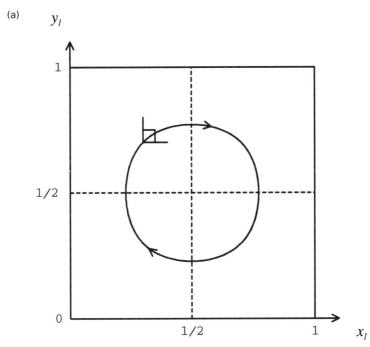

(b)

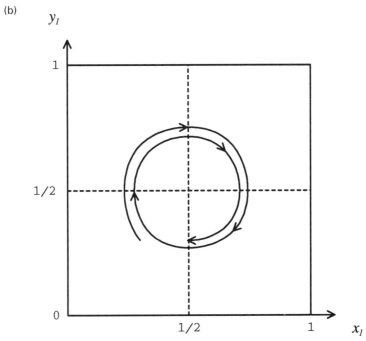

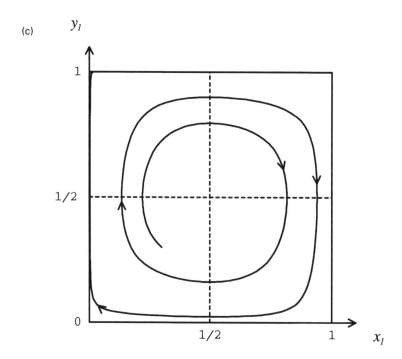

Figure 5.5
Payoff-linear two-population replicator dynamics in the Matching Pennies Game of examples 1.5, 5.3, and 5.5: (a) The $90°$ cone for the vector field, (b) solution curve when $a(x, y) = [u_1(x, y) + c]^{-1}$ and $b(x, y) = [u_2(x, y) + c]^{-1}$, (c) solution curves when $a(x, y) = u_1(x, y) + c$ and $b(x, y) = u_2(x, y) + c$.

that earn above average have positive growth rates, as under payoff positivity, or if, say, some pure *best* reply has a positive growth rate whenever such a strategy gives a payoff above average in its player population. By the same argument as was used in the single-population setting, it can be verified that every payoff-monotonic growth-rate function is weakly payoff positive also in the present multipopulation setting.

More exactly, suppose that $g : X \to R^m$ is some regular growth-rate function with open domain X containing Θ. For any population state x and player position i, let $B_i(x)$ denote the (possibly empty) subset of pure strategies, available to that player position, which earn above average

$$B_i(x) = \left\{ h \in S_i : u_i(e_i^h, x_{-i}) > u_i(x) \right\}. \tag{5.45}$$

Definition 5.8   *A regular growth-rate function g is* weakly payoff-positive *if for all $x \in \Theta$ and $i \in I$: $B_i(x) \neq \emptyset \Rightarrow g_{ih}(x) > 0$ for some $h \in B_i(x)$.*

Denoting the set of weakly payoff monotonic growth-rate functions G^w, we have

$$G^m \cup G^p \subset G^w. \tag{5.46}$$

It turns out that this property of weak positivity is sufficient when it concerns implications for aggregate Nash equilibrium behavior. This property does not suffice, however, to weed out strictly dominated strategies along nonconvergent solution paths.

5.6   Implications of Evolutionary Dynamics for Noncooperative Solution Concepts

5.6.1   Dominated Strategies

Just as in the single-population setting, it is not difficult to show that a pure strategy that is strictly dominated by another *pure* strategy vanishes in the long run, along any interior solution path to a payoff-monotonic selection dynamics (see proposition 4.5). The present multipopulation version of the result is due to Samuelson and Zhang (1992):

Proposition 5.6   *Suppose that $g \in G^m$. A pure strategy that is strictly dominated by some pure strategy vanishes along all interior solution paths to the associated dynamics (5.37).*

Proof   Suppose that $u_i(e_i^k, x_{-i}) < u_i(e_i^h, x_{-i})$ for all $x \in \Theta$. Then $g_{ik}(x) - g_{ih}(x) < 0$ for all $x \in \Theta$, by (5.41). By continuity of g and compactness of Θ, there exists some $\epsilon > 0$ such that $g_{ik}(x) - g_{ih}(x) < -\epsilon$ for all $x \in \Theta$. Suppose that $x^o \in \text{int}(\Delta)$. By (5.39),

$$\frac{d}{dt}\left[\frac{\xi_{ik}(t, x^o)}{\xi_{ih}(t, x^o)}\right] < -\epsilon \cdot \frac{\xi_{ik}(t, x^o)}{\xi_{ih}(t, x^o)} \qquad \forall t \geq 0,$$

and hence $\xi_{ik}(t, x^o) \to 0$, for the same reason as in the proof of proposition 4.5.   ∎

Example 4.4 suggests how, in a certain payoff-monotonic single-population-selection dynamics, a strictly dominated strategy not dominated by any pure strategy may survive in the long run, along nonconvergent interior solution paths. This example also suggests that survival of such strategies is possible in payoff-monotonic *multi*population dynamics. For we may apply the same dynamics as there to each of two populations separately, where each population takes one of the player positions in the symmetric two-player game in question. In such a symmetric setup the diagonal D of Θ is invariant, and the two-population dynamics induces the same solution trajectories on D as the single-population dynamics.

In *payoff-linear* selection dynamics, however, all strictly dominated strategies vanish, not only those that are strictly dominated by *pure* strategies. This result, also due to Samuelson and Zhang (1992), can be proved along the same lines as proposition 3.1 was established for the single-population case:

Proposition 5.7 *Suppose that $g \in G^l$. A strictly dominated strategy vanishes along any interior solution path to the associated dynamics (5.37).*

Proof Suppose that $k \in S_i$ is strictly dominated by $y_i \in \Delta_i$, and let

$$\epsilon = \min_{x \in \Theta} u_i(y_i - e_i^k, x_{-i}).$$

By continuity of u_i and compactness of Θ, $\epsilon > 0$. As in the proof of proposition 3.1, define $v_{ik} : \text{int}(\Theta) \to R$ by

$$v_{ik}(x) = \log(x_{ik}) - \sum_{h \in S_i} y_{ih} \log(x_{ih}).$$

Suppose that $g \in G^l$, and let a_i be the associated rescaling function of time for player $i \in I$. Since $\Theta \subset X$ is compact and a_i continuous, $a_i(x) \geq \alpha_i$ for some $\alpha_i > 0$. Clearly v_{ik} is differentiable, and its time derivative along any interior solution path $\xi : R \times \text{int}(\Theta) \to \text{int}(\Theta)$ is, at any point $x = \xi(t, x^o) \in \text{int}(\Theta)$,

$$\dot{v}_{ik}(x) = \left[\frac{dv_{ik}(\xi(t, x^o))}{dt} \right]_{\xi(t,x^o)=x} = \sum_{h \in S_i} \frac{\partial v_{ik}(x)}{\partial x_{ih}} \dot{x}_{ih}$$

$$= \frac{\dot{x}_{ik}}{x_{ik}} - \sum_{h \in S_i} \frac{y_{ih} \dot{x}_{ih}}{x_{ih}}$$

$$= a_i(x) u_i(e_i^k - y_i, x_{-i}) \leq -\epsilon \alpha_i < 0.$$

Hence $v_{ik}\left[\xi(t, x^o)\right]$ is strictly decreasing toward minus infinity as $t \to \infty$. By definition of v_{ik}, this implies that $\xi_{ik}(t, x^o) \to 0$. ∎

In fact Samuelson and Zhang (1992) go one step further and show that the conclusion above can be extended to all pure strategies that are *iteratively strictly dominated*:

Theorem 5.1 *Suppose that* $g \in G^l$. *If a pure strategy is iteratively strictly dominated, then its population share converges to zero along any interior initial solution path to (5.37).*

(For a formal proof, see Samuelson and Zhang 1992; for an intuitive argument, see the discussion preceding theorem 3.1.)

For the single-population replicator dynamics in symmetric two-player games, it was shown that if a pure strategy i is weakly dominated, and this strategy does not vanish in the long run, then all pure strategies vanish against which strategy i performs worse than the dominating strategy. Suitably reformulated, this result can be extended to the present setting, provided that the selection dynamics is payoff linear. However, now the result involves one pure strategy for each player position. For the sake of notational clarity, the result will be established only for two-player games (the extension to games with more players should be clear from the proof). The result then is as follows: If a pure strategy k in one of the two-player positions i is weakly dominated by some strategy $y_i \in \Delta_i$ and strategy k does not vanish from its player population over time, then all those pure strategies h in the other player position, j, against which y_i is better than k, vanish from that player population j (see subsection 3.2.2). With some abuse of notation:

Proposition 5.8 *Suppose that* $n = 2$ *and* $g \in G^l$. *If* $k \in S_i$ *is weakly dominated by* $y_i \in \Delta_i$, *and* $u_i(y_i, e_j^h) > u_i(e_i^k, e_j^h)$, *where* $j \neq i$ *and* $h \in S_j$, *then*

$$x^o \in \text{int}(\Delta) \Rightarrow \xi_{ik}(t, x^o) \to 0 \quad \text{or} \quad \xi_{jh}(t, x^0) \to 0 .$$

Proof Let $v_{ik} : \text{int}(\Delta) \to R$ be as in the proof of proposition 5.7. Then

$$\dot{v}_{ik}(x) = a_i(x)u_i\left(e_i^k - y_i, x_j\right)$$

for all $x \in \text{int}(\Delta)$. Since y_i weakly dominates e_i^k and x is interior, $v_{ik}(\xi(t, x^o))$ decreases monotonically over time along any solution $\xi(t, x^o)$ through an interior initial state x^o.

Now suppose that $j \neq i$ and that $h \in S_j$ is such that $u_i(y_i - e_i^k, e_j^h) = \varepsilon > 0$. Since y_i weakly dominates e_i^k,

$$u_i(y_i - e_i^k, x_j) = \sum_l u_i(y_i - e_i^k, e_j^l) x_{jl} \geq u_i(y_i - e_i^k, e_j^h) x_{jh} \geq \varepsilon x_{jh}$$

for any $x \in \Delta$. Since $\Theta \subset X$ is compact and a_i continuous, $a_i(x) \geq \alpha_i$ for some $\alpha_i > 0$. Hence at all times $t \geq 0$,

$$\frac{d}{dt} v_{ik}\left(\xi(t, x^o)\right) \leq -\varepsilon \alpha_i \xi_{jh}(t, x^o) \leq 0.$$

The rest of the argument is identical with that in the proof of proposition 3.2. ∎

The following example illustrates the possibility that a weakly dominated pure strategy survives along interior solution trajectories to a payoff-linear selection dynamics, the standard replicator dynamics (5.4).

Example 5.6   Reconsider the Entry Deterrence Game of examples 1.6 and 5.4. The second pure strategy to player position 2 (fight) is weakly dominated (by any mixed strategy), and performs worse against the first player's first pure strategy (enter). Hence, along the solution trajectory to any payoff-linear selection dynamics, $\xi_1\left[t, (x^o, y^o)\right] \eta_2\left[t, (x^o, y^o)\right] \to 0$ by proposition 5.8. Solution orbits to the standard replicator dynamics (5.4) were analyzed in example 5.4; see figure 5.3. Indeed we see that in the notation of the present section and along any interior solution trajectory, either $\xi_1\left[t, (x^o, y^o)\right] \to 1$ and $\eta_2\left[t, (x^o, y^o)\right] \to 0$ (when the solution converges to the subgame perfect equilibrium) or $\xi_1\left[t, (x^o, y^o)\right] \to 0$ and $\eta_2\left[t, (x^o, y^o)\right]$ converges to a value above $\frac{1}{2}$ (when the solution converges to a point in the other Nash equilibrium component). In the latter case the weakly dominated second strategy (fight) does thus not vanish in the long run.

5.6.2   Nash Equilibrium

It turns out that payoff-monotonic and payoff-positive selection dynamics have similar implications for aggregate Nash equilibrium behavior. Indeed the most important of these are valid for any weakly payoff-positive selection dynamics.

We begin by noting that all payoff-monotonic and payoff-positive dynamics have the *same* set of stationary states. Since the standard replicator dynamics (5.4) is payoff monotonic, this set must be the set Θ^o defined in equation (5.6):

Proposition 5.9 *If $g \in G^m \cup G^p$, then the associated set of stationary states in (5.37) is*

$$\Theta^o = \left\{ x \in \Theta : u_i(e_i^h, x_{-i}) = u_i(x) \ \forall i \in I, \ h \in C(x_i) \right\}.$$

Proof   First, suppose that $x \in \Theta^o$. Then x is clearly stationary if $g \in G^p$, since (5.42) then requires that $g_{ih}(x) = 0$ for all $i \in I$, $h \in C(x_i)$. Likewise, for any $g \in G^m$, (5.41) implies that for each player population i, there exists some $\mu_i \in R$ such that $g_{ih}(x) = \mu_i$ for all $h \in C(x_i)$. But then $g_i(x) \cdot x_i = \mu_i$, and so $\mu_i = 0$ by (5.38). Hence x again is stationary in (5.37).

Second, suppose that $x \in \Theta$ is stationary in some regular selection dynamics (5.37). Then $g_{ih}(y) = 0$ for all $i \in I$ and $h \in C(x_i)$. For $g \in G^p$ this implies that $u_i(e_i^h, x_{-i}) = u_i(x)$ for all $i \in I$, $h \in C(x_i)$, so $x \in \Theta^o$. Likewise for $g \in G^m$ this implies that for each player population i there exists some $\alpha_i \in R$ such that $u_i(e_i^h, x_{-i}) = \alpha_i$ for all $h \in C(x_i)$. But then $u_i(x) = \sum_h x_{ih} u(e_i^h, x_{-i}) = \alpha_i$, and thus $x \in \Theta^o$. ∎

An immediate implication of this result is that all interior stationary states are Nash equilibria and all Nash equilibria are stationary, in any payoff-monotonic or payoff-positive selection dynamics (5.37). The first implication, that interior stationarity implies Nash equilibrium, is valid also for any weakly payoff-positive selection dynamics (see below). Not all Nash equilibria need to be stationary in such a dynamics, though. The reason is that, in contrast to the two other criteria, weak payoff positivity does not impose any condition on growth rates in a player population where everyone earns the same payoff. Individuals in such a population may switch from one pure strategy to another, and such drift may take the population away from a Nash equilibrium. The following simple example illustrates that it is sufficient with one such player population.

Example 5.7   Consider the symmetric 2×2 game with payoff matrices

$$A = \begin{pmatrix} 1 & 0 \\ 0 & 1 \end{pmatrix}, \quad B = \begin{pmatrix} 0 & 0 \\ 0 & 0 \end{pmatrix}.$$

It is as if player 1 wants to do whatever player 2 does, but player 2 is completely indifferent. The set of Nash equilibria in this (nongeneric) game consists of a single connected (but nonconvex) component; see figure 5.6 (a). Due to 2's indifference, weak payoff positivity imposes no restriction, beyond regularity, on the growth-rate function g_2 for that player population. Let, for instance, g_2 represent a general drift toward pure strategy 1, and suppose that the growth-rate function for player population 1 is as in the standard replicator dynamics. In the notation in subsection 5.2.2,

$$\dot{x}_1 = (2y_1 - 1)(1 - x_1)x_1,$$

$$\dot{y}_1 = (1 - y_1)y_1.$$

The only stationary states in this dynamics are the four vertices, but the only dynamically stable state is when both populations play their first pure strategy, namely when both players always do what the indifferent player 2 tends to do; see figure 5.6 (b).

What about stationary states that are not Nash equilibria? In the context of the single-population replicator dynamics in symmetric two-player games, studied in detail in chapters 3 and 4, it was shown that such symmetric stationary states are not Lyapunov stable. In its most general form this was shown for weakly payoff-positive single-population selection dynamics (subsection 4.3.4). It turns out that this implication holds also in the present multipopulation setting, again under weak payoff positivity. Note, however, that while the single-population approach only dealt with symmetric Nash equilibria in symmetric two-player games, we here consider arbitrary Nash equilibria in arbitrary (finite) n-player games. Moreover a symmetric Nash equilibrium in a symmetric two-player game may be dynamically stable in the single-population standard replicator dynamics (3.5) without being stable in the corresponding two-population dynamics (5.4). Indeed we saw in section 5.2 that the symmetric Nash equilibrium of the Hawk-Dove Game, which is asymptotically stable in the single-population standard replicator dynamics, constitutes an unstable (saddle-point) state in the two-population standard replicator dynamics. Instead, the game's two asymmetric and strict Nash equilibria were seen to be asymptotically stable in the latter dynamics, as shown in figure 5.4 (c). That Lyapunov stability does imply Nash equilibrium also in multipopulation *payoff-monotonic* selection dynamics was suggested in Nachbar (1990).

In chapters 3 and 4 we also showed that even if a stationary state is not Lyapunov stable in certain single-population dynamics in a symmetric two-player game, it may still be a symmetric Nash equilibrium, namely if there is some interior solution path that converges to the state. This result was established for the single-population standard replicator dynamics (3.5) in subsection 3.3.3, and in its most general form for weakly payoff-monotonic single-population selection dynamics in subsection 4.3.4. Nachbar (1990) suggested that this

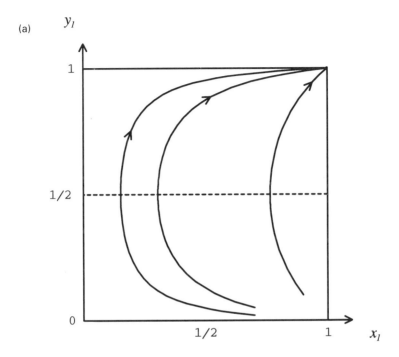

(a)

result holds also for payoff-monotonic multipopulation selection dynamics. Here it is established for all weakly payoff-positive selection dynamics. Again, moving from single-population dynamics to multipopulation dynamics allows also for nonsymmetric population states and Nash equilibria.

We summarize these implications in one theorem. Although the proofs are straightforward extensions of the corresponding proofs for single-population dynamics in symmetric games, we here give them in full. In view of proposition 5.4 this result generalizes these earlier discussed implications from dynamic evolutionary selection to aggregate Nash equilibrium behavior.

Theorem 5.2 *Suppose that $g \in G^w$, and consider the associated dynamics (5.37):*

a. If $x \in \text{int}(\Theta)$ is stationary, then $x \in \Theta^{NE}$.

b. If $x \in \Theta$ is Lyapunov stable, then $x \in \Theta^{NE}$.

c. If $x \in \Theta$ is the limit to some interior solution, then $x \in \Theta^{NE}$.

(b)

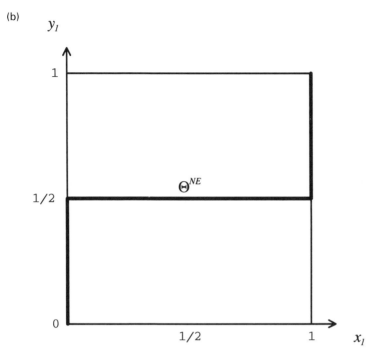

Figure 5.6
(a) The set Θ^{NE} in the game of example 5.7. (b) Solution curves to the dynamics in example 5.7.

Proof (a) Suppose that $x \in \mathrm{int}(\Theta)$ is stationary in (5.37). Then $g_{ih}(x) = 0$ for all $i \in I$ and $h \in S_i$, so $B_i(x) = \emptyset$ for all $i \in I$, by weak payoff positivity. Thus $x \in \Theta^{NE}$. (b) Suppose that $x \in \Theta$ is stationary in (5.37). Then $g_{ih}(x) = 0$ for all $i \in I$ and $h \in C(x_i)$. If $x \notin \Theta^{NE}$, then $B_i(x) \neq \emptyset$ for some $i \in I$, and hence, by weak payoff positivity, $g_{ih}(x) > 0$ for some $h \in B_i(x)$. By stationarity, $h \notin C(x_i)$, that is, $x_{ih} = 0$. By continuity of g_{ih}, there is a $\delta > 0$ and a neighborhood U of x such that $g_{ih}(y) \geq \delta$ for all $y \in U \cap \Theta$. But then $\xi_{ih}(t, x^o) \geq x_{ih}^o \exp(\delta t)$ for any $x^o \in U \cap \Theta$ and all times $t > 0$ such that $\xi(t, x^o) \in U \cap \Theta$. Thus $\xi_{ih}(t, x^o)$ initially increases exponentially from any $x^o \in U \cap \mathrm{int}(\Theta)$. Yet $x_{ih} = 0$, so x is not Lyapunov stable. (c) Suppose that $x^o \in \mathrm{int}(\Theta)$ and $\xi(t, x^o)_{t \to \infty} \to x$, in some weakly payoff-positive dynamics (5.37). Then x is stationary, by proposition 6.3, and $g_{ih}(x) = 0$ for all $i \in I$ and $h \in C(x_i)$. If $x \notin \Theta^{NE}$, then $B_i(x) \neq \emptyset$ for some $i \in I$, and hence, by weak payoff positivity, $g_{ih}(x) > 0$ for some $h \in B_i(x)$ with $x_{ih} = 0$. By continuity of g_{ih}, there is a $\delta > 0$ and a neighborhood U of x such that

$g_{ih}(y) \geq \delta$ for all $y \in U \cap \Theta$. However, this contradicts the hypothesis that $\xi(t, x^o)$ converges to x. The latter implies that there exists a time $T > 0$ such that $\xi(t, x^o) \in U \cap \text{int}(\Delta)$ for all $t \geq T$. Since $x_{ih} = 0$, there must be some $t \geq T$ such that $d\xi_{ih}(t, x^o)/dt < 0$, a contradiction to g_{ih} being positive on $U \cap \Theta$. Hence $x \in \Theta^{NE}$. ∎

The extensive-form game in the following example has two Nash equilibrium components. One is a continuum of Nash equilibria, and all but one of these are Lyapunov stable in the standard replicator dynamics. Hence as a set this component is not even Lyapunov stable. However, it does attract a fairly large set of interior solution trajectories. The other Nash equilibrium component is a singleton, consisting of a strict Nash equilibrium. This Nash equilibrium is asymptotically stable. In the extensive form this game has three subgame perfect equilibria, two in the continuum component, and the mentioned strict equilibrium. Only the latter is compatible with "forward induction."

Example 5.8 Consider the extensive-form game in figure 5.7 (a). In this game player 1 may take an outside option that gives both players payoff 2, or else play a simultaneous-move 2×2 game of the Battle of the Sexes type. The Battle of the Sexes subgame has three Nash equilibria: each of the two symmetric and strict equilibria, and one mixed-strategy equilibrium. Since precisely one of these subgame Nash equilibria results in a higher payoff to player 1 than the outside option gives her, the game has three subgame perfect Nash equilibria. In two of these, player 1 takes the outside option, and in the third she enters the Battle of the Sexes subgame and earns payoff 3. However, as has been argued by van Damme (1989), the first two subgame perfect equilibria can be rejected by forward induction. The intuitive argument is that these equilibria break down if player 2, upon seeing 1's deviation from the equilibrium action of taking the outside option, maintains the hypothesis that player 1 is "rational." Then player 1 should be expected not to use her strictly dominated strategy db, so player 2 should deviate as well.

The pure-strategy sets of this game are $S_1 = \{dt, db, at, ab\}$ and $S_2 = \{l, r\}$, and the associated payoff matrices are

$$A = \begin{pmatrix} 3 & 0 \\ 0 & 1 \\ 2 & 2 \\ 2 & 2 \end{pmatrix}, \quad B = \begin{pmatrix} 1 & 0 \\ 0 & 3 \\ 2 & 2 \\ 2 & 2 \end{pmatrix}.$$

(a)

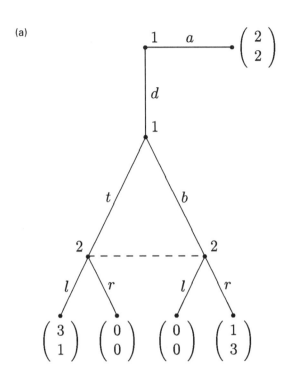

(b)

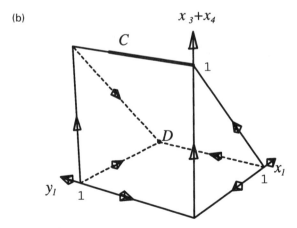

Figure 5.7
(a) The extensive form of the Outside Option Game of example 5.8. (b) The (reduced form) polyhedron Θ in this game, with Nash equilibrium components C and D.

The set Θ^{NE} has two components, $C = \{(x, y) \in \Theta : x_3 + x_4 = 1 \text{ and } y_1 \leq \frac{2}{3}\}$ and $D = \{(e_1^1, e_2^1)\}$. The singleton component D consists of the game's unique strict equilibrium; this corresponds to the only forward inductive sub-game perfect equilibrium in the extensive form. Since the last two pure strategies of player 1 are behaviorally undistinguishable, we will plot the sum $x_3 + x_4$ of their population shares (probabilities) on one axis. The resulting polyhedron of (reduced form) mixed-strategy profiles, with Nash equilibrium components, is given in figure 5.7 (b). The second pure strategy of player 1, $x \prime = e_1^2 = db$, is strictly dominated by her third (and also fourth) pure strategy, $x \prime = e_1^3 = at$. Hence, by proposition 5.6, the second strategy vanishes along all interior solution trajectories, to any payoff monotonic dynamics. Geometrically this means that interior solution trajectories converge to the boundary face B of the polyhedron Θ where $x_2 = 0$. (In figure 5.7 (b), this is the square and sloping boundary face farthest from the viewer.) The arrows along the edges of the polyhedron in that diagram give the associated directions of the vector field of any payoff-monotonic dynamics. Note in particular the movement out from the boundary face B at the vertex where $x_1 = 1$ and $y_1 = 0$, along the edge to the origin. Near this edge, the strictly dominated strategy e_1^2 temporarily grows along interior solution trajectories, finally to fall down to zero at the Nash equilibrium component C. The reason is that initially individuals in population 2 rarely use their first pure strategy, and since virtually all individuals in population 1 initially enter the Battle of the Sexes Subgame, the selection against their strictly dominated second pure strategy is very weak in the beginning. All interior solution trajectories starting near this edge converge to some point on the Nash equilibrium component C. The standard replicator dynamics on the boundary face B (where $x_2 = 0$) is given by

$$\dot{x}_1 = (3y_1 - 2)(1 - x_1)x_1$$

$$\dot{y}_1 = x_1(1 - y_1)y_1$$

This is qualitatively the same as that in the Entry Deterrence Game of example 5.4. In particular, all but one point in the component C are Lyapunov stable, C is not Lyapunov stable, and the strict Nash equilibrium component D is, as expected, asymptotically stable. In this weak sense evolution selects the forward inductive equilibrium (see Nöldeke and Samuelson 1993).

5.6.3   Strategically Stable Sets of Nash Equilibria

A closed set $X \subset \Theta$ of Nash equilibria is *strategically stable* in the sense of Kohlberg and Mertens (1986) if it is robust with respect to any sequence of small trembles in strategies and contains no proper subset with this property (see subsection 1.4.5). Since such sets consist of perfect Nash equilibria, and asymptotic stability in the single-population replicator dynamics implies (symmetric) perfect equilibrium (section 3.4), one may ask if there is a similar connection between setwise asymptotic stability in n-population selection dynamics and strategic stability.

While some games possess no asymptotically stable population state, there is always at least one (closed) *set* of states that is asymptotically stable in any given, regular dynamics, namely the whole polyhedron Θ itself. Moreover sometimes an asymptotically stable proper subset of Θ can be identified, in which case the evolutionary dynamic paradigm does have some predictive power. If the initial population state belongs to such a subset, or is near to it, then the population state will remain in the set, or near to it, at all future times—even in the presence of (unmodeled) occasional small shocks to the population state such as those due to mutations, experimentation, or mistakes in individual behavior.

Suppose that a (nonempty and closed) proper subset X of the polyhedron Θ of strategy profiles has been found to be asymptotically stable in some payoff-monotonic or payoff-positive selection dynamics. In the special case where X is a singleton, we have earlier seen that the unique strategy profile (at least) has to be a Nash equilibrium (theorem 5.2). Swinkels (1993) has established a result with the implication that if X is convex, then it must contain some strategically stable subset. In the special case of a singleton $X = \{x\}$, it follows that $x \in \Theta$ has to be strictly perfect; see subsection 1.4.3.

Proposition 5.10 *Suppose that $g \in G^m \cup G^p$ and $X \subset \Theta$ is nonempty, closed, and convex. If X is asymptotically stable in (5.37), then X contains a strategically stable subset $Y \subset \Theta^{NE}$.*

Proof We here only restate Swinkels's (1993) result and verify that it applies to the present setting. The result in question (his theorem 2) concerns the class of regular selection dynamics (5.37) such that

$$\sum_{h \in S_i} u_i(e_i^h, x_{-i}) g_{ih}(x) x_{ih} \geq 0 \qquad \forall x \in \Theta, i \in I .$$

It is not difficult to show that all payoff-positive selection dynamics meet this condition. For by orthogonality (5.38) we may rewrite the left-hand side in the desired inequality as $\sum_h [u_i(e_i^h, x_{-i}) - u_i(x)] g_{ih}(x) x_{ih}$, a quantity that is nonnegative by definition of payoff positivity (5.42). Likewise, for any $x \in \Theta$ and $i \in I$, a payoff-monotonic growth-rate function g_i ranks the growth rates $\{g_{ih}(x) : h \in S_i\}$ in the same order as the corresponding payoffs $\{u_i(e_i^h, x_{-i}) : h \in S_i\}$ are ranked. For any $x \in \Theta$ and $i \in I$, let $S_i^+ \subset S_i$ be the subset of pure strategies with nonnegative growth rates, and let α_i be the lowest payoff among these. With S_i^- denoting the set of remaining pure strategies in S_i, we have

$$\sum_{h \in S_i} u_i(e_i^h, x_{-i}) g_{ih}(x) x_{ih} \geq \sum_{h \in S_i^+} \alpha_i g_{ih}(x) x_{ih} + \sum_{h \in S_i^-} \alpha_i g_{ih}(x) x_{ih}$$

$$= \alpha_i \left[g_i(x) \cdot x_i \right] = 0 .$$

Swinkels establishes that if a nonempty closed set $X \subset \Theta$ is asymptotically stable in a selection dynamics meeting the above condition, and X has a basin of attraction that contains a (relative) neighborhood U of X such that the closure of U is homeomorphic to Θ, then X contains a set $Y \subset \Theta^{NE}$ that is strategically stable in the sense of Kohlberg and Mertens (1986). (By his theorem 1, the set Y can in the present context be taken to be hyperstable in the sense of Kohlberg and Mertens 1986.) The topological condition on the basin of attraction is clearly met if X is convex. ■

It may seem surprising that asymptotic stability in evolutionary selection dynamics, which presumes no rationality whatsoever, has any connection with such a stringent noncooperative refinement as strategic stability. Intuitively this connection is possible because both criteria rely on the data of the game in a similar way; they are both robust to small strategy perturbations and depend positively on payoffs (in the sense that players strive for high payoffs). Note, however, the convexity requirement on the set X in the statement of the above result. The significance of this restriction is apparent from the earlier analysis of the Matching Pennies Game of example 5.2; for certain payoff-linear dynamics the boundary of the polyhedron Θ is asymptotically stable and yet does not contain any Nash equilibrium.

5.7   Robust Criteria for Evolutionary Dynamic Stability

In many applications only broad qualitative features concerning the selection dynamics are known or assumed. Then it is desirable that predictions, in terms of strategy profiles or sets of strategy profiles, be dynamically stable in a fairly wide class of selection dynamics. At the present stage of research in this field this robustness desideratum concerning the details of the dynamics appears mandatory. Just think of how slight modifications of imitation processes can change the dynamics from, say, the standard replicator dynamics to the adjusted replicator dynamics, as well as to other payoff-linear or payoff-monotonic selection dynamics. Such robustness clearly imposes restrictions on the stability criterion to be used. In particular, as pointed out in chapter 3, Lyapunov stability is not satisfactory. This property is structurally nonrobust in that it can be destroyed by arbitrarily small perturbations of the vector field generating the dynamics.[20] In contrast, asymptotic stability is preserved under such small perturbations, such as those due to occasional mutations, experimentations, or mistakes in small population fractions.[21] As will be shown later, robustness of predictions also imposes restrictions on the class of strategy profiles or sets of strategy profiles. In particular, it will be shown that such stringent robustness disqualifies all mixed-strategy profiles (i.e., where at least one player randomizes) and all sets of strategy profiles in the (relative) interior of any face of the polyhedron of mixed strategies.[22]

5.7.1 Evolutionary Stability

In chapter 3 it was shown that evolutionary stability of a strategy in a symmetric two-player game implies asymptotic stability in the associated single-population replicator dynamics (3.5) (proposition 3.10). The corresponding implication for the present context, namely from evolutionary stability of a strategy profile in an arbitrary (finite) n-player game to its asymptotic stability in the associated standard (5.4) and adjusted (5.5) n-population replicator dynamics, is also valid. In fact the implication holds for a very wide class of

---

20. For instance, the unique Nash equilibrium in the Matching Pennies Game was seen in example 5.2 to be Lyapunov, but not asymptotically, stable in the standard replicator dynamics (5.4). However, as can be seen from the analysis in example 5.5 of the same game in terms of payoff-linear selection dynamics, an arbitrarily small perturbation of the standard replicator vector field can turn the Nash equilibrium unstable (and an opposite perturbation can turn it asymptotically stable).

21. More precisely, for sufficiently small perturbations of the vector field in question, there will be some arbitrarily nearby asymptotically stable point or set. However, in some examples, asymptotic stability seems unnecessarily stringent for robust predictions; see, for instance, set C in example 5.10.

22. Recall (from subsection 1.1.1) that a set $X \subset \Theta$ is a *face* of Θ if it is the cartesian product of faces of the players' mixed-strategy simplexes, where a face of a simplex Δ_i is the set of all randomizations over some nonempty subset of pure strategies available to the player position.

selection dynamics. In view of the fact that evolutionary stability of a strategy profile is equivalent to it being a strict Nash equilibrium (proposition 5.1),
this is not so surprising. What may be surprising, though, is that unlike in the
single-population context, here the converse holds for a class of selection dynamics containing the standard replicator dynamics: Asymptotic stability is
equivalent with strict Nash equilibrium. We begin by establishing:

Proposition 5.11 *Every strict Nash equilibrium $x \in \Theta$ is asymptotically stable in all weakly payoff-positive selection dynamics (5.37).*

Proof   Suppose that $x \in \Theta$ is a strict Nash equilibrium. Then x is a vertex
of Θ, say, $x_i = e_i^{h_i}$ for each $i \in I$, and $u_i\left(e_i^k, x_{-i}\right) < u_i(x)$ for all $i \in I$ and
$k \neq h_i$. By continuity of u (and finiteness of the pure strategy sets) these strict
inequalities hold also for all nearby profiles. Formally x is contained in an
open set U such that

$$u_i\left(e_i^k, y_{-i}\right) < u_i(y) \qquad \forall i \in I, \ k \neq h_i, y \in U \cap \Theta.$$

Without loss of generality, U can be taken to contain no other vertex of Θ.
Thus $h_i \in C(y_i)$ for all $i \in I$ and $y \in U \cap \Theta$, and so

$$u_i\left(e_i^{h_i}, y_{-i}\right) > u_i(y) \qquad \forall i \in I, y \neq x, \ y \in U \cap \Theta.$$

Thus, for any weakly payoff-positive growth-rate function g, $g_{ih_i}(y) > 0$
for all $y \neq x$, $y \in U \cap \Theta$. Here proposition 5.5 comes in handy. Its sufficient
condition (5.40) for asymptotic stability (in any regular selection dynamics) is
clearly met in the present case:

$$\sum_{i \in I} x_i \cdot g_i(y) = \sum_{i \in I} g_{ih_i}(y) > 0 \qquad \forall y \neq x, \ y \in U \cap \Theta. \quad \blacksquare \qquad (5.47)$$

It is not difficult to establish the following partial converse to this result:
If a *pure*-strategy profile $x \in \Theta$ is not a strict Nash equilibrium, then x is not
asymptotically stable in any payoff-monotonic or payoff-positive selection dynamics (5.37) (see Samuelson and Zhang 1992). We know from theorem 5.2
that an asymptotically stable profile x is a Nash equilibrium. Suppose that
$x \in \Theta^{NE}$ is pure but not a strict Nash equilibrium. Then there is some player
i who has an alternative pure best reply $h \in S_i$. The edge of the polyhedron Θ
that connects the vertex x with the vertex $y = \left(e_i^h, x_{-i}\right)$ is invariant under any
regular selection dynamics. Along this edge the payoff to player i is constant,
and hence no movement takes place in a payoff-monotonic or payoff-positive

selection dynamics. (However, some movement may well take place in a selection dynamics that is only weakly payoff positive; see example 5.7.)

Another negative result for pointwise asymptotic stability is that no Nash equilibrium that belongs to a nonsingleton component of the set Θ^{NE} of Nash equilibria is asymptotically stable in any payoff-monotonic or payoff-positive selection dynamics. The obvious reason for this is that all Nash equilibria are stationary in such dynamics, and hence such nearby points, which exist in a nonsingleton component of Θ^{NE}, are not attracted toward the Nash equilibrium in question. This failure of (pointwise) asymptotic stability arises easily in extensive-form games. If a Nash equilibrium in such a game does not reach all information sets of the game, then some player can alter her (local) strategy at an unreached information set without affecting her own payoff, and if the game is generic in the sense that there are no payoff ties at its end nodes, such a local strategy deviation, if sufficiently small, can be made without affecting the best replies of the other players. Thus in such a game the Nash equilibrium in question belongs to a nonsingleton component of Θ^{NE} and is not asymptotically stable.

We have established:

Proposition 5.12 *Suppose that $g \in G^m \cup G^p$. If $x \in \Theta^{NE}$ is pure but not a strict equilibrium, or x belongs to a nonsingleton component of Θ^{NE}, then x is not asymptotically stable in (5.37).*

Recall that asymptotic stability in the single-population replicator dynamics (3.5) in symmetric two-player games implies perfection (proposition 3.9). In one of its two multipopulation counterparts, the standard n-population replicator dynamics (5.4), the implication of asymptotic stability is even stronger: If a profile $x \in \Theta$ is asymptotically stable in that dynamics, then $x \in \Theta^{NE}$ is strict (Hofbauer and Sigmund 1988; Ritzberger and Vogelsberger 1990). In view of proposition 5.11, we have the following striking equivalence:

Proposition 5.13 *A profile $x \in \Theta$ is asymptotically stable in the standard replicator dynamics (5.4) if and only if x is a strict Nash equilibrium.*

Proof The "if" part follows immediately from proposition 5.11, and the "only if" part follows from proposition 5.12 in conjunction with proposition 5.14 below. ∎

In view of the fact that the standard replicator dynamics appears as a first-order approximation to a range of other selection dynamics (e.g., see the discussion in subsection 4.4.2), this result, together with proposition 5.12, suggests that few population states $x \in \Theta$ are asymptotically stable in n-population selection dynamics.

5.7.2   Relatively Interior Sets

Example 5.3 shows that interior Nash equilibria do exist that are asymptotically stable in *some* payoff-linear selection dynamics. However, as shown by Hofbauer and Sigmund (1988), no such equilibrium is asymptotically stable in the benchmark case of the standard replicator dynamics (5.4). The proof of this claim uses a deep and general property of the standard replicator dynamics, namely that it induces the same solution orbits in the interior of the polyhedron Θ as a certain divergence-free vector field. Hence, since a divergence-free dynamics on an open set is volume preserving, by Liouville's formula, it has no compact asymptotically stable set (proposition 6.6). In particular, no interior population state is asymptotically stable in the standard replicator dynamics. Since this argument also applies to the *relative* interior of every face of Θ (each face being invariant in the dynamics), only pure-strategy profiles can be asymptotically stable. Consequently, if $x \in \Theta$ is asymptotically stable in the standard replicator dynamics, then x must be a strict Nash equilibrium, by proposition 5.12.

It is easily shown that the result extends to any *constant* player-specific rescaling of time in the standard replicator dynamics, and thus for first-order approximations of a wide class of evolutionary dynamics:[23]

Proposition 5.14   *If a closed set $X \subset \Theta$ belongs to the relative interior of some face of Θ, then X is not asymptotically stable in (5.48), for any scalars $\alpha_i > 0$:*

$$\dot{x}_{ih} = \alpha_i u_i(e_i^h - x_i, x_{-i}) x_{ih} \tag{5.48}$$

This result can be proved by an extension of the technique used in subsection 5.2.2 for 2×2 games; see the appendix (subsection 5.8.2) at the end of this chapter for details. Hence, if one requires predictions to be robust across a class of selection dynamics that contains any constant rescaling of time in

---

23. Ritzberger and Weibull (1993) show that the result is valid for all payoff-linear selection dynamics in which each player-specific proportionality factor $a_i(x)$ is a nondecreasing function of the associated average payoff $u_i(x)$. (Note that the adjusted replicator dynamics (5.5) does not belong to this subclass.)

the standard replicator dynamics, then one can disregard all relatively interior (closed) sets.

5.7.3   Pure-Strategy Subsets Closed under Better Replies

One class of (closed and convex) sets which are *not* relatively interior are the *faces* of Θ (see subsection 1.1.1). For any nonempty subset $H_i \subset S_i$ of player i's pure strategies, let $\Delta_i(H_i) \subset \Delta_i$ be the face of the simplex Δ_i spanned by H_i:

$$\Delta_i(H_i) = \{x_i \in \Delta_i : C(x_i) \subset H_i\} . \tag{5.49}$$

Note that $\Delta_i(H_i) = \Delta_i$ if $H_i = S_i$, and $\Delta_i(H_i) = \left\{e_i^h\right\}$ if H_i is the singleton $\{h\}$.

Likewise, for any collection of such subsets $H_i \subset S_i$ of pure strategies, one for each player position $i \in I$, let $H = \times_{i \in I} H_i \subset S$, and let $\Theta(H)$ be the face of the polyhedron Θ spanned by H:

$$\Theta(H) = \times_{i \in I} \Delta_i(H_i). \tag{5.50}$$

In particular, if $H = S$, then $\Theta(H) = \Theta$. This is the *maximal* face of Θ. At the opposite extreme end of the spectrum of faces of Θ are the *pure* strategy profiles, each of which, viewed as a singleton set, is a *minimal* face of Θ.

It turns out that all payoff-positive selection dynamics agree concerning asymptotic stability of sets $X \subset \Theta$ that are faces; a face $X \subset \Theta$ is either asymptotically stable in all such dynamics or in none. Hence the details of the dynamics are irrelevant as long as it is payoff positive. Evolutionary dynamic predictions in terms of faces are thus highly robust. More exactly, such predictions are robust to arbitrarily large perturbations of the vector field of the dynamics as long as the perturbed vector field also results in a payoff-positive selection dynamics. In contrast, perturbations that result in a (regular) selection dynamics that is not payoff positive have to be small; if the face in question is asymptotically stable in the original dynamics, then it will remain so for *all* sufficiently small perturbations. In contrast to the case in the single-population setting, asymptotic stability of a face can be *characterized* in terms of weakly better replies (Ritzberger and Weibull 1993).

In the spirit of sections 3.7 and 4.3.3 we call a pure strategy $h \in S_i$ a *weakly better reply* to a strategy profile $x \in \Delta$ if h does not give a lower payoff to its player position, against x, than x_i does. In terms of player populations, the weakly better replies are those pure strategies that do not earn below average. Formally:

Definition 5.9 *A subset of pure-strategy profiles $H = \times_{i \in I} H_i \subset S$ is closed under weakly better replies if $\alpha_i(H) \subset H_i$ for all player positions $i \in I$ where*

$$\alpha_i(H) = \{h \in S_i : u_i(e_i^h, x_{-i}) \geq u_i(x) \text{ for some } x \in \Theta(H)\}. \tag{5.51}$$

The maximal subset $H = S$ clearly meets this condition, since, by definition, there is no pure strategy profile outside S. Also a singleton set $H = \{s\}$ is closed under weakly better replies if and only if each pure strategy s_i is the unique *best* reply to $s \in S$, that is, if and only if the profile s constitutes a strict Nash equilibrium. In this sense closure under weakly better replies is a setwise generalization of strict Nash equilibrium.

Moreover a necessary condition for a set $H = \times H_i$ to be closed under weakly better replies is that it be closed under *best* replies. The latter property is that $\beta_i(x) \subset H_i$ for all strategy profiles $x \in \Theta(H)$ and player positions $i \in I$ (see Basu and Weibull 1991 for an analysis of such sets).

The following result (Ritzberger and Weibull 1993) generalizes the earlier observation that in any payoff-positive selection dynamics, asymptotic stability of a pure-strategy profile is equivalent with it being a strict Nash equilibrium (propositions 5.11 and 5.12):[24]

Theorem 5.3 *Suppose that $g \in G^p$. A face $\Delta(H) \subset \Theta$ is asymptotically stable in the associated selection dynamics (5.37) if and only if $H = \times_{i \in I} H_i \subset S$ is closed under weakly better replies.*

To prove this, we proceed just as in the single-population setting (sections 3.7 and 4.3.3) by first establishing that if a subset $H = \times_{i \in I} H_i$ of pure strategy profiles is closed under weakly better replies, then H also contains the weakly better replies to all population states *near* the face it spans:

Lemma 5.1 *If $H = \times_{i \in I} H_i \subset S$ is closed under weakly better replies, then $\Delta(H) \subset U$ for some open set U such that*

$$\left[y \in U \cap \Theta \text{ and } u_i(e_i^h, y_{-i}) \geq u_i(y) \right] \Rightarrow [h \in H_i]. \tag{5.52}$$

---

24. Ritzberger and Weibull establish this for a somewhat larger class of regular growth-rate functions g, namely those that assign negative growth rates to pure strategies that earn below average.

Proof   Suppose that $H = \times_{i \in I} H_i \subset S$ is closed under weakly better replies. Thus, if, for some $i \in I$, $h \notin H_i$, then $u_i(e_i^h, x_{-i}) < u_i(x)$ for all $x \in \Delta(H)$. By continuity of u_i and compactness of $\Delta(H)$, there is an open set U_{ih} such that $\Delta(H) \subset U_{ih}$ and $u_i(e_i^h, y_{-i}) < u_i(y)$ for all $y \in U_{ih} \cap \Delta$. Let $U_i = \cap_{h \notin H_i} U_{ih}$. Doing likewise for all player positions $i \in I$, and taking the finite intersection $U = \cap_{i \in I} U_i$ of open sets containing $\Delta(H)$, one obtains an open set U that contains $\Delta(H)$ and meets condition (5.52). (The case $H = S$ is trivial.) ∎

The first part of the following proof is essentially the same as in the single-population setting (proposition 4.10b). The second part, establishing that closure under weakly better replies is necessary for asymptotic stability, is unique to the present setting. Indeed in example 3.15 it was shown that this claim is false in the single-population replicator dynamics.

Proof of Theorem 5.3   Suppose that $g \in G^p$. First, assume that $H = \times_{i \in I} H_i \subset S$ is closed under weakly better replies. Let U be as in the lemma. There then is some $\bar{\varepsilon} > 0$ such that for any $\varepsilon \in (0, \bar{\varepsilon})$ and each player position $i \in I$, the ε-slice,

$$B_i(\varepsilon) = \{x_i \in \Delta_i : x_{ih} < \varepsilon \ \forall h \notin H_i\} \, ,$$

contains the corresponding face $\Delta_i(H_i)$ and $B(\varepsilon) = \times_{i \in I} B_i(\varepsilon)$ is contained in U. By payoff positivity, $g_{ih}(x) < 0$ for all profiles $x \in U \cap \Theta$, player positions $i \in I$, and pure strategies $h \notin H_i$. By continuity of the growth rate functions g_i, we may assume that for any $x \in B(\varepsilon) \cap \Theta$, $i \in I$ and $h \notin H_i$, $g_{ih}(x) < -\delta$ for some $\delta > 0$. Hence $\dot{x}_{ih} = g_{ih}(x)x_{ih} < -\delta x_{ih}$ for any such x, i, and h, and this implies that $\xi_{ih}(t, x^o)$ decreases monotonically to zero from any initial state x^o in $B(\varepsilon) \cap \Theta$. Thus $\Theta(H)$ is asymptotically stable.

Second, assume that $H = \times_{i \in I} H_i \subset S$ is *not* closed under weakly better replies. There then exists some pure-strategy profile $s \in H$, player position $i \in I$ and pure strategy $k \notin H_i$ such that $u_i(e_i^k, s_{-i}) \geq u_i(s)$. If this were not the case, then we would have $u_i(e_i^h, s_{-i}) - u_i(s) < 0$ for all $s \in H$, $i \in I$, and $h \notin H_i$. Consequently we would have $u_i(e_i^h, x_{-i}) - u_i(x) < 0$ for all $x \in \Theta(H)$, $i \in I$, and $h \notin H_i$, implying that H would be closed under weakly better replies. Now consider the one-dimensional face E of Θ spanned by the two pure-strategy profiles $s \in H$ and $s^* = (e_i^k, s_{-i}) \notin H$. Being a face, E is invariant in any regular selection dynamics (5.37). Moreover, since $u_i(s^*) \geq u_i(s)$ and u_i is linear in x_i, we have $u_i(e_i^k, x_{-i}) \geq u_i(x)$ for all $x \in E$, and thus $\dot{x}_{ik} = g_{ik}(x)x_{ik} \geq 0$ for all such x, by payoff positivity. Hence for no $x^o \in$

$E \cap \sim \Theta(H)$ do we have $\xi_i(t, x^o) \to \Delta_i(H_i)$. Since the two faces E and $\Theta(H)$ intersect at the vertex s of Θ, this implies that $\Theta(H)$ is not asymptotically stable. ∎

Lemma 5.1 also has an important implication for the connection between evolutionary and noncooperative criteria: If a subset $H = \times H_i$ of pure-strategy profiles is closed under weakly better replies, then the associated face $\Theta(H)$ of the polyhedron of mixed-strategy profiles contains an essential component of Nash equilibria (see subsection 1.4.5). In view of theorem 5.3 this means that robust evolutionary dynamic stability of a face $\Theta(H)$ implies that the face contains a closed and connnected set of Nash equilibria that is robust to payoff perturbations of the game. This follows from a more general result in Ritzberger and Weibull (1993):

Proposition 5.15   *If a (nonempty) set of pure strategy profiles $H = \times_{i \in I} H_i \subset S$ is closed under weakly better replies, then $\Theta(H)$ contains an essential component of the set Θ^{NE}.*

The concept of a long-run survivor set, in the context of single-population dynamics in a symmetric two-player game (sections 3.7 and 4.3.3) can be readily extended to the present n-population setting for n-player games. Let a regular selection dynamics (5.37) be given:

Definition 5.10   *A (nonempty) set of pure-strategy profiles $H = \times_{i \in I} H_i \subset S$ is a* long-run survivor set *if $\Theta(H)$ is asymptotically stable and does not properly contain a (nonempty) subset $K = \times_{i \in I} K_i$ for which $\Theta(K)$ is asymptotically stable.*

Since the number of pure strategy profiles is finite in the class of games considered, existence of at least one long-run survivor set is guaranteed. By theorem 5.3 all payoff-positive selection dynamics have the same collection of long-run survivor sets, in any given game, and each such set is minimal with respect to the property of being closed under weak better replies. Moreover, if a set is minimal in this sense, then it is *fixed* under weak best replies (Ritzberger and Weibull 1993). Formally:

Definition 5.11   *A (nonempty) set of pure-strategy profiles $H = \times_{i \in I} H_i \subset S$ is* fixed under weakly better replies *if $\alpha_i(H) = H_i$ for all player positions $i \in I$.*

A (nonempty) set $H = \times_{i \in I} H_i \subset S$ is a *minimal* fixed set under weakly better replies if it contains no proper (nonempty) subset $K = \times_{i \in I} K_i$ that is fixed under weakly better replies. In this terminology theorem 5.3 has the following implication:

Corollary 5.3.1 *If a set $H = \times_{i \in I} H_i \subset S$ is a minimal fixed set under weakly better replies, then H is a long-run survivor set in all payoff-positive selection dynamics. Conversely, if $H = \times_{i \in I} H_i \subset S$ is a long-run survivor set in some payoff-positive selection dynamics, then H is a minimal fixed set under weakly better replies.*

Proof   It only remains to prove that if a set $H = \times_{i \in I} H_i \subset S$ is minimal with respect to the property of being closed under weakly better replies, then it is fixed under weakly better replies. Suppose that $H = \times_{i \in I} H_i \subset S$ is closed but not fixed under weakly better replies. Then there is some player position $i \in I$ and pure strategy $h \in H_i$ such that $u_i(e_i^h, x_{-i}) < u_i(x)$ for all $x \in \Theta(H)$. But then also $K = \times_{j \in I} K_j$, where $K_i = \{k \in H_i : k \neq h\}$ and $K_j = H_j$ for all $j \neq i$, is closed under weakly better replies, so H is not minimal with respect to this property. ∎

The following two examples show how these criteria can be used to identify long-run survivor sets in the Outside Option Game of example 5.8 and the Beer-Quiche Game of example 5.1.

Example 5.9   Reconsider the Outside Option Game of example 5.8. Inspection of the payoff matrices show that the game has (only) two sets that are closed under weakly better replies, $H = S$ and $K = \{1\} \times \{1\}$. Only K is fixed under weakly better replies, so this is the only long-run survivor set. This finding, based only on the data of the game, conforms with the findings in example 5.8 based on the standard replicator dynamics. (Note that the set K corresponds to the Nash equilibrium component D, in the notation of example 5.8, which consists of the game's unique strict Nash equilibrium.)

Example 5.10   Reconsider the Beer-Quiche Game of example 5.1. Inspection of the payoff matrices shows that the game has (only) two sets which are closed under weakly better replies, $H = S$ and $K = \{1, 2\} \times \{1, 2\}$. Of these only K is fixed under weakly better replies, so this is the unique long-run survivor set, in any payoff-positive selection dynamics. This is the set where player 1 either always sends the strong signal or always sends the true signal,

and player 2 either retreats only when seeing the strong signal or always retreats. The corresponding face $\Theta(K)$ contains the intuitive Nash equilibrium
component C.

Note that $\Theta(K)$ is two-dimensional and contains the one-dimensional face
$\Theta(L)$, where $L = \{1\} \times \{1, 2\}$ and $C \subset \Theta(L)$. However, L is not closed under
weakly better replies. In fact, there is nothing to stop drift in population 2
toward always retreat, and once this pure strategy is used by more than half
of population 2, player 1's pure strategy 2 is a better reply for her than her
equilibrium pure strategy 1. But once population 1 starts to drift toward its
pure strategy 2, the second player's pure strategy 1 becomes a better reply
than his pure strategy 1, and so on. There thus seems to be a possibility for
evolutionary drift inside the whole face $\Theta(K)$.[25] See figure 5.8 for computer
simulations of solution curves in the face.

In example 3.15 it was shown that, in the single-population replicator dynamics (3.5) a subset of pure strategies in a (doubly) symmetric two-player
game may be asymptotically stable without being closed under weakly better
replies, as defined in the single-population context. How can this be reconciled with theorem 5.3? The following example reconsiders the game in example 3.15 in terms of the present multipopulation approach.

Example 5.11   The payoff matrix of the game in example 3.15 is

$$A = \begin{pmatrix} 2 & 0 & 1 \\ 0 & 2 & 1 \\ 1 & 1 & 0 \end{pmatrix} .$$

Hence $B = A$, and the first two pure strategies for each player together constitute a coordination game. In the present two-population setup, let $x \in \Delta$ denote the first population's state and $y \in \Delta$ that of the second population, where
Δ is the unit simplex in R^3. The subset of pure-strategy profiles $H = \{1, 2\} \times$
$\{1, 2\} \subset S$ is not closed under weakly better replies. For instance (as noted already in example 3.15), when $x = y = (\frac{1}{2}, \frac{1}{2}, 0)$, we have $(x, y) \in \Theta(H)$, and
yet $u_i(x) = 1 = u_i(e_i^3, x_{-i})$ for $i = 1, 2$. More strikingly perhaps, for $x' = e_1^1$
and $y' = e_2^2$, we have $u_1(x', y') = 0 < 1 = u_1(e_1^3, y')$. Accordingly $\Theta(H)$ is
not asymptotically stable in any payoff-positive two-population selection dynamics, a fact that also can be deduced from precisely the last observation:

---

25. For discussions of "evolutionary drift," see Gale, Binmore, and Samuelson (1993) or Binmore
and Samuelson (1994).

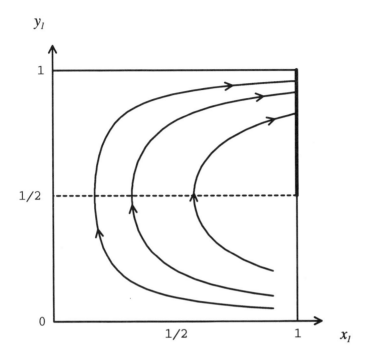

Figure 5.8
Solution orbits to the standard two-population replicator dynamics on the face $\Theta(K)$ of the polyhedron Θ in the Beer-Quiche Game of examples 5.1 and 5.10.

Along the edge of Θ which connects the vertex (x', y') with the vertex (e_1^3, y'), any payoff-positive dynamics moves the population state *away* from the face $\Theta(H)$. Suppose that $y_3 = 0$. The associated boundary face of Θ looks as in figure 5.9, where $\Theta(H)$ is the sloping square (sub-)face. The arrows along the edges indicate the direction of movement in any payoff-positive dynamics. In contrast, the asymptotically stable face of Δ, in the single-population setting of example 3.15, corresponds to the dotted diagonal line D in figure 5.9.

5.8   Appendix

5.8.1   Aggregate Monotonicity

The following payoff-monotonicity criterion was introduced by Samuelson and Zhang (1992):

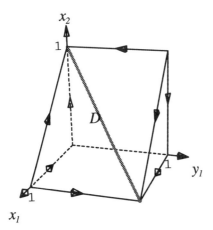

Figure 5.9
The boundary face $y_3 = 0$ of the polyhedron Θ in the game of examples 3.15 and 5.11.

Definition 5.12 $g \in G$ *is* aggregate monotonic *if, for all population states* $x \in \Theta$, *player populations* $i \in I$, *and mixed strategies* $y_i, z_i \in \Delta_i$:

$$u_i(y_i, x_{-i}) > u_i(z_i, x_{-i}) \Leftrightarrow g_i(x) \cdot y_i > g_i(x) \cdot z_i. \tag{5.53}$$

This criterion is more stringent than payoff monotonicity, since an application of (5.53) to pure strategies $y_i = e_i^h$ and $z_i = e_i^k$ is identical with condition (5.41).

Note that if the payoff to a mixed strategy y_i is above the current average payoff in player population i, then the growth vector $g_i(x)$ is required to make an acute angle with y_i. To see this, let $z_i = x_i$, and apply (5.53):

$$u_i(y_i, x_{-i}) > u_i(x) \Rightarrow g_i(x) \cdot y_i > g_i(x) \cdot x_i = 0, \tag{5.54}$$

where the equality follows by orthogonality (5.38). In particular, this equality holds for all vertices $y_i = e_i^h \in \Delta_i$, that is, pure strategies $h \in S_i$, showing that every aggregate monotonic dynamics is also payoff positive.[26] Conversely, every payoff-linear growth rate is clearly aggregate monotonic, since then

$$g_i(x) \cdot y_i = a_i(x) \sum_h \left[u_i(e_i^h, x_{-i}) - u_i(x) \right] y_{ih} = a_i(x)[u_i(y_i, x_{-i}) - u_i(x)],$$

and likewise for $g_i(x) \cdot z_i$.

---

26. The validity of equation (5.42) in the other two cases ($=$ and $<$) follows by similar arguments.

The following representation result is due to Samuelson and Zhang (1992):

Proposition 5.16 *If $g \in G$ is aggregate monotonic, then there exists a positive function $a_i : \Theta \to R$ for each player population $i \in I$ such that, for all $x \in \Theta$ and $h \in S_i$,*

$$g_{ih}(x) = a_i(x) \left[u_i(e_i^h, x_{-i}) - u_i(x) \right]. \tag{5.55}$$

Thus aggregate monotonicity implies a property just slightly weaker than payoff linear; the result does not state that the player-specific time-rescaling functions a_i can be taken to be Lipschitz continuous.

This result can be proved along the following lines: Suppose that $g \in G$ is aggregate monotonic, and consider a point $x_i \in \text{int}(\Delta_i)$ at which $g_i(x) \neq 0$ (the claim is trivial if $g_i(x) = 0$). For $\varepsilon > 0$ sufficiently small, Δ_i contains a circle C with center x_i and radius $\varepsilon > 0$. On this circle the inner product $g_i(x) \cdot y_i$ is maximized at precisely one point $\hat{y}_i$. On the same circle $u_i(y_i, x_{-i})$ also is maximized at precisely one point; we denote it $\tilde{y}_i$. (Uniqueness follows again from $g_i(x) \neq 0$, now via (5.53).) However, aggregate monotonicity implies that $g_i(x) \cdot y_i$ and $u_i(y_i, x_{-i})$ are maximized at the same point on C, that is, $\tilde{y}_i = \hat{y}_i$. Using standard Lagrangian techniques to characterize $\tilde{y}_i$ and $\hat{y}_i$, respectively, this results in the multiplier representation (5.55).

5.8.2 Proof of Proposition 5.14

First, we reformulate the dynamics (5.48) so that its orbits move in a full-dimensional subset of a euclidean space. In such a space any neighborhood of the set in question has positive volume, and hence Liouville's formula can be used (an approach developed in Ritzberger and Vogelsberger 1990).

This reformulation can be done in several ways. Here we write $x_{i1} = 1 - \sum_{h>1} x_{ih}$ for each player population $i \in I$, and represent each population state $x \in \Theta$ by vectors $(x_{i2}, x_{i3}, \ldots, x_{im_i}) \in R^{m_i - 1}$, one for each player position $i \in I$. The vector field φ in (5.48) can then be written, for each $i \in I$ and pure strategy $h \in S_i$ with $h > 1$,

$$\varphi_{ih}(x) = \alpha_i \left[u(e_i^h, x_{-i}) - (1 - \sum_{k>1} x_{ik}) u_i(e_h^1, x_{-i}) - \sum_{k>1} x_{ik} u(e_i^k, x_{-i}) \right] x_{ih}$$

We now divide every component $\varphi_{ih}(x)$ by the product

$$p(x) = \prod_{i \in I} \prod_{h \in S_i} x_{ih} = \left(\prod_{j \neq i} \prod_{k \in S_i} x_{jk} \right) \left(1 - \sum_{l>1} x_{il} \right) \prod_{l>1} x_{il}$$

of all population shares. On $\mathrm{int}(\Theta)$, these shares are all positive, so the new vector field $\psi_{ih}(x) = \varphi_{ih}(x)/p(x)$ is well-defined for all $x \in \mathrm{int}(\Theta)$. Since all components of φ have been multiplied by the same positive factor, no solution orbit of (5.48) in $\mathrm{int}(\Theta)$ is affected by this transformation. What remains is to compute $\mathrm{div}\left[\psi(x)\right] = \sum_{i \in I} \sum_{h>1} \partial \psi_{ih}(x)/\partial x_{ih}$ at any point $x \in \mathrm{int}(\Theta)$. For this purpose, we rewrite each $\psi_{ih}(x)$, for any $i \in I$ and $h \in S_i$ with $h > 1$, as

$$\psi_{ih}(x) = b_{ih}(x) \left[\frac{u_i(e_i^h, x_{-i}) - \sum_{k>1} x_{ik} u_i(e_i^k, x_{-i})}{\left(1 - \sum_{l>1} x_{il}\right)} - u_i(e_i^1, x_{-i}) \right],$$

where $b_{ih}(x) = \alpha_i \left[\left(\prod_{j \neq i} \prod_{k \in S_i} x_{jk} \right) \prod_{l>1, l \neq h} x_{il} \right]^{-1}$. We obtain

$$\frac{\partial \psi_{ih}(x)}{\partial x_{ih}} = \frac{\alpha_i}{p(x)} \left[u_i(e_i^h, x_{-i}) - \frac{u_i(x) - u_i(e_i^1, x_{-i}) x_{i1}}{1 - x_{i1}} \right] \left(\frac{1 - x_{i1}}{x_{i1}} \right) x_{ih}.$$

Hence

$$\sum_{h>1} \frac{\partial \psi_{ih}(x)}{\partial x_{ih}} = \frac{\alpha_i}{p(x)} \left[u_i(x) - u_i(e_i^1, x_{-i}) x_{i1} \right.$$

$$\left. - \frac{u_i(x) - u_i(e_i^1, x_{-i}) x_{i1}}{1 - x_{i1}} (1 - x_{i1}) \right] \left(\frac{1 - x_{i1}}{x_{i1}} \right).$$

The expression in square brackets is equal to zero, so the rescaled vector field ψ is indeed divergence free at all interior states x. ∎

6 Elements of the Theory of Ordinary Differential Equations

To write down a system of ordinary differential equations (ODEs) is a classical way to represent mathematically a deterministic dynamic process in continuous time. This approach is also used in evolutionary game theory, where the dynamic process in question concerns the change over time in the distribution of behaviors (strategies) in a large population of interacting individuals. In the standard setting the interaction takes the form of random matchings of pairs of individuals from a single large population, where the interaction is modeled as a symmetric two-player game in normal form. This approach is taken in chapters 3 and 4. An alternative setting for explicit dynamic analysis along these lines considers random matchings of n-tuples of individuals from n large populations, each population representing a player role in an n-player game in normal form (the topic of chapter 5).

The first question in such dynamic models is whether the system of ordinary differential equations uniquely determines how the state (i.e., in the present case the population distribution of strategies) evolves over time. Given that this question has been answered in the affirmative, one may ask whether the state (strategy distribution) converges over time toward some limit state, and if so, what properties such a limit state has. One may also ask whether a given state is stable in the given dynamics, where a few distinct criteria for stability may be relevant that ask for some robustness property with respect to perturbations of the state in question. The present chapter introduces some of the mathematical machinery for such dynamic analyses, focusing on the concepts and techniques used in chapters 3 through 5.

Section 6.1 examines whether a system of ODEs uniquely determines the dynamic evolution of the state vector in question, the central result being the classical so-called Picard-Lindelöf theorem. Section 6.2 moves the focus from the system of ODEs to the solution mapping that it induces. Much of the relevant qualitative analysis of solutions to ODEs actually depends only on three general properties that such solutions have. In fact some of the modern and abstract dynamic systems literature takes these three conditions as *axioms* (e.g., see Bhatia and Szegö 1970), and we follow this route. Section 6.3 explains and studies the concepts of invariance and stationarity in this light, section 6.4 provides definitions and basic results for different notions of stability, and section 6.5 gives a short account of the so-called direct Lyapunov method. Section 6.6 concludes with a brief presentation of the so-called Liouville formula, a result used in physics that turns out to be useful also in certain multipopulation evolutionary selection dynamics (analyzed in chapter 5).

An excellent introduction to the basic theory of ordinary differential equations is given in Hirsch and Smale (1974). For a more technical and far-reaching treatment, Hale (1969) is recommended, and for a more abstract and general approach, the beautiful book by Bhatia and Szegö (1970). Many of the examples in this chapter have been borrowed from the latter source.

6.1   Differential Equations and Vector Fields

In general, the differential equations may themselves change with (calendar) time, examples being the dependency of biological and economic growth processes on such external but time-varying factors as weather. A system of differential equations that does not depend on time is called *autonomous* (or time homogeneous). In this book we will focus exclusively on such dynamics. Hence the external environment in which the studied evolutionary selection processes take place is presumed to be fixed and constant over time.[1] Moreover we will only consider *first-order* differential equations, namely differential equations that contain first-order derivatives but no derivatives of higher order.[2] All derivatives will be derivatives with respect to time (and not with respect to some state variable) so the differential equations are *ordinary* (as opposed to *partial*).

In sum, we focus on systems of *autonomous, first-order, ordinary differential equations*. Using dots for time derivatives, such a system of k equations will be written in vector form as

$$\dot{x} = \varphi(x), \tag{6.1}$$

where

$$\dot{x} = (\dot{x}_1, \ldots, \dot{x}_k) = \frac{dx}{dt} = \left(\frac{dx_1}{dt}, \ldots, \frac{dx_k}{dt} \right), \tag{6.2}$$

and φ is a mapping from an open set $X \subset R^k$ to R^k. Here $x = (x_1, \ldots, x_k) \in X$ is the *state vector*, X is the *state space*, and the right-hand side of (6.1)

---

1. By introducing such time-varying external factors as state variables, with associated differential equations for their time dependence, we can transform a time-dependent system of ODEs into an autonomous system.

2. Again this is no real restriction, since, by introducing first-order derivatives as state variables, any second-order differential equation can be turned into a first-order equation, and so on (e.g., see Hirsch and Smale 1974).

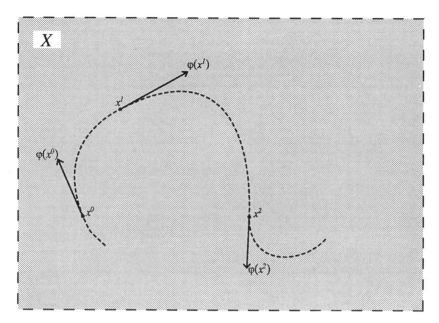

Figure 6.1
Geometric connection between a vector field and solution orbits.

specifies the *direction and velocity of change* of the state, at each point x in the *state space* X. The function φ is called a *vector field*, defining at each point x the direction and velocity of the flow at x. For each component x_i of the state x, $\varphi_i(x) \in R$ is its time derivative; see figure 6.1 for an illustration of a vector field in R^2.

The first issue that arises, once a system of differential equations (6.1) has been written down, is whether it has, in some precise sense, a *solution* (see the dotted curve in figure 6.1), and if so, whether the solution is unique. Moreover there is the question of whether the solution is *global* in the sense of defining the state at *all* (past and future) times. Formally:

Definition 6.1 *A (local) solution through a point $x^o \in X$ to a system (6.1) is a function $\xi(\cdot, x^o) : T \to X$, where T is an open interval containing $t = 0$, such that $\xi(0, x^o) = x^o$, and such that (6.3) below holds for all $t \in T$. The solution is* global *if $T = R$.*

$$\frac{d}{dt}\xi(t, x^o) = \varphi\left[\xi(t, x^o)\right]. \tag{6.3}$$

It turns out that the existence and uniqueness of a (local) solution is guaranteed for all vector fields φ that are sufficiently smooth in a precise sense. The condition, called *Lipschitz continuity*, is somewhat more stringent than continuity. Recall that both the states $x \in X$ and the associated values $\varphi(x)$ of the vector field are points in the same euclidean space R^k. Hence the difference in strength and direction of the vector field φ may be meaningfully measured at any two points $x, y \in X$ by the same euclidean metric as used when measuring distance in $X \subset R^k$. Lipschitz continuity essentially requires that there exist some constant $\lambda \in R$ such that the difference in strength and direction of φ at any two states $x, y \in X$ be less than the λ-fold distance between the states x and y. More precisely, and in a slightly weaker, local, version:

Definition 6.2 *A function $\varphi : X \to R^k$, where $X \subset R^k$, is (locally)* Lipschitz continuous *if for every compact subset $C \subset X$ there exists some real number λ such that (6.4) holds for all $x, y \in C$:*

$$\|\varphi(x) - \varphi(y)\| \leq \lambda \|x - y\| . \tag{6.4}$$

In this book the studied vector fields will always meet this continuity condition.

It is not difficult to show that if the vector field φ has continuous first partial derivatives, then it is Lipschitz continuous. Clearly, if φ is Lipschitz continuous, then it is indeed continuous.

Example 6.1 The continuously differentiable function $\varphi : R \to R$ defined by $\varphi(x) = x^2$ is Lipschitz continuous, and so is the continuous but not (everywhere) differentiable function $\varphi(x) = |x|$. In contrast, the continuous but not (everywhere) differentiable function $\varphi : R \to R$, defined by $\varphi(x) = 0$ for $x < 0$ and $\varphi(x) = \sqrt{x}$ for $x \geq 0$, is not Lipschitz continuous. Its right-hand slope at $x = 0$ is $+\infty$, and hence no $\lambda \in R$ can be found that meets (6.4) for all y near $x = 0$.

The claimed implication for the uniqueness and existence of a (local) solution to a system (6.1) is a classical result, called the *Picard-Lindelöf theorem:*[3]

---

3. We have here included the continuity of the solution mapping. This is usually stated and proved as a separate result.

Theorem 6.1 *If $X \subset R^k$ is open and the vector field $\varphi : X \to R^k$ Lipschitz continuous, then the system (6.1) has a unique solution $\xi(\cdot, x^o) : T \to X$ through every state $x^o \in X$. Moreover $\xi(t, x^o)$ is continuous in $t \in T$ and $x^o \in X$.*

(For a proof, see Hirsch and Smale 1974 or Hale 1969.)

It is well-known that if φ meets the slightly more stringent condition of having continuous first partial derivatives, then $\xi(t, x^o)$ is continuously differentiable in t and x^o (e.g., see theorem 6.3 in chapter 1 of Hale 1969). The following example shows that an ordinary differential equation may have multiple solutions if the vector field is not Lipschitz continuous.

Example 6.2 Consider the (not Lipschitz continuous) function $\varphi : R \to R$ defined by $\varphi(x) = 0$ for $x < 0$ and $\varphi(x) = \sqrt{x}$ for $x \geq 0$. One (global) solution through the initial state $x^o = 0$ is the function $\xi(\cdot, x^o) : T \to X$, defined by $\xi(t, x^o) = 0$ for all $t \in R$. Another (global) solution through the same initial state is the function $\eta(\cdot, x^o) : T \to X$, defined by $\eta(t, x^o) = 0$ for all $t < 0$ and $\eta(t, x^o) = t^2/4$ for all $t \geq 0$. See figure 6.2.

The next example shows that even if the vector field is Lipschitz continuous, equation (6.1) may have a (local) solution (i.e., with $T \neq R$) that explodes in finite time.

Example 6.3 Consider the Lipschitz continuous function $\varphi : R \to R$ defined by $\varphi(x) = x^2$, and let the initial state (at time $t = 0$) be $x^o = 1$. The function $\xi(\cdot, x^o) : T \to X$, defined by $\xi(t, x^o) = 1/(1 - t)$ for all $t < 1$ is a solution to the associated differential equation (6.1) through $x^o = 1$. Note that the solution is not global; it is defined only on the interval $T = (-\infty, 1)$, and $\xi(t, x^o) \to +\infty$ as $t \to 1$. See figure 6.3.

Example 6.4 Consider the system of linear differential equations

$$\dot{x}_1 = \varphi_1(x) = \alpha x_1 - x_2,$$

$$\dot{x}_2 = \varphi_2(x) = x_1 + \alpha x_2,$$

where $\alpha \in R$. Since any linear function is Lipschitz continuous, this system has a unique solution through every point $x^o = (x_1^o, x_2^o) \in R^2$. Using techniques from linear algebra (based on eigenvalues and eigenvectors, e.g., see Hirsch and Smale 1974), one can show that the solution $\xi(\cdot, x^o)$ is given by the pair of equations

(a)

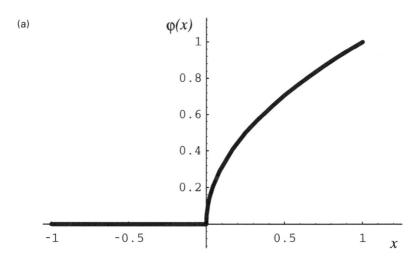

(b)

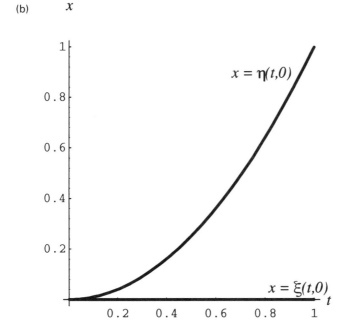

Figure 6.2
(a) The vector field in example 6.2. (b) Two solution trajectories to the differential equation in the same example.

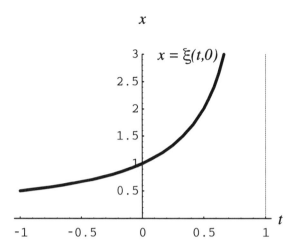

Figure 6.3
A solution trajectory that "explodes" in finite time in example 6.3.

$$\xi_1(t, x^o) = \left[x_1^o \cos t - x_2^o \sin t\right] e^{\alpha t},$$

$$\xi_2(t, x^o) = \left[x_1^o \sin t + x_2^o \cos t\right] e^{\alpha t}.$$

The vector field $\varphi : R^2 \to R^2$ is indicated in figure 6.4. Two associated solutions, one for $\alpha > 0$ and one for $\alpha < 0$ are indicated in figure 6.5 (a) and (b). Expressed in polar coordinates (r, θ), the dynamics is simply $\dot{r} = \alpha r$ and $\dot{\theta} = 1$, where r is the distance from the origin, and θ the angle with the x_1-axis, measured counterclockwise in radians. From these polar-coordinate differential equations, we see that all solutions swirl counterclockwise around the origin, $\dot{\theta} > 0$, moving outward ($\dot{r} > 0$) when α is positive, staying on circles when α is zero ($\dot{r} = 0$), and moving inward ($\dot{r} < 0$) when α is negative. (Note that $r = \|x\|$, $\theta = \arctan(y/x)$, or conversely, that $x = r \cos \theta$ and $y = r \sin \theta$.)

Example 6.5   Consider the pair of nonlinear differential equations

$$\dot{x}_1 = \varphi_1(x) = x_1 - \|x\|(x_1 + x_2),$$

$$\dot{x}_2 = \varphi_2(x) = x_2 + \|x\|(x_1 - x_2).$$

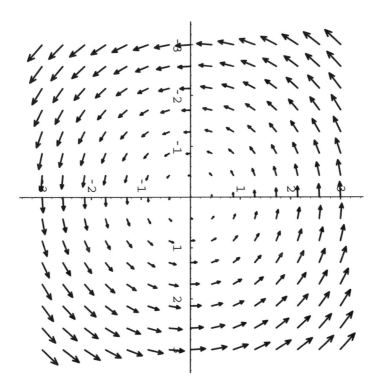

Figure 6.4
The vector field in example 6.4.

This vector field φ is clearly Lipschitz continuous, so this system also has a unique solution through every point $x^o = (x_1^o, x_2^o) \in R^2$. The vector field is indicated in figure 6.6 (a), and two solution curves are indicated in figure 6.6 (b). Expressed in polar coordinates (r, θ), the dynamics is $\dot{r} = r(1 - r)$ and $\dot{\theta} = r$. From these equations we see that solutions indeed swirl counterclockwise around the origin toward the unit circle where $r = \|x\| = 1$.

6.2   The Induced Solution Mapping

In all applications in the preceding chapters, all *relevant* states belong to some compact subset C of the domain X of the vector field φ. More exactly, we always have $x^o \in C$ and $\xi(t, x^o) \in C$ for all $t \in T(x^o)$, where $T(x^o) \subset R$ is the open time interval on which the solution through x^o is defined. Usually

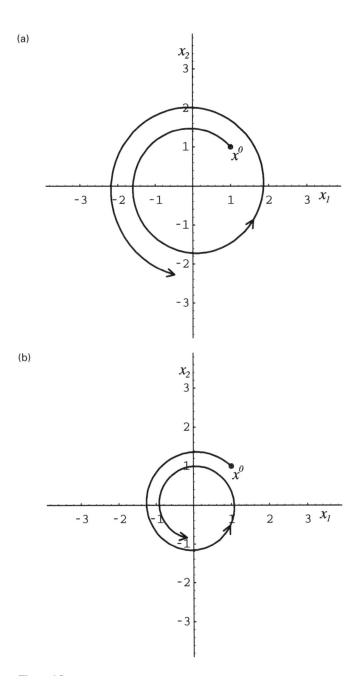

Figure 6.5
Solution orbits to the dynamics in example 6.4: (a) When $\alpha > 0$, (b) when $\alpha < 0$.

(a)

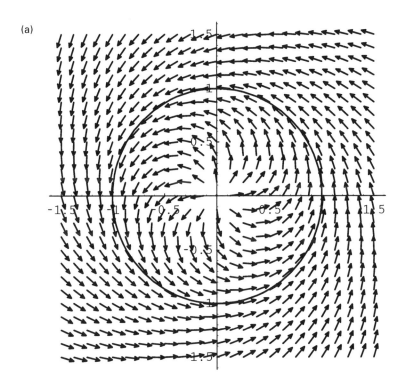

$X = R^k$, and C is either a simplex Δ of mixed strategies for a player or C is the polyhedron Θ of mixed-strategy profiles in the game in question. In such a setting one could show that the solution through any point $x^o \in C$ is global (e.g., see theorem 2.1 in chapter 1 of Hale 1969). In fact we have the following important result:

Proposition 6.1 *Suppose that $X \subset R^k$ is open, that $\varphi : X \to R^k$ is Lipschitz continuous, and that C is a compact subset of X such that $\xi(t, x^o) \in C$ for all $x^o \in C$ and $t \in T(x^o)$. Then $T(x^o)$ can be taken to be R, and the induced solution mapping $\xi : R \times C \to C$ will meet the three conditions*

$$\xi(0, x) = x \qquad \forall x \in C ,\tag{6.5}$$

$$\xi\left[t, \xi(s, x)\right] = \xi(t + s, x) \qquad \forall x \in C, \forall s, t \in R ,\tag{6.6}$$

$$\xi \text{ is continuous} .\tag{6.7}$$

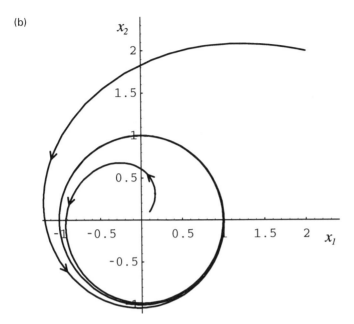

Figure 6.6
(a) The vector field in example 6.5. (b) Two solution orbits to the associated differential equations.

The first condition says that the state after $t = 0$ time units is identical with the initial state. The second condition says that the state after $t + s$ time units is identical with the state obtained by first following the solution through the initial state for s time units, arriving at the state $y = \xi(s, x)$, and then following the solution through the initial state y for another t units. The third condition says that solutions are continuous functions over time, as well as with respect to the initial state. The latter property simply means that when observed at any fixed time $t \in R$, the solution trajectory through any initial state y^o near x^o is near to the solution trajectory through x^o. Since in practice it may be difficult (or perhaps even impossible) to obtain precise information about the exact initial state, this property is clearly a desirable robustness property.

Just as a triplet $G = (I, S, \pi)$ formally defines a normal-form game, a triplet $D = (R, C, \xi)$ defines a *dynamic system* on the (compact) *state-space* $C \subset X$ over *continuous time* $t \in R$, with *solution mapping* ξ meeting the three conditions (6.5), (6.6), and (6.7).[4] From now on we will require the studied systems of ordinary differential equations to induce such a dynamic system D.

When studying such dynamic systems, the concepts of *trajectory, orbit, invariance, stationarity*, and *stability* are of central importance. The (solution) *trajectory* (or *path*) through a state $x^o \in C$ is the *graph* of the solution $\xi(\cdot, x^o)$. Formally, it is the following subset of time-state pairs:

$$\tau(x^o) = \{(t, x) \in R \times C : x = \xi(t, x^o)\} . \tag{6.8}$$

In other words, the trajectory $\tau(x^o)$ contains all the data of how the state evolves over time. In contrast, the *orbit* through a point tells *which* states are reached but not *when*. Formally, the orbit $\gamma(x^o)$ through an initial state x^o is the image of the whole time axis under the solution mapping $\xi(\cdot, x^o)$:

$$\gamma(x^o) = \{x \in C : x = \xi(t, x^o) \text{ for some } t \in R\} . \tag{6.9}$$

Equivalently one may think of $\gamma(x^o)$ as the projection of the trajectory $\tau(x^o)$ to the state-space C. For any subset $A \subset C$, one writes $\gamma(A) \subset C$ for the union of all orbits $\gamma(x^o)$ with $x^o \in A$.

In many applications we are interested in the set of states reached *after* the system has been in some state x^o. For this purpose we define the *forward (semi-)orbit* through a state x^o as the image of the nonnegative time axis under the solution mapping $\xi(\cdot, x^o)$:

$$\gamma^+(x^o) = \{x \in C : x = \xi(t, x^o) \text{ for some } t \geq 0\} \tag{6.10}$$

The set $\gamma^+(A)$ is defined as the union of all semi-orbits $\gamma^+(x^o)$ with $x^o \in A$.

Example 6.6   The curves shown in figures 6.5 (a) and (b) are parts of the forward (semi-)orbits of solutions to the differential equations in example 6.4. Each of the two curves in figure 6.6 is part of the forward orbit of a solution to the differential equations in example 6.5.

6.3   Invariance and Stationarity

A subset $A \subset C$ of states is *invariant* under some given solution mapping ξ if the *entire* orbit through any point in A lies in A. In other words, if the state is

---

4. More generally, the set R may be replaced by a time set $T \subset R$, where, for instance, T may be the set of integers, resulting in a dynamical system over discrete time.

known to be in A at some point in time, then it must have always been in A, and will always remain in A. The set is *forward (or positively) invariant* if the solution through any point in A *remains* forever in A. Formally:

Definition 6.3   *A subset $A \subset C$ is invariant if $\gamma(x^o) \subset A$ for all $x^o \in A$. The set is* forward invariant *if $\gamma^+(x^o) \subset A$ for all $x^o \in A$.*

A simple example of an invariant set is the orbit $A = \gamma(x^o)$ through any state x^o. Indeed this is the *minimal* invariant set containing x^o (and likewise for forward semi-orbits). It follows immediately from the definitions that a set $A \subset C$ is (forward) invariant if and only if $\gamma(A) = A$ ($\gamma^+(A) = A$).

The following properties of invariant sets are more or less immediate consequences of the three "axioms"(6.5), (6.6), and (6.7):

Proposition 6.2   *Unions and intersection of invariant sets are invariant. If $A \subset C$ is invariant, then so is its closure $\bar{A} \subset C$, complement $B = C \cap \sim A$, interior int$(A) \subset C$ and boundary bd $(A) \subset C$.*

Proof   First, let $\{A_\lambda\}$ be a collection of invariant subsets of C. Suppose that $x \in D = \cup_\lambda A_\lambda$ and that $t \in R$. Then there exists some λ such that $x \in A_\lambda$. Since A_λ is invariant, $\xi(t, x) \in A_\lambda$, and therefore $\xi(t, x) \in D$, that is, $D = \cup_\lambda A_\lambda$, is invariant. Similarly one verifies that $E = \cap_\lambda A_\lambda$ is invariant. Second, let $A \subset C$ be invariant. First, suppose that $x \in \bar{A}$ and that $t \in R$. Then there is a sequence $(x^i)_{i=1}^\infty$ from A converging to x. By invariance of A, $y^i = \xi(t, x^i) \in A$ for each i. By (6.7), $\lim_{i \to \infty} \xi(t, x^i) = \xi(t, x)$ and thus $y = \xi(t, x) \in \bar{A}$, proving that $\bar{A}$ is invariant. To see that also $B = C \cup \sim A$ is invariant, suppose that it is not. Then there is some $x \in B$ and $t \in R$ such that $y = \xi(t, x) \in A$. But then A would not be invariant, since $\xi(-t, y) = \xi(-t, \xi(t, x)) = \xi(t - t, x) = \xi(0, x) = x$ by (6.6) and $\xi(0, x) = x$ by (6.5). (The established equation $\xi(-t, y) = x \in B$ shows that the orbit $\gamma(y)$ is not a subset of A, and thus A is not invariant if B is not.) The invariance of $F = \text{int}(A)$ and $G = \text{bd}(A)$ follows from the already demonstrated results combined with the observations that F is the complement of the closure of B and G is the intersection of the closure of A and the closure of B.   ∎

Note that the above statements are not generally valid for sets that are only *forward* invariant. For instance, the unit interval $A = [0, 1] \subset R$ is forward invariant in the one-dimensional dynamics $\dot{x} = -x$, so is its interior $(0, 1)$ but not its boundary $\{0, 1\}$: The solution through $x = 1$ moves into the interior of A.

An important class of invariant sets are the stationary states (i.e., states of no motion):

Definition 6.4 A stationary state *under a solution mapping ξ is a state $x \in C$ such that $\xi(t, x) = x$ for all $t \in R$.*

Alternatively, stationary states are sometimes referred to as *rest points, critical points,* or (dynamic) *equilibria*.

Hence a state $x \in X$ is stationary if and only if the orbit $\gamma(x)$ through x is the singleton set $\{x\}$ or, equivalently, if and only if the set $A = \{x\}$ is invariant. Expressed in terms of a system of ordinary differential equations (6.1), a state $x \in C$ is stationary if and only if the vector field φ vanishes at x, namely $\varphi(x) = 0$. To see this, just note that if the vector field vanishes at $x \in C$, then one solution to (6.1) through x is $\xi(t, x) = x$ for all t. By the Picard-Lindelöf theorem this is the only solution through x, so x is stationary. Conversely, suppose that $\xi(t, x) = x$ for all t is the solution through x. Then clearly $d\xi(t, x)/dt = 0$ for all t, and $\varphi(x) = 0$ by (6.3).

A useful consequence of axioms (6.5), (6.6), and (6.7) is that if a solution converges over time, then the limit state is necessarily stationary. Intuitively this is not surprising for solutions to differential equations. If a solution through some initial state x settles down over time toward some state y, then the vector field should be weak near y and thus vanish at y (by continuity of φ):

Proposition 6.3 *If $x, y \in C$, and $\lim_{t \to +\infty} \xi(t, x) = y$, then y is stationary.*

Proof Suppose that $x, y \in C$ and that $\lim_{t \to +\infty} \xi(t, x) = y$. Then for every neighborhood B of y there exists some time $t_B \geq 0$ such that $\xi(t, x) \in B$ for all $t \geq t_B$. Let $x^B = \xi(t_B, x)$, and suppose that y is not stationary. Then there exists some moment $\hat{t} \in R_+$ when $\xi(\hat{t}, y) = z \neq y$. By (6.7) there then exists a neighborhood A of y such that z is not in A, nor are any $z' = \xi(\hat{t}, y')$ with $y' \in A$. But for $B = A$ we have $x^A \in A$ and $\xi(t, x^A) \in A$ for all $t \geq t_A$, which, by (6.6), is equivalent to $\xi(s, x^A) = \xi(s, \xi(t_A, x)) = \xi(s + t_A, x) \in A$ for all $s \geq 0$. This causes a contradiction when $s = \hat{t}$. ∎

Note, however, that convergence of a solution toward a point does *not* imply that the point is ever reached (in finite time). In fact, unless the system initially is in a stationary state, it will *never* be in a stationary state: If $x \neq y$ and y is stationary, then $\xi(t, x) \neq y$ for all t. If y is stationary, then a solution through y is the constant solution $\xi(t, y) = y$ for all t, and by the Picard-Lindelöf theorem, this is the only solution through y.

Example 6.7 As figures 6.5 (a) and (b) suggest, the origin $x = (0, 0)$ is the only stationary state of the dynamics induced by the differential equations in example 6.4. Equivalently, the set $A = \{(0, 0)\}$ is the only invariant *singleton* set. For all values of α the full space $X = R^2$ is, of course, invariant. Every disc $D_\lambda = \{x \in R^2 : \|x\| \leq \lambda\}$, for any $\lambda \in R_+$, is forward invariant when $\alpha \leq 0$ (since then $\dot{r} \leq 0$; see example 6.4), and the complement to D_λ is forward invariant when $\alpha > 0$. Note also that the fact that at least one solution (in fact, any solution) converges to the origin when α is negative implies, by proposition 6.3, that the origin is a stationary state.

Example 6.8 The origin is the only stationary *state* in the dynamics of example 6.5, but also the unit circle $A = \{x : \|x\| = 1\}$ is invariant. In fact every closed ring-shaped set $E = \{x : \alpha \leq \|x\| \leq \beta\}$ such that $\alpha \leq 1 \leq \beta$ is forward invariant in this dynamics.

6.4 Stability Concepts

Let $D = (R, C, \xi)$ be a dynamic system. We will use two distinct (classical) notions of stability: Lyapunov and asymptotic stability, respectively, as applied to individual states $x \in C$ or to sets of states $A \subset C$. The most basic notion is that of *Lyapunov stability,* frequently referred to as "stability" for short. Intuitively, a state $x \in C$ is Lyapunov stable if no small perturbation of the state induces a movement away from x. While Lyapunov stability thus requires there to be no push away from the state, asymptotic stability requires there to be a (local) pull toward the state: a state $x \in C$ is *asymptotically stable* if it is Lyapunov stable and all sufficiently small perturbations of the state induce a movement back toward x. By definition, then, asymptotic stability implies Lyapunov stability. Formally:

Definition 6.5 *A state $x \in C$ is* Lyapunov stable *if every neighborhood B of x contains a neighborhood B^o of x such that $\xi(t, x^o) \in B$ for all $x^o \in B^o \cap C$ and $t \geq 0$. A state $x \in C$ is* asymptotically stable *if it is Lyapunov stable and there exists a neighborhood B^* such that (6.11) holds for all $x^o \in B^* \cap C$.*

$$\lim_{t \to \infty} \xi(t, x^o) = x \tag{6.11}$$

Note that the criterion for Lyapunov stability is equivalent to the requirement that all forward orbits from B^o are contained in B: $\gamma^+(B^o \cap C) \subset B$.

Clearly a state x has to be stationary in order to be (Lyapunov or asymptotically) stable, since otherwise the solution ξ would lead away from x even in the absence of a perturbation:

Proposition 6.4   *If a state is Lyapunov stable, then it is stationary.*

Proof   Suppose that $x \in C$ is not stationary. Then there exists some $y \neq x$ and $t \in R$ such that $\xi(t, x) = y$. The point y is at some finite distance from x, and so there exists some neighborhood B of x that the system leaves in finite time if started at x.   ∎

The preceding definitions of diverse stability properties of individual states $x \in C$ are readily generalized to properties of *sets* $A \subset C$ of states. For technical reasons the studied subsets A will be taken to be *closed* (and hence compact, since they are subsets of the compact set C). The reader should verify that the pointwise and setwise stability definitions coincide in the special case of a singleton set $A = \{x\}$. Since we need to consider convergence to a closed set, rather than to a point, three more pieces of mathematics are needed. First, we measure the *distance* between a point $y \in C$ and a closed set $A \subset C$ as the *minimal* distance between y and *any* point a in A: $d(y, A) = \min_{a \in A} d(y, a)$. Second, we say that a solution $\xi(\cdot, x^o)$ *converges* to a closed set $A \subset C$, written $\xi(t, x^o)_{t \to \infty} \to A$, if the distance $d(\xi(t, x^o), A)$ converges to zero as $t \to \infty$. Note that this does not require the solution to be convergent. Third, by a *neighborhood* of a closed set A we mean an open set B containing A.

Definition 6.6   *A closed set $A \subset C$ is Lyapunov stable if every neighborhood B of A contains a neighborhood B^o of A such that $\gamma^+(B^o \cap C) \subset B$. A closed set $A \subset C$ is asymptotically stable if it is Lyapunov stable and if there exists a neighborhood B^* of A such that $\xi(t, x^o)_{t \to \infty} \to A$ for all $x^o \in B^* \cap C$.*

Examples 6.9 through 6.11 illustrate these properties.

Proposition 6.5   *If a closed set $A \subset C$ is Lyapunov stable, then it is forward invariant.*

Proof   Suppose that $A \subset C$ is not forward invariant. Then there exists some $x \in A$, $y \notin A$, and $t \in R$ such that $\xi(t, x) = y$. The point y is at some positive distance from A, and so there exists some neighborhood B of A that the system leaves in finite time if started at x. In particular, if $B^o \subset B$ is a neighborhood of A, then $x \in B^o$ and $\gamma^+(B^o)$ is *not* a subset of B. Thus A is not Lyapunov stable.   ∎

A useful concept closely related to those of asymptotic stability is that of *basin of attraction* of a state $x \in C$ or a closed set $A \subset C$ of states. As the name suggests, this basin is the set of initial states that the dynamics pulls toward the point x or set A in question. More precisely, the basin of attraction of a state x is the set of states x^o such that the solution through x^o converges over time to x, and likewise for the basin of attraction of a set A. Note, however, that in the latter case the solution need not be convergent; it suffices that its *distance* to the set A in question converges to zero. Formally, one may treat individual states and sets of states with the same mathematical machinery:

Definition 6.7   *The* basin of attraction *of a closed set $A \subset C$ is the set* $\{x^o \in C : \xi(t, x^o)_{t \to \infty} \to A\}$. *A set $A \subset C$ is called an* attractor *if its basin of attraction is a neighborhood of A.*

It follows that a Lyapunov stable state or set is *asymptotically* stable if and only if it is an attractor.

6.5   Lyapunov's Direct Method

A general method to establish stability properties of individual states or closed sets of states is the *direct Lyapunov method*. The idea is intuitively simple, and we will apply it to three distinct contexts.

First, let $A \subset C$ be a closed set which we want to show is Lyapunov stable in some given dynamics ξ on (a compact set) C. Suppose that we have found some real-valued continuous function v, defined on a neighborhood D of the set A, such that $v(x)$ is zero on A and positive outside A. Suppose furthermore that v, evaluated along any solution path in its domain D, is *not* increasing over time. Then we would be tempted to guess that, at least for initial states sufficiently near A, the system does not move away from A. There are some subtleties, of course, involving the possibility that the system instead moves toward some local minimum $y \notin A$ of v and/or toward the boundary of the domain D of v. However, Lyapunov stability of A can actually be proved. We will refer to this first of three related results as *Lyapunov's first theorem*.

In results like this one usually calls the involved value function v a local *Lyapunov function*:[5]

Theorem 6.2 *Suppose that $A \subset C$ is closed. If there exists a neighborhood D of A and a continuous function $v : D \to R_+$ meeting conditions (6.12) and (6.13) below, then the set A is Lyapunov stable:*

$$v(x) = 0 \qquad \text{if and only if } x \in A, \tag{6.12}$$

$$v\left(\xi(t, x)\right) \leq v(x) \qquad \text{if } x \notin A, \ t > 0, \text{ and } \xi(s, x) \in D \ \ \forall s \in [0, t]. \tag{6.13}$$

Proof   Let $B \subset D$ be any neighborhood of A such that its boundary $E = \partial B$ is contained in D. Clearly E is compact (since it is a closed subset of the compact set C), and v is positive on E. Since v is continuous, its minimum value on E is positive: $\min_{y \in E} v(y) = \alpha > 0$. Let $B' = \{x \in B : v(x) < \alpha\}$. Then B' is a forward invariant neighborhood of A. First, $B\prime$ contains A and $B\prime$ is open by continuity of v. Second, if $x \in B'$, and at some $T > 0$, $\xi(T, x) \notin B'$, then, by (6.7), there exists some $t \in [0, T]$ such that $\xi(s, x) \in D \ \forall s \in [0, t]$ and $y = \xi(s, x) \in E = \partial B'$ for at least one such time s. But this implies that $v(y) \geq \alpha$, contradicting (6.13). ∎

Strengthening the weak inequality in (6.13), one usually calls the associated function a *strict* local Lyapunov function, and we obtain that the studied set A is *asymptotically* stable. In fact, it can be shown that this *characterizes* asymptotic stability. We will refer to this result as *Lyapunov's second theorem*:

Theorem 6.3 *Suppose that $A \subset C$ is closed. There exists a neighborhood D of A and a continuous function $v : D \to R_+$ meeting conditions (6.12) and (6.14) if and only if A is asymptotically stable:*

$$v\left(\xi(t, x)\right) < v(x) \qquad \text{if } x \notin A, t > 0, \text{ and } \xi(s, x) \in D \ \ \forall s \in [0, t]. \tag{6.14}$$

(For a proof, see theorem 2.2 in chapter 5 of Bhatia and Szegö 1970.)

There are two drawbacks with these results, however. The most apparent is that no method is given for how to find a Lyapunov function! Indeed this is a matter of intuition and luck, though there is a class of entropy functions that

---

5. In physics one usually takes some form of energy or entropy as a candidate Lyapunov function. In some dynamic economic models of so-called nontatonnement adjustement processes, certain utilitarian welfare functions may serve this purpose. In evolutionary game theory the best-known Lyapunov functions are relative-entropy functions; see subsection 3.5.1.

has turned out to work well in many contexts of evolutionary game dynamics (see chapters 3 and 5).

The second drawback is that monotonicity conditions such as (6.13) and (6.14) are in general hard to verify. However, if the dynamics ξ is the solution of a system of ordinary differential equations (6.1), and the associated vector field φ is continuously differentiable, then each of the two monotonicity conditions can be replaced by an intuitive and operational sufficient condition. In this alternative approach we use the contour maps of the value function v and the vector field φ, respectively, and no knowledge of the explicit solutions to the system of differential equations is needed.

Again, the basic idea is simple: At any state x in the domain $D \subset C$ of the value function v, the direction of *steepest ascent* of v is given by its *gradient* $\nabla v(x) = (\partial v(x)/\partial x_1, \ldots, \partial v(x)/\partial x_k)$, a vector orthogonal to the level curve (or isoquant) of v through the point x. Likewise the vector $\varphi(x)$ points in the (tangent) direction of the solution curve $\xi(\cdot, x)$ through x. Consequently v is decreasing along the solution ξ if the negative gradient $-\nabla v(x)$ makes an acute angle with the tangent of motion $\varphi(x)$ or, equivalently, if the inner product $\nabla v(x) \cdot \varphi(x)$ is negative.

By the chain rule of differentiation, this inner product equals the time derivative of the value function at $x = \xi(t, x^0)$:

$$\frac{d}{dt}\left[v\left(\xi(t, x)\right)\right] = \sum_{h=1}^{k} \frac{\partial v(x)}{\partial x_h}\left[\frac{d\xi_h(t, x)}{dt}\right]$$

$$= \sum_{h=1}^{k} \frac{\partial v(x)}{\partial x_h}\varphi_h(x) = \nabla v(x) \cdot \varphi(x). \tag{6.15}$$

Granted the solution remains in the domain D during some time interval $[0, t]$, integration of (6.15) gives

$$v\left(\xi(t, x^0)\right) - v\left(x^0\right) = \int_0^t \nabla v\left(\xi(s, x^0)\right) \cdot \varphi\left(\xi(s, x^0)\right) ds. \tag{6.16}$$

Hence, if the inner product $\nabla v(x) \cdot \varphi(x)$ is negative for all $x \notin A$ in the domain D, then clearly (6.14) holds. Likewise one can show that if $\nabla v(x) \cdot \varphi(x)$ is nonpositive for all $x \notin A$ in the domain D, and A is a connected set, then (6.13) holds.[6] In sum:

---

6. This second claim is essentially Lyapunov's original statement of his now classic result.

Theorem 6.4 *Suppose that $A \subset C$ is closed. If there exists a neighborhood D of A and a continuously differentiable function $v : D \rightarrow R_+$ meeting conditions (6.12) and (6.17) below, then A is asymptotically stable. Suppose that $A \subset C$ is closed and connected. If there exists a neighborhood D of A and a continuously differentiable function $v : D \rightarrow R_+$ meeting conditions (6.12) and (6.18) below, then A is Lyapunov stable.*

$$\nabla v(x) \cdot \varphi(x) < 0 \quad \forall x \notin A, \tag{6.17}$$

$$\nabla v(x) \cdot \varphi(x) \leq 0 \quad \forall x \notin A. \tag{6.18}$$

Note that the topological requirements on the set A of states in question are trivially met in the important special case of a single state; if $A = \{x\}$ for some $x \in C$, then A is certainly both closed and connected.[7]

Example 6.9 The origin $x_1 = x_2 = 0$ is a stationary state in the two-dimensional dynamics in example 6.4. This state is clearly unstable when $\alpha > 0$. Moreover it is Lyapunov stable but not asymptotically stable when $\alpha = 0$. Finally, the origin is asymptotically stable when $\alpha < 0$. The continuously differentiable function $v : R^2 \rightarrow R$ defined by $v(x) = \|x\|^2$, the square of the distance to the origin, changes along any solution according to the equation

$$\dot{v}(x) = \frac{d}{dt}\|x\|^2 = 2x_1\dot{x}_1 + 2x_2\dot{x}_2 = 2\alpha\|x\|^2.$$

Clearly v vanishes at the origin and nowhere else, so it is a Lyapunov function when α is negative. The inner product between its gradient $\nabla v(x) = 2x \in R^2$ and the vector field $\varphi(x) \in R^2$ is $2\alpha\|x\|^2$, indeed a negative (nonpositive) number whenever α is negative (nonpositive); see the three Lyapunov theorems above.

Example 6.10 A Lyapunov function for the dynamics of example 6.5 is $v(x) = (\|x\| - 1)^2$, the square distance from the unit circle. To see this, just observe that this function is continuously differentiable, vanishes on the unit circle, and only there, and that its time derivative along solutions, $\dot{v}(x) = \nabla v(x) \cdot \varphi(x) = -2\|x\|(\|x\| - 1)^2$, is negative except at the origin and on the unit circle. Any open ring $D = \{x : \alpha < \|x\| < \beta\}$, for $\alpha \in (0, 1)$ and $\beta > 1$,

---

7. For a rigorous proof of theorem 6.4 in this special case, see theorem 1.1 in section X.1 of Hale (1969). For a full proof of the second claim of the theorem, in the general case, see corollary 3.5 in chapter III of Bhatia and Szegö (1970).

thus meets the requirements for the domain for v as a Lyapunov function for this dynamics (see theorem 6.4).

Example 6.11   To provide an example of a stationary state that is an attractor but not Lyapunov stable, we modify the equations in example 6.5 as follows:

$$\dot{x}_1 = \varphi_1(x) = x_1 - \|x\| \left(x_1 + x_2 \arctan \frac{x_2}{x_1} \right),$$

$$\dot{x}_2 = \varphi_2(x) = x_2 - \|x\| \left(x_2 - x_1 \arctan \frac{x_2}{x_1} \right).$$

In polar coordinates (r, θ) this is simply $\dot{r} = r(1 - r)$ and $\dot{\theta} = r\theta$. Typical orbits are shown in figure 6.7. The origin $(r = 0)$ and the unit circle $(r = 1)$ are still invariant, but now the origin is no longer the unique stationary state. Also the point $x^* = (1, 0)$ (or, equivalently, $(r, \theta) = (1, 0)$) is stationary. The diagram suggests that x^* has the whole plane, except the origin, as its basin of attraction. Yet x^* is not Lyapunov stable, since any neighborhood of x^* contains some segment of the unit circle, along which the state moves counterclockwise.

To *prove* that the singleton x^* is not *asymptotically* stable, we invoke theorem 6.3. Suppose that there is a neighborhood D of x^* and a function v meeting conditions (6.12) and (6.14). Then v would be discontinuous at x^*. A movement counterclockwise around the unit circle, starting just above x^*, would lead v toward lower positive values, and yet $v(x^*) = 0$. Hence there exists no continuous function meeting the conditions in theorem 6.3 and x^* is not asymptotically stable. However, the diagram suggests that the unit circle is an asymptotically stable set. Indeed it is, since there is a Lyapunov function for this set, the same as in example 6.10.

6.6   Liouville's Formula

For certain questions in stability analysis there is available a handy mathematical formula that is used in physics in studies of flows of liquids and gases. It has to do with the possibility that such flows may locally or globally contract, preserve, or expand the volume of the liquid or gas as it moves along the flow. This formula relates a certain characteristic of a vector field, its so-called *divergence*, to the rate of change of *volume* in the dynamics. The formula is hence of general interest for studies of dynamic systems, and it has important

(a)

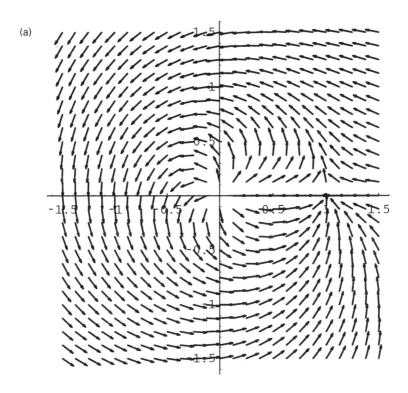

(b)

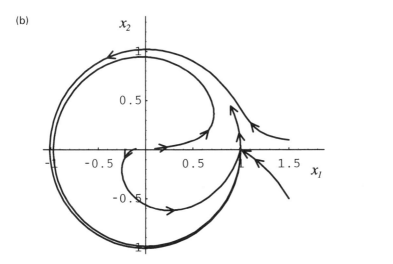

Figure 6.7
(a) The vector field of the dynamics in example 6.11. (b) Solution orbits to the same dynamics.

implications for our stability analysis of multipopulation evolutionary dynamics in chapter 5.

The Liouville formula applies to any system of autonomous ordinary differential equations (6.1) in which the vector field φ is continuously differentiable on an open domain $X \subset R^k$. The *divergence* of φ at any point $x \in X$ is defined as the trace of its Jacobian at the point

$$\text{div}\left[\varphi(x)\right] = \sum_{i=1}^{k} \frac{\partial \varphi_i}{\partial x_i}(x). \tag{6.19}$$

In particular, a vector field for which the divergence is everywhere zero is called *divergence free,* a property that turns out to imply that the associated flow is volume preserving.

Equation (6.19) defines the divergence as a continuous function on the domain of the vector field φ, and hence we can compute its integral over measurable sets $A \subset X$. Given any such set A and time $t \in R$ such that the solution $\xi(\cdot, x^o)$ through any point $x^o \in A$ is defined at time t: $\xi(t, x^o) \in X$, let $A(t)$ be the image of A under the solution mapping ξ:

$$A(t) = \left\{\xi(t, x^o) : x^o \in A\right\}.$$

Then $A(t)$ is measurable, and its *volume* is $\text{vol}\left[A(t)\right] = \int_{A(t)} dx$.

The *Liouville formula* states that the time derivative of the volume of $A(t)$ exists and equals the integral of the divergence over $A(t)$:

$$\frac{d}{dt}\text{vol}\left[A(t)\right] = \int_{A(t)} \text{div}\left[\varphi(x)\right] dx. \tag{6.20}$$

In particular, as indicated above, any divergence-free vector field keeps all volumes constant over time. In physics this corresponds to the flow of an incompressible liquid (e.g., water at constant temperature and pressure).

Intuitively we expect a divergence-free vector field to have no asymptotically stable state. If $x \in X$ is asymptotically stable, then there is some neighborhood $B \subset X$ of x that is contracted toward the point x over time, implying that the volume of the neighborhood shrinks to zero as time increases toward infinity. By Liouville's formula, this is not possible in a divergence-free vector field. (The most we can hope for in such dynamics is Lyapunov stability.)

The following result is the slightly stronger claim that a vector field that has nonnegative divergence has no compact asymptotically stable set:

Proposition 6.6 *If $X \subset R^k$ is open and $\varphi : X \to R^k$ is continuously differentiable with $\mathrm{div}\big[\varphi(x)\big] \geq 0$ for all $x \in X$, then the dynamics (6.1) has no compact asymptotically stable set $A \subset X$.*

Proof   Suppose that $\emptyset \neq A \subset X$ is compact and asymptotically stable. Then $\mathrm{vol}\,[A] \in R_+$ and there exists a neighborhood $B \subset X$ of A with compact closure $\bar{B}$ in X, such that $\xi(t, x^o)_{t \to \infty} \to A$ for all $x^o \in \bar{B}$. Let $B(t) = \big\{\xi(t, x^o) : x^o \in \bar{B}\big\}$. It is shown below that for every $\varepsilon > 0$, there exists a time T_ε such that each point x in $B(t)$ is within (Hausdorff) distance $d(x, A) < \varepsilon$ from the set A at all times $t \geq T_\varepsilon$. Thus $\mathrm{vol}\,\big[B(t)\big]_{t \to \infty} \to \mathrm{vol}\,[A]$. Since $\mathrm{vol}\,[A] < \mathrm{vol}\,\big[B(0)\big]$, $d/dt\,\mathrm{vol}\,\big[B(t)\big] < 0$ for some t, and hence we do not have $\mathrm{div}\,\big[\varphi(x)\big] \geq 0$ for all $x \in X$, by (6.20).

To complete the proof, suppose that there is *no* finite time after which each point $x \in B(t)$ is within arbitrarily small distance from the set A and remains there. Then there exists some $\varepsilon > 0$ and an increasing sequence of times $t^k \to +\infty$, with accompanying initial states $x^k \in \bar{B}$, such that $d\,\big[\xi(t^k, x^k), A\big] \geq \varepsilon$ for all k. Since $\bar{B}$ is compact, the sequence $(x^k)_{k=1}^\infty$ contains a convergent subsequence (by the Bolzano-Weierstrass theorem), so without loss of generality we may assume that $x^k \to x^*$ for some $x^* \in \bar{B}$. By hypothesis, A is Lyapunov stable, and hence there exists a neighborhood C of A such that $x^0 \in C \Rightarrow d(\xi(t, x^0), A)) < \epsilon\ \forall t \leq 0$. Let D be another neighborhood of A such that its closure $\bar{D}$ is contained in C, and let $t^* = \min\{t \geq 0 : \xi(t, x^*) \in \bar{D}\}$. By continuity of ξ, there exists a neighborhood E of x^* such that $x^0 \in E \Rightarrow \xi(t^*, x^0) \in C$. But for k sufficiently large $t_k > t^*$ and $x^k \in E$, so $d(\xi(t^k, x^k), A)) < \epsilon$, a contradiction. ∎

Example 6.12   The pair of ordinary differential equations

$$\dot{x} = -(1 - x)\,x,$$

$$\dot{y} = -(1 - y)\,y,$$

arises in the standard two-population replicator dynamics as applied to the Prisoner's Dilemma Game (with normalized payoffs $a_1 = -1$ and $a_2 = 1$). The relevant state space is the unit square $C = [0, 1]^2$. The vector field is a continuously differentiable function on R^2 that has negative divergence on the interior of C: $\mathrm{div}\big[\varphi(x, y)\big] = 2x + 2y - 2 < 0$ for all $(x, y) \in \mathrm{int}(C) = (0, 1)^2$. Hence, according to Liouville's formula, the volume of any measurable set A of initial states in $\mathrm{int}(C)$ shrinks over time in this dynamics. In fact both variables decrease monotonically over time in int(C), and all solution orbits in int(C) converge to the origin. The set C is invariant, so is int(C), and the origin is asymptotically stable relative to the state space C.

Division by both right-hand sides in the above differential equations by the same positive and Lipschitz continuous function $\psi : (0, 1)^2 \to R_{++}$ does not alter the solution orbits in int(C). For instance, let $\psi(x, y) = (1 - x)(1 - y)xy$. Then the new dynamics on int(C) is given by

$$\dot{x} = -\frac{1}{(1 - y)y} ,$$

$$\dot{y} = -\frac{1}{(1 - x)x} .$$

The new vector field is still continuously differentiable on int(C), but it is clearly divergence free, since the diagonal of its Jacobian consists of zeros. Hence, in this new dynamics, volumes do *not* shrink over time, although the solution orbits are the same as in the first pair of differential equations!

The explanation is that although orbits are unchanged, *velocities* along these orbits are changed. In particular, velocities along orbits near the boundary of C are increased a lot (to $+\infty$ at the boundary). Hence forward images of sets look very different in the two dynamics. Moreover, while the origin is not reached in finite time from any interior initial state in the original dynamics, this point is reached in finite time by all interior initial states in the modified dynamics. Consequently, for any given set $A \subset$ int(C), there is a finite time t at which the solution through some initial state in A leaves the domain int(C) of the vector field in the new dynamics. Accordingly Liouville's formula no longer applies. However, as long as the image $A(t)$ belongs to int(C), its volume is indeed constant by Liouville's formula.

Bibliography

Akin, E. 1980. Domination or equilibrium. *Mathematical Biosciences* 50: 239–50.

Akin, E. 1982. Exponential families and game dynamics. *Canadian Journal of Mathematics* 34: 374–405.

Amann, E., and J. Hofbauer. 1985. Permanence in Lotka-Volterra and replicator equations. In W. Ebeling and M. Peschel (eds.), *Lotka-Volterra Approach to Cooperation and Competition in Dynamic Systems*. Berlin: Akademie-Verlag.

Aumann, R. 1987. Correlated equilibrium as an expression of Bayesan ratinonality. *Econometrica* 55: 1–18.

Aumann, R., and A. Brandenburger. 1991. Epistemic conditions for Nash equilibrium. Mimeo. Hebrew University.

Balkenborg, D., and K. Schlag. 1994. On the interpretation of evolutionary stable sets in symmetric and asymmetric games. Mimeo. Bonn University Economics Department.

Banerjee, A., and J. Weibull. 1992. Evolution and rationality: Some recent game-theoretic results. *Proceedings from the Tenth World Congress of the International Economic Association*. Oxford: Blackwell (forthcoming).

Banerjee, A., and J. Weibull. 1993. Evolutionary selection with discriminating players. WP 1637. Department of Economics, Harvard University.

Banerjee, A., and J. Weibull. 1995. Evolutionary selection and rational behavior. In A. Kirman and M. Salmon (eds.), *Learning and Rationality in Economics*. Oxford: Blackwell, pp. 343–63.

Basu, K., and J. Weibull. 1991. Strategy subsets closed under rational behavior. *Economics Letters* 36: 141–46.

Bhaskar, V. 1991. Noisy communication and the evolution of cooperation. Mimeo. Delhi School of Economics.

Bhatia, N. P., and G. P. Szegö. 1970. *Stability Theory for Dynamical Systems*. Berlin: Springer Verlag.

Binmore, K., and L. Samuelson. 1992. Evolutionary stability in repeated games played by finite automata. *Journal of Economic Theory* 57: 278–305.

Binmore, K., and L. Samuelson. 1994. Evolutionary drift. *European Economic Review* 38: 859–67.

Binmore, K., L. Samuelson, and R. Vaughan. 1993. Musical chairs: Modelling noisy evolution. SSRI WP 9324. University of Wisconsin.

Björnerstedt, J. 1993. Experimentation, imitation and evolutionary dynamics. Mimeo. Department of Economics, Stockholm University.

Björnerstedt, J., Dufwenberg, M., Norman, P., and J. W. Weibull. 1993. Evolutionary selection dynamics and irrational survivors. Mimeo. Department of Economics, Stockholm University.

Björnerstedt, J., and J. Weibull. 1993. Nash equilibrium and evolution by imitation. In K. Arrow and E. Colombatto (eds.), *Rationality in Economics*. New York: Macmillan (forthcoming).

Blume, A. 1993a. Equilibrium refinements in sender-receiver games. WP 93-06. University of Iowa.

Blume, A. 1993b. Neighborhood stability in sender-receiver games. Mimeo. Department of Economics, University of Iowa.

Blume, A., Y.-G. Kim, and J. Sobel. 1993. Evolutionary stability in games of communication. *Games and Economic Behavior* 5: 547–75.

Bomze, I. 1986. Non-cooperative two-person games in biology: A classification. *International Journal of Game Theory* 15: 31–57.

Bomze, I. 1991. Cross entropy minimization in uninvadable states of complex populations. *Journal of Mathematical Biology* 30: 73–87.

Bomze, I., and E. van Damme. 1992. A dynamical characterization of evolutionarily stable states. *Annals of Operations Research* 37: 229–44.

Bomze, I., and B. Pötscher. 1989. *Game Theoretical Foundations of Evolutionary Stability*. Berlin: Springer Verlag.

Bomze, I., and J. Weibull. 1994. Does neutral stability imply Lyapunov stability? Mimeo. Department of Economics, Stockholm University (forthcoming in *Games and Economic Behavior*).

Boylan, R. 1992. Laws of large numbers for dynamical systems with randomly matched individuals. *Journal of Economic Theory* 57: 473–504.

Cabrales, A., and J. Sobel. 1992. On the limit points of discrete selection dynamics. *Journal of Economic Theory* 57: 407–19.

Cannings, C. 1987. Topics in the theory of ESS's. In S. Lessard (ed.), *Mathematical and Statistical Developments of Evolutionary Theory*. Dordrecht: Kluwer.

Cannings, C., and G. T. Vickers. 1988. Patterns of ESS's II. *Journal of Theoretical Biology* 132: 409–20.

Cho, I.-K., and D. Kreps. 1987. Signaling games and stable equilibria. *Quarterly Journal of Economics* 102: 179–221.

Crawford, V. 1990a. Nash equilibrium and evolutionary stability in large- and finite-population "Playing the Field" Models. *Journal of Theoretical Biology* 145: 83–94.

Crawford V. 1990b. An "Evolutionary" interpretation of Van Huyck, Battalio, and Beil's experimental results on coordination. *Games and Economic Behavior* 3: 25–59.

Cressman, R. 1990. Strong stability and density-dependent evolutionarily stable strategies. *Journal of Theoretical Biology* 145: 319–30.

Cressman, R. 1992a. *The Stability Concept of Evolutionary Game Theory*. Berlin: Springer Verlag.

Cressman, R. 1992b. Evolutionarily stable sets in symmetric extensive two-person games. *Mathematical Biosciences* 108: 179–201.

van Damme, E. 1984. A relation between prefect equilibria in extensive-form games and proper equilibria in normal-form games. *International Journal of Game Theory* 13: 1–13.

van Damme, E. 1987. *Stability and Perfection of Nash Equilibria*. Berlin: Springer Verlag (2nd ed. 1991).

van Damme, E. 1989. Stable equilibria and forward induction. *Journal of Economic Theory* 48: 476–96.

van Damme, E. 1994. Evolutionary game theory. *European Economic Review* 38: 847–58.

Dawkins, R. 1976. *The Selfish Gene*. Oxford: Oxford University Press.

Dekel, E., and S. Scotchmer. 1992. On the evolution of optimizing behavior. *Journal of Economic Theory* 57: 392–406.

Fischer, R. A. 1930. *The Genetical Theory of Natural Selection*. Oxford: Clarendon (2nd ed. 1958).

Fort, M. 1950. Essential and non essential fixed points. *American Journal of Mathematics* 72: 315–22.

Foster, D., and P. Young. 1990. Stochastic evolutionary game dynamics. *Theoretical Population Biology* 38: 219–32.

Friedman, D. 1991. Evolutionary games in economics. *Econometrica* 59: 637–66.

Friedman, M. 1953. The methodology of positive economics. In *Essays in Positive Economics*. Chicago: University of Chicago Press.

Fudenberg, D., and E. Maskin. 1990. Evolution and cooperation in noisy repeated games. *AEA Papers and Proceedings* 80 (2): 274–79.

Fudenberg, D., and J. Tirole. 1991. *Game Theory*. Cambridge: MIT Press.

Gale, J., K. Binmore, and L. Samuelson. 1993. Learning to be imperfect: the ultimatum game. Mimeo. Department of Economics, University of Wisconsin.

Gaunersdorfer, A., J. Hofbauer, and K. Sigmund. 1991. On the dynamics of asymmetric games. *Theoretical Population Biology* 39 (3): 345–57.

Gilboa, I., and A. Matsui. 1991. Social stability and equilibrium. *Econometrica* 59 (3): 859–67.

Haigh, J. 1975. Game theory and evolution. *Advances in Applied Probability* 7: 8–11.

Hale, J. 1969. *Ordinary Differential Equations*. New York: Wiley.

Hamilton, W. D. 1967. Extraordinary sex ratios. *Science* 156: 477–88.

Hammerstein, P., and R. Selten. 1993. Game theory and evolutionary biology. Mimeo. Max-Planck-Institute, Seewiesen, and Department of Economics, Bonn University.

Harsanyi, J., and R. Selten. 1988. *A General Theory of Equilibrium Selection in Games*. Cambridge: MIT Press.

Hirsch, M., and S. Smale. 1974. *Differential Equations, Dynamical Systems, and Linear Algebra*. San Diego: Academic Press.

Hofbauer, J. 1981. A general cooperation theorem for hypercycles. *Monatshefte für Mathematik* (Vienna) 91: 233–40.

Hofbauer, J., P. Schuster, and K. Sigmund. 1979. A note on evolutionary stable strategies and game dynamics. *Journal of Theoretical Biology* 81: 609–12.

Hofbauer, J., and K. Sigmund. 1988. *The Theory of Evolution and Dynamical Systems*. Cambridge: Cambridge University Press.

Hofbauer, J., and K. Sigmund. 1989. On the stabilizing effect of predators and competitors on ecological communities. *Journal of Mathematical Biology* 27: 537–48.

Hurkens, S. 1993. An evolutionary foundation of curb retracts and related solution concepts. Mimeo. Tilburg University, Netherlands.

Jansen, W. 1986. A permanence theorem for replicator and Lotka-Volterra systems. *Journal of Mathematical Biology* 25: 411–22.

Jiang, J.-H. 1963. Essential equilibrium points of n-person non-cooperative games. *Sci. Sinica* 12: 651–71.

Kandori, M., G. Mailath, and R. Rob. 1993. Learning, mutation, and long-run equilibria in games. *Econometrica* 61: 29–56.

Kim, Y.-G., and J. Sobel. 1991. An evolutionary approach to pre-play communication. Mimeo. University of Iowa.

Kohlberg, E., and J.-F. Mertens. 1986. On the strategic stability of equilibria. *Econometrica* 54: 1003–37.

Kreps, D., and R. Wilson. 1982. Sequential equilibrium. *Econometrica* 50: 863–94.

Kuhn, H. 1953. Extensive games and the problem of information. In H. Kuhn and A. Tucker (eds.), *Contributions to the Theory of Games II*. Princeton: Princeton University Press, pp. 193–216.

Kullback, S. 1959. *Information Theory and Statistics*. New York: Wiley.

Leonard, R. 1994. Reading Cournot, reading Nash or the creation and stabilisation of the Nash equilibrium. *Economic Journal* 104: 492–511.

Losert, V., and E. Akin. 1983. Dynamics of games and genes: Discrete versus continuous time. *Journal of Mathematical Biology* 17: 241–51.

Lu, X., and D. Stahl II. 1993. An evolutionary process for a little more clever population and its implications. WP 9303. Department of Economics, University of Texas.

Mailath, G. 1992. Introduction: Symposium on evolutionary game theory. *Journal of Economic Theory* 57: 259–77.

Matsui, A. 1991. Cheap-talk and cooperation in a society. *Journal of Economic Theory* 54: 245–58.

Matsui, A. 1992. Best response dynamics and socially stable strategies. *Journal of Economic Theory* 57: 343–62.

Matsui, A., and R. Rob. 1991. The roles of uncertainty and preplay communication in evolutionary games. Mimeo. University of Pennsylvania.

Maynard Smith, J. 1974. The theory of games and the evolution of animal conflicts. *Journal of Theoretical Biology* 47: 209–21.

Maynard Smith, J. 1982. *Evolution and the Theory of Games*. Cambridge: Cambridge University Press.

Maynard Smith, J. 1988. Can a mixed strategy be stable in a finite population? *Journal of Theoretical Biology* 132: 247–60.

Maynard Smith, J., and G. R. Price. 1973. The logic of animal conflict. *Nature* 246: 15–18.

Myerson, R. B. 1978. Refinements of the Nash equilibrium concept. *International Journal of Game Theory* 7: 73–80.

Nachbar, J. 1990. "Evolutionary" selection dynamics in games: Convergence and limit properties. *International Journal of Game Theory* 19: 59–89.

Nash, J. 1950a. Non-cooperative games. Ph.D. dissertation. Princeton University.

Nash, J. 1950b. Equilibrium points in *n*-person games. *Proceedings of the National Academy of Sciences* (USA) 36: 48–49.

Nash, J. 1951. Non-cooperative games. *Annals of Mathematics* 54: 286–95.

Nöldeke, G., and L. Samuelson. 1993. An evolutionary analysis of backward and forward induction. *Games and Economic Behavior* 5: 425–54.

Okada, A. 1981. On stability of perfect equilibrium points. *International Journal of Game Theory* 10: 67–73.

Pearce, D. 1984. Rationalizable strategic behavior and the problem of perfection. *Econometrica* 52: 1029–50.

Reiss, R.-D. 1989. *Approximate Distributions of Order Statistics*. Berlin: Springer Verlag.

Riley, J. 1979. Evolutionarily equilibrium strategies. *Journal of Theoretical Biology* 76: 109–23.

Ritzberger, K., and K. Vogelsberger. 1990. The Nash field. RR 263. Institute for Advanced Studies, Vienna.

Ritzberger, K., and J. W. Weibull. 1993. Evolutionary selection in normal-form games. WP 383. The Industrial Institute for Economic and Social Research, Stockholm (forthcoming in *Econometrica*).

Robson, A.J. 1990. Efficiency in evolutionary games: Darwin, Nash and the secret handshake. *Journal of Theoretical Biology* 144: 379–96.

Samuelson, L. 1991a. Limit evolutionarily stable strategies in two-player, normal form games. *Games and Economic Behavior* 3: 110–28.

Samuelson, L. 1991b. How to tremble if you must. WP 9122. University of Wisconsin.

Samuelson, L. 1993. Does evolution eliminate dominated strategies? In K. Binmore, A. Kirman, and P. Tani (eds.), *Frontiers of Game Theory*, Cambridge: MIT Press.

Samuelson, L., and J. Zhang. 1992. Evolutionary stability in asymmetric games. *Journal of Economic Theory* 57: 363–91.

Savage, L. 1954. *The Foundations of Statistics*. New York: Wiley.

Schlag, K. 1993a. Cheap talk and evolutionary dynamics. Discussion Paper B-242. University of Bonn.

Schlag, K. 1993b. Dynamic stability in the repeated prisoners' dilemma played by finite automata. Discussion Paper B-243. Department of Economics, University of Bonn.

Schlag, K. 1993c. Why imitate, and if so, how? Mimeo. Department of Economics, University of Bonn.

Schuster, P., and K. Sigmund. 1983. Replicator dynamics. *Journal of Theoretical Biology* 100: 533–38.

Schuster, P., K. Sigmund, J. Hofbauer, and R. Wolff. 1981a. Selfregulation of behaviour in animal societies I. *Biological Cybernetics* 40: 1–8.

Schuster, P., K. Sigmund, J. Hofbauer, and R. Wolff. 1981b. Selfregulation of behaviour in animal societies II. *Biological Cybernetics* 40: 9–15.

Selten, R. 1965. Spieltheoretische Behandlung eines Oligopolmodells mit Nachfrageträgheit. *Zeitschrift für die gesamte Staatswissenschaft* 12: 301–24.

Selten, R. 1975. Re-examination of the perfectness concept for equilibrium points in extensive games. *International Journal of Game Theory* 4: 25–55.

Selten, R. 1978. The chain-store paradox. *Theory and Decision* 9: 127–59.

Selten, R. 1980. A note on evolutionarily stable strategies in asymmetric animal conflicts. *Journal of Theoretical Biology* 84: 93–101.

Selten, R. 1983. Evolutionary stability in extensive-form two-person games. *Mathematical Social Sciences* 5: 269–363.

Selten, R. 1991. Evolution, learning, and economic behavior. *Games and Economic Behavior* 3: 3–24.

Shaffer, M. E. 1988. Evolutionarily stable strategies for a finite population and a variable contest size. *Journal of Theoretical Biology* 132: 469–78.

Sigmund, K. 1992. Time averages for unpredictable orbits of deterministic systems. *Annals of Operations Research* 37: 217–28.

Stahl, D. O. 1993. Evolution of smart n players. *Games and Economic Behavior* 5: 604–17.

Swinkels, J. 1992a. Evolutionary stability with equilibrium entrants. *Journal of Economic Theory* 57: 306–32.

Swinkels, J. 1992b. Evolution and Strategic Stability: From Maynard Smith to Kohlberg and Mertens. *Journal of Economic Theory* 57: 333–42.

Swinkels, J. 1993. Adjustment dynamics and rational play in games. *Games and Economic Behavior* 5: 455–84.

Tan, T., and S. R. Werlang. 1988. The Bayesian foundations of solution concepts of games. *Journal of Economic Theory* 45: 370–91.

Taylor, P. 1979. Evolutionarily stable strategies with two types of player. *Journal of Applied Probability* 16: 76–83.

Taylor, P., and L. Jonker. 1978. Evolutionary stable strategies and game dynamics. *Mathematical Biosciences* 40: 145–56.

Thomas, B. 1985a. On evolutionarily stable sets. *Journal of Mathematical Biology* 22: 105–15.

Thomas, B. 1985b. Evolutionarily stable sets in mixed-strategist models. *Theoretical Population Biology* 28: 332–41.

Ullmann-Margalit, E. 1978. Invisible-hand explanations. *Synthese* 39: 263–91.

Vickers, G., and C. Cannings. 1987. On the definition of an evolutionarily stable strategy. *Journal of Theoretical Biology* 129: 349–53.

Vickers, G. T., and C. Cannings. 1988. Patterns of ESS's I. *Journal of Theoretical Biology* 132: 387–408.

Wärneryd, K. 1991. Evolutionary stability in unanimity games with cheap talk. *Economics Letters* 36: 375–78.

Wärneryd, K. 1994. Transactions cost, institutions, and evolution. Mimeo. Stockholm School of Economics (forthcoming in *Games and Economic Behavior*).

Weibull, J. 1992. An introduction to evolutionary game theory. WP 347. The Industrial Institute for Economic and Social Research, Stockholm.

Weibull, J. 1994. The "as if" approach to game theory: Three positive results and four obstacles. *European Economic Review* 38: 868–81.

Weissing, F. 1991. Evolutionary stability and dynamic stability in a class of evolutionary normal form games. R. Selten (ed.), *Game Equilibrium Models I*. Berlin: Springer Verlag.

Winter, S. 1971. Satisficing, selection, and the innovating remnant. *Quarterly Journal of Economics* 85: 237–61.

Wu, W., and J. Jian. 1962. Essential equilibrium points of *n*-person non-cooperative games. *Sci. Sinica* 11: 1307–22.

Young, P. 1993. Evolution of conventions. *Econometrica* 61: 57–84.

Zeeman, E. 1981. Dynamics of the evolution of animal conflicts. *Journal of Theoretical Biology* 89: 249–70.

Index